LATIN-AMERICAN
WOMEN WRITERS

SUNY Series in Feminist Criticism and Theory
Michelle A. Massé, Editor

LATIN-AMERICAN WOMEN WRITERS

Class, Race, and Gender

Myriam Yvonne Jehenson

STATE UNIVERSITY
OF NEW YORK
PRESS

Published by
State University of New York Press, Albany

© 1995   State University of New York

Production by Susan Geraghty
Marketing by Fran Keneston

Printed in the United States of America

For information, address State University of New York
Press, State University Plaza, Albany, N.Y., 12246

Library of Congress Cataloging-in-Publication Data

Jehenson, Myriam Yvonne.
    Latin-American women writers : class, race, and gender / by Myriam
Yvonne Jehenson.
        p.   cm.—(SUNY Series in feminist criticism and theory)
    Includes bibliographical references and index.
    ISBN 0-7914-2559-2 — ISBN 0-7914-2560-6 (pbk.)
    1. Latin American fiction—Women authors—History and criticism.
2. Latin American fiction—20th century—History and criticism.
3. Feminism in literature. 4. Women in literature. 5. Race in
literature. 6. Social classes in literature.   I. Title.
II. Series.
PQ7082.N7J4   1995
863—dc20   94-33936
                                                                        CIP

10 9 8 7 6 5 4 3 2 1

*To my son Roger and my husband,
Peter, with love*

CONTENTS

ABOUT THE AUTHOR

Myriam Yvonne Jehenson is professor and chair of Modern Languages and Literary and Cultural Studies at the University of Hartford in Connecticut. She held a fellowship at the Five College Women's Studies Research Center at Mount Holyoke College in South Hadley, Massachusetts, in 1993. At the State University of New York at Oswego she was associate professor and professor of Foreign Languages and English as well as coordinator of the Spanish and Latin-American Programs from 1986–1993. She was director of the Honors Program at the University of Albuquerque from 1975–1986. Born in Belize, British Honduras, she has a doctorate in Comparative Literature from Columbia University. She is the author of a book on the Renaissance pastoral, *The Golden World of Pastoral: A Comparative Study of Philip Sidney's "Arcadias" and Honoré d'Urfé's "L'Astrée"* (1981), and articles and book reviews on Spanish, French, and Latin-American literature in numerous journals.

PREFACE

The French critic Roger Caillois once remarked: "When the second half of the twentieth century is remembered, it will be for its Latin American literature."[1] That statement, evidenced by the vast amount of critically acclaimed books, plays, short stories, and poetry written by Latin Americans, has proved accurate. Postmodernist critics such as Michael Collins, Ihab Hassan, and Linda Hutcheon, discuss Latin American works as avatars of postmodern experimentation.[2] French feminists use them as models of "écriture féminine," as is the case of Hélène Cixous and Brazilian Clarice Lispector.[3] But a greater reality makes the work of Latin American authors, especially that of the women in the second half of the twentieth century, memorable. It is their transgressive and contestatorial nature, and their critical reconsideration of hierarchical oppositions, that make their texts revolutionary, conflictual, and dialectic in the sense expounded by Monique Wittig: "For as long as oppositions . . . appear as given, already there, before all thought, 'natural'—as long as there is no conflict and no struggle—there is no dialectic, there is no change, no movement."[4]

This book constitutes a representative sampling of the fiction of Latin-American women. It focuses primarily on authors who belong to the second half of the twentieth century, but also includes earlier writers to show a network of relationships, illustrating, in the words of Myriam Díaz-Diocaretz, that the "strategic discursive consciousness" of contemporary Latin-American women writers is part of a continuum. It emerges from a feminine tradition in Latin America that focuses on the formation of the woman's voice as a collective as well as an individual subject, what Díaz-Diocaretz felicitously calls the "matriheritage of founding discourses."[5] The women introduced in these pages are from diverse cultural backgrounds and socioeconomic conditions, and employ various literary strategies, ranging from the sophisticated, postmodernist experimentation of Cuban/Mexican Julieta Campos, Argentine Luisa Valenzuela, Uruguayan Cristina Peri

Rossi, and Brazilian Helena Parente Cunha, to the "direct testimony" of Guatemalan and Bolivian Indians Rigoberta Menchú
and Domitila Barrios de Chungara, and black Brazilian *favelana*,
Carolina María de Jesús.

Not all these authors profess to be feminists. Some resolutely
resist association with a feminism whose capitalist values, in their
view, emphasize the good of the individual over the collective
good.[6] Others are as suspicious of the "inbuilt colonialism of First
World feminism toward the Third" (Spivak) as they are of their
indigenous *machismo*. Chungara expresses their belief well: "Our
position is not like the feminists' position. We think our liberation
consists primarily in our country being freed forever from the
yoke of imperialism . . . I think that *machismo* is a weapon of
imperialism just like feminism is . . . the basic fight isn't between
the sexes. . . ."[7] Such a viewpoint, however, has its own pitfalls.
The oppression of women cannot be regarded as secondary to or
distinguishable from socioeconomic oppression because, in the
words of Costa Rican Carmen Naranjo, "the fight to improve
women's condition is identical with the fight to improve society."[8]
Third World women are, in fact, oppressed *as women*. The humble Chungara's own account makes this clear, as does the experience of the upper class Victoria Ocampo of Argentina: "Privileges
of fortune," Ocampo explains, do "not change at all the injustices
to which women [are] subjected . . . Such advantages [hide] serious disadvantages, which rarely are taken into account."[9] Catego-
rizing oppressions hierarchically tends to discount issues affecting
women in particular, but it also constitutes a clear example of
what Debra Castillo has called "the latest version of a masculinist
theory of emancipation."[10]

All the writers in this book are women-identified in Adrienne
Rich's sense of the term: they embrace many "forms of primary
intensity between and among women, including the sharing of a
rich inner life . . . the giving and receiving of practical and political
support," and the undermining of masculinist clichés.[11] Speaking
through a woman's voice, each of these authors humorously
undermines such time-honored commonplaces as women's
"appropriation" of discourse or their "trespassing" into exclusively male domains.[12] The female narrator of Luisa Valenzuela's
The Lizard's Tail, for example, laughingly asks: "A woman
writer? Don't be funny, women don't know how to write" (259).
Rosario Ferré's *Sitio a Eros* (*Besieging Eros*) repeats Virginia

Woolf's ironic denunciation of the same cliché. If a woman wants to write, she tells us, the world mockingly asks: "Write: Why would *you* want to write?" (149; emphasis mine). And the marvelously self-assured narrator of Clarice Lispector's novel, *The Stream of Life*, ironically writes to her lover: "I write this facsimile of a book, the book of one who does not know how to write" (43). These writers are women and they concentrate on the experiences and relationships of women in Latin America, thereby providing a rich field in which to discuss the issues of gender, race, and class. Their writing, in the words of Francine Masiello, constitutes a "double discourse," a conscious recognition of the "structures of power at the same time that it offers an alternative."[13] These women are less interested in singling out male/female polarities in their work than they are in exploring a genuine Latin-American understanding of feminism. Griselda Gambaro remarks: ". . . as far as I'm concerned, a work is feminist insofar as it attempts to explain the mechanics of cruelty, oppression, and violence through a story that is developed in a world in which men and women exist."[14] But these authors are not satisfied with merely explaining the mechanics of oppression: their goal is to change taken-for-granted views. Through biting and/or humorous irony—Angeles Mastretta accomplishes this with the popular song the *bolero*, and Rosario Ferré with the subversive use of proverbs—they reveal and reduce to humor the otherwise harmful power of the "givens" of popular forms, that is, their power to universalize stereotypical assumptions of male/female oppositions. The conflictual nature of such polarities is prominent in the work of these women. In addition to the most obvious opposition, that of male/female, hetero-/homosexual, binarisms of all kinds are confused, blurred, and burlesqued. Luisa Valenzuela, for example, simply renders the polarities of sex nonexistent in her depiction of transsexuality, bisexuality, and cross-dressing. For Marta Traba and Cristina Peri Rossi, homoeroticism is valued in a world otherwise permeated with hatred. Yet none of these women privileges a particular kind of love. They show, in fact, the pitfalls of too readily romanticizing love in any of its forms. Heterosexual love is treated ironically in the works of Teresa de la Parra, Marta Brunet, and María Luisa Bombal. The "Latin-American *Bovarisme*" these writers describe, to quote Parra, is seen to be allied with women's internalizations of the romanticized conventions of the sentimental novel. These conventions either cause suffering in the case of Parra, Brunet, and Bombal, or are sub-jected to ridicule in Carmen Naranjo's *Ondina*. Homosexual love is treated in similar fashion. Lesbianism simply becomes another form of love for Reina Roffé, whose depictions of lesbian relation-ships exhibit the same joy and suffering as heterosexual ones. Griselda Gambaro's lesbian scenes are as humorously written as are Naranjo's more "conventional" romantic portrayals. Gam-baro's irony, however, is more deliberate. She seeks to reduce to bathos traditional literary scenes of erotic titillation—both hetero-sexual and homosexual—that have been traditionally aimed at a male audience and have perpetuated *machista* views of sexual domination.

The same critical reconsideration is given to racist and classist binarisms. Ferré and Nélida Piñón transform the racial polarities of white/black into examples of tender bonding between women of different races. Classist polarities are blurred in the texts of Vic-toria Ocampo and of Isabel Allende, and in the *testimonios* of Domitila Barrios de Chungara, Rigoberta Menchú, Elvia Alva-rado, and Elena Poniatowska, where both educated interlocutors and undereducated native informants are united in a common endeavor.

Lydia Cabrera, Elena Garro, and Rosario Castellanos focus on the elasticity of the polarities of victimizer/victim and, further, on alternating supposedly fixed power situations. Nothing is beyond their ironic critique. Armonía Somers challenges religious taboos, while Gambaro, Valenzuela, Roffé, and Orphée question so-called norms of decency and unmask unwarranted self-righ-teousness. These women expose the hidden but real danger of tor-ture by debunking the idea that cruelty is to be attributed to a monstrous "other" or that torture is inherently repulsive. Instead, by allying torture with eroticism, they expose both assumptions. They show the power that cruelty has to fascinate its perpetrators, and they demonstrate that the resultant release of tension, what Georges Bataille calls the "orgy of annihilation," may actually prove humanly satisfying. Therein, they emphasize, resides the insidious danger of torture.

The traditional male-centered world of the hero is also con-tested and transformed into one that is woman-identified. Alba-lucía Angel shows convincingly in *Estaba la pájara pinta sentada en el verde limón* that the masculine genre of the *Bildungsroman* simply does not work for the female hero. She invents, instead, a new "herland" in *Las andariegas*. Angeles Mastretta, conversely, consciously restructures the *Bildungsroman* to make it work for the female hero. Whereas the male protagonist of the traditional genre acquires wisdom, maturity, his lady, and reintegration into society as a result of his arduous trials, Mastretta's female hero experiences freedom only after she has paid her dues to society through marriage and widowhood. Finally able to realize her independence, her orientation is on the future rather than on the present, which—contrary to the male's—is for her an existing order that must be overthrown.[15] Besides their transgressive and contestatorial nature, the woman-authored texts investigated in this book are memorable for yet another reason: they are *sui generis*. They are neither derivative nor paradigmatic, but quintessentially Latin American. They refuse to be circumscribed by any abstracted assumptions, whether these take the form of the "natural" roles assigned to women or of such Euro-American labels as "postmodernist" or "écriture féminine" ascribed to their work. In this respect, the authors would indubitably respond as did Frida Kahlo to André Breton's effort to "internationalize" her by labelling her a surrealist: "I never painted dreams. I painted my own reality."[16] These women too paint their own reality, but do not remain within it. Theirs is more than a mimetic representation of their restrictive worlds, it is an attempt to construct alternatives. Whether they critique literary notions such as *mimesis*, as do Julieta Campos and Helena Parente Cunha, or whether they focus on *poesis*, the making of new worlds, as do the texts of Albalucía Angel and Cristina Peri Rossi, they have in common a part in that ongoing continuum labelled the "matriheritage of founding discourses." Deliberately or obliquely, the early and the later writers alike emphasize a dual reality: that is, that the oppression of women is not a specifically "feminist" concern but a problem that affects all of society, "that supposedly 'subjective', 'individual', 'private' problems are in fact social problems, class problems" (Wittig, 19); and that until a new order can be effected, the goal of the writer is to use irony to represent the old. It is irony, above all, which affords these women a critical perspective on reality as a "given." They concur with Georg Lukács' view that irony is the highest category of expression: "Irony sees the lost utopian home of the idea that has become an ideal, and yet at the same time it understands that the ideal is subjectively and psychologically conditioned, because that is its only possible existence."[17] Irony in depicting an empirical world where divisions of sex, class, and race still exist becomes for these women, to cite Lukács again, "the highest freedom that can be achieved."

A final word about the title of the book. Any attempt to postulate ahistorical, universalistic assumptions about either "Latin-American" literature or Latin-American "women" is simply incorrect. It consitutes what Fredric Jameson has termed "strategies of containment," which "construct their objects of study and . . . project the illusion that their readings are somehow complete and self-sufficient."[18] In fact, such reductive and homogeneous notions of both "Latin America" and "women" differ little from similar colonializing and paternalistic/patriarchical paradigms rejected in the very works analyzed in this book. Therefore, my title, *Latin-American Women Writers: Class, Race, and Gender,* is purely descriptive, designating authors who are women and who come from countries where Spanish or Portuguese is spoken. The aim of this book is threefold. First, it acquaints the English-speaking reader with an overview of both the sociohistorical context that has shaped these women and the part women have played in shaping it (chapter one). Secondly, it offers an exposure to women whom I consider especially important in the "matriheritage of founding discourses" (chapters two and three). My third aim is to discuss fictional works of women from as many Latin-American countries, races, and classes as possible. Chapters four, five, and six emphasize the richness and innovation of individual texts of later writers. I have given more space to Argentine writers because of the diversity of their narratives. Some readers may wonder at my exclusion of so well-known a writer as Brazilian Clarice Lispector. The reason is that she has already received extensive scholarly attention. I have, instead, given my attention to such lesser known Brazilian women as Carolina María de Jesús, Helena Parente Cunha, and Nélida Piñón, whose works deserve increased exposure and more critical attention. My approach, therefore, which may be best described as eclectic, is meant to serve as a basis for continued discussion and debate. All quotations are given in English. If adequate translations are not available for the work under discussion, I provide my own.

ACKNOWLEDGMENTS

I would like to thank the librarians of Penfield Library at SUNY Oswego, especially Ms. Mary Bennett and Ms. Adele Mangano, for their invaluable patience and assistance; and the SUNY Oswego Scholarly and Creative Committee for a summer grant to conduct my research. For their intelligent suggestions for improving a large portion of the manuscript, I am especially grateful to Peter N. Dunn and to Virginia L. Radley. Special thanks are extended to Carola F. Sautter and Susan Geraghty of SUNY Press and to Eileen Dunn. I also thank Natalie J. Woodall, who at first undertook to type the manuscript, but who ultimately became an invaluable research assistant. My debts to many writers are apparent throughout the book, especially to the translators and the critics of the texts considered in these pages. Their work has made the fiction of these talented women readily available. Without them, the present book would not have been possible.

CHAPTER 1

Latin-American Women/
Women in Latin America

Women were essential to the development of the new culture in the centuries that witnessed the conquest of Latin America. Emigration to the "New World," however, was tightly controlled by the Spanish Crown and few Spanish women, particularly the unmarried, were granted permission to depart.[1] Isabel de Guevara's 1556 letter to the Spanish queen, referring to an attempt to establish a settlement in the Rio de la Plata area of Argentina in 1536–7, describes the arduous nature such a journey required of women who emigrated to the New World:

> So great was the famine that at the end of three months a thousand [men] perished. . . . The men became so weak that the poor women had to do all their work; they had to wash their clothes, and care for them when sick, cook the little food they had; stand sentinel, care for the watch-fires and prepare the cross-bows when the Indians attacked, and even fire the petronels; to give the alarm, crying out for all our strength, to drill and put the soldiers in good order, for at that time we women, as we did not require so much food, had not fallen into the same state of weakness as the men. Your Highness will understand that had it not been for the care and the solicitude that we had for them they would have all died.[2]

Since most of the settlers did not have their wives available either as sexual partners or as helpers in daily domestic chores, they began to mate with Indian women and to place them in their homes as concubines or unpaid servants.[3] Though nominally free and under royal protection, Indians generally enjoyed a status not much different from slavery. Women, in particular, suffered the indignities of being bought and sold like property, even rented to sailors making journeys to and from Peru. They were sexually assaulted by blacks and whites, and abducted by government officials and priests.[4] Used for heavy labor, Indian women were sepa-

1

rated from their villages and families for long periods of time. These enforced absences from their husbands and children destroyed family life and undermined Indian culture. Injuries suffered when they were forced to carry heavy loads for long distances resulted in complete physical breakdowns, resulting in a high rate of suicide (Sherman, 313–5). Indian women often acted as wet nurses for Spanish women who could not or did not wish to nurse their own children. In her novel *Balún Canán*, Rosario Castellanos describes the tragic contemporaneity of this colonial situation: an Indian woman's child dies because the mother has only enough milk to nurse her mistress's child.[5]

The lot of the black woman was more severe since imported African slaves did not enjoy even the nominal protection afforded the indigenous population. Much harsher treatment, including flogging for all kinds of offenses, was customary for both female and male slaves.[6] Sexual exploitation of female slaves was an everyday occurrence, and its effects were compounded when children were forcibly separated from their mothers to be sold (Williams, 302; Bush, 108–9).[7] The abolition of slavery brought the black woman little improvement in status: she continued to occupy the lowest rung of the social ladder, discriminated against because of her race, class, and sex.

Women's role in Latin-American warfare is beyond the scope of this introduction, but three brief references should suffice to illuminate the extent of their participation in Latin America's almost constant fascination with organized bloodshed. The first conflict, between Brazil, Argentina, and Uruguay (the "Triple Alliance") on one side and Paraguay on the other, lasted from 1864–1870. The war commenced when Francisco Solano López, dictator of Paraguay, threatened to attack Brazil should that nation invade Uruguay.[8] When the invasion did occur, Solano López declared war, initiating a struggle that devastated Paraguay. A census taken in 1863 showed a total population of 1,337,489. Another, taken in 1871, recorded 221,079. Of that figure, only 28,746 were men (Akers, 195). This drastic shortage of men led to active participation by the Paraguayan women. Historical documents record the women's active involvement in the fighting during the final battle at Peribebuy in August 1869 (Akers, 192). Lacking adequate arms, they used broken bottles as weapons, and in acts of extreme desperation, reportedly flung sand in the eyes of the enemy.[9] The massive loss of soldiers was compounded by the deaths of the women pressed into service as porters. If unable to keep pace with the military forces because of illness or exhaustion, they simply "were left to die by the roadside" (Akers, 195). The battlefield death of General López ended the war, but the reconstruction of Paraguay entailed a slow process. With so few able-bodied men left to rebuild the nation, the women undertook the task.

> They set to work to raise foodstuffs for themselves and their families, selling surplus to purchase the scanty clothing they needed . . . This action wrought a rapid alteration in the economic conditions. The women cultivated such crops as Indian corn, mandioca, and similar products to meet their own necessities. They made long journeys afoot to market, and where manual work on the farms was impossible they manufactured lace and other articles for disposal in Asunción (Akers, 200–1).

Scarcely sixty years later Paraguay was fighting again, this time against Bolivia in what is commonly called the Chaco War. The Paraguayans were victorious, but at the cost of another 30,000 soldiers. Bolivia fared worse, sacrificing 230,000 men (Fogelquist, 603). Once more, the women were an important factor, providing clothes, food, and weapons to the fighting forces (Fogelquist, 612). Paraguayan Josefina Plá, who lived through the Chaco War, is one of the women whose artistic efforts helped revitalize the country after it drained itself a second time of both human and material resources. Art, Plá reminded a devastated country, was not a mirror of reality but a beacon for the future: "Poetry," she said, "begins where reality ends, its mission is to create new realities . . . to show what can still be actualized."[10]

Lastly, well known is the account of the "mamitas" of Peru, which comes out of the war of independence from Spain. These women traveled with the army to cook for the soldiers and frequently tricked the royalists by entering a city while crying that the patriots had been defeated. At times they resorted to drastic measures, appearing nude and pretending to be insane so as to disconcert the royalist army and thereby give the patriots time to prepare their assault.[11]

Given these documented realities, why are Latin-American women systematically stereotyped as lovely, dependent decorations? The reasons are historical. Influenced by a Hispanic-Arab, Roman Catholic heritage, Latin America has perpetuated several received traditions that have effectively served to marginalize women. One is the widespread and well-known cult of *machismo*, which glorifies the aggressive, sexually promiscuous male.[12] The second, equally powerful, cultural phenomenon is that of *marianismo* (Stevens, 91). Referring to the Virgin Mary, after whom the practice is named, *marianismo* glorifies the long-suffering, self-sacrificing female, pure and chaste, devoted to homemaking and motherhood. In her short story, "The Fall," the Uruguayan Armonía Somers exposes the oppressiveness inherent in the phenomenon of *marianismo*, and makes the Virgin Mary its first victim. In the story, the Virgin appeals to an oppressed human being, a black runaway slave, begging him to free her from her unnatural pedestal. Conventionally represented in an upright position, with her arms extended and her face frozen in a perpetual smile, the Virgin has, throughout the centuries, been dehumanized, transformed into a long-suffering and self-sacrificing being.[13] Only when represented as Our Lady of the Seven Dolors is she even allowed to cry over the death of her son. Nicaraguan Doris Tijerino explains how *marianismo* is translated into the daily life of Latin-American women: "The nuns told us that . . . woman's cross was marriage and she had to bear it."[14] Her father frequently asserted that a woman "is something that can be dominated, something he could do what he wanted with . . ." (Randall, 34). Domitila Barrios de Chungara comments: "We women were raised from the cradle with the idea that women were made only to cook and take care of the kids, that we are incapable of assuming important tasks . . ." (40). The notion that marriage and childbearing are woman's destiny is deeply rooted in Mediterranean culture generally and certainly in Spanish culture.[15] The Pauline tenet of man as the head of woman and Christ as the head of man has consistently supported and promoted both the image of women as mothers and homemakers and its corollary, that if a woman leaves her home she is to be considered "loose." This belief may provoke laughter, as in Rosario Castellanos's humorous parody in *The Eternal Feminine*, but it can still elicit severe criticism.[16] Victoria Ocampo, for example, was vilified for driving her own car on the streets of Buenos Aires in the 1920s. In rural areas of Latin America today, a young woman can still be denied the opportunity to work on coffee plantations for the same reason.[17]

Since women of all social classes were perceived as homemakers and mothers, little thought was given to providing formal education even to those of the upper classes.[18] This prejudice still prevails among the poorer classes. Chungara tells of the Bolivian miners' contemptuous reaction when the *compañeras* formed the Housewives Committee: "The men weren't used to hearing a woman speak on the same platform as them. So they shouted: 'Go back home! Back to the kitchen! Back to the washing! Back to your housework!' And they jeered and booed them" (74). As a result, peasant women have great difficulty initiating change and are especially courageous when they do, as exemplified by the cases of Guatemalan Rigoberta Menchú, Bolivian Chungara, and Honduran Elvia Alvarado, who are among many included in this book.[19] So ingrained is the notion that they must be mothers that Latin-American women often internalize the need for large families. Abortion and birth control, disapproved of by the Roman Catholic Church, are generally unavailable. Women either suffer the effects of frequent pregnancies or resort to the horrors of illegal abortion and infanticide. In 1980, for example, 30 to 50 percent of all maternal deaths in Latin America resulted from botched, illegal abortions (Shapiro, 7). In the poorer classes, rearing of children is primarily the mother's responsibility and this problem is aggravated, as Honduran Elvia Alvarado points out, because many men refuse to give their wives enough money for food. The women are thus compelled to obtain outside employment, no matter how low-paying, while still being held responsible for the domestic chores of cooking, cleaning, and mending.[20] Since servants and nannies take care of household chores in the upper classes, class and not sex often determines the division of labor. Rosario Castellanos focuses on this issue in "Herlinda se va" ("Herlinda Leaves"), where she discusses women's exploitation of other women in this regard. Generally, however, there is no question that household chores are associated with women regardless of class. The Argentine author Marta Lynch recounts a conversation with a fellow professor:

> One day we went to lunch together, and in the middle of the explanations which I was giving him concerning my work, I heard [him] asking me: "Do you know how to cook?" I believed that I was hearing things, but I wasn't; in effect, my colleague, in order to place me where he believed I belonged as a woman, *had to know if I knew how to cook.* . . . [21]

The novelist Silvina Bullrich further illustrates this attitude toward women:

It amuses me that when someone calls and asks me if I am busy, I respond, "I was writing." Ah, in that case, my caller thinks, I can continue speaking. It is a much stronger argument to say, "My toast is burning . . . I have something in the oven and have to take it out." The unavoidable immediacy of manual labor justifies feminine tasks. Her intellectual work makes her suspect.[22]

Some readers may object to the reactions of Lynch and of Bullrich as overly sensitive. After all, in Lynch's case, the very question precludes the assumption that all women know how to cook. In Bullrich's case, it is the urgency of the task rather than its gendered associations that affects the response. Whether such reactions are created as stereotypical in feminist writings or whether they indicate a subtle but real *machismo* that is ubiquitous, but cleverly disguised, women are reappropriating household metaphors to revalorize them for serious critical purposes. Rosario Castellanos employs this technique in "Lección de cocina" ("Cooking Lesson") in *Album de familia* (1971; *Family Album*). An excellent collection of feminist writings bears the title *El sartén por el mango: encuentro de escritoras latinoamericanas* (1985; *The Frying Pan by the Handle: Meeting of Latin-American Women Writers*). Debra Castillo's *Talking Back: Toward a Latin-American Feminist Literary Criticism* (1992) begins and ends with culinary and household metaphors. Cooking is the central trope of Laura Esquivel's best-selling book and even more successful movie, "Como agua para chocolate" ("Like Water For Chocolate").

The common perception that "men's work" is separate and different from "women's work" also contributes to the lack of economic opportunity for women. In some cases women are denied access to jobs because they are married, or, as with women worldwide, they are paid substantially less for the same work (Shapiro, 9–11). The flower industry and the coffee plantations provide graphic examples of the exploitation of Latin-American women. The workers in the flower industry are generally young women in their first job or those over thirty-five. They are regularly exposed to the chemicals used on the plants and they work under extreme conditions, either in the hot sun or in refrigerated rooms. Statistics show that over half these workers suffer from occupational maladies ranging from intense pain to chemical poisoning and muscular paralysis (León and Viveros, 9). The coffee plantations exploit both women and men. Rigoberta Menchú's brother, to cite one instance, died of pesticide intoxication on the plantation where the family worked.[23] Additionally, the birth of a girl is often perceived by parents as an event to be mourned rather than celebrated.[24] Sexual molestation of little girls by male relatives is not uncommon, nor are instances of financial exploitation.[25] Poor women "rent out" their small daughters to haul water. Rural youngsters are often lured from their villages and "sold" into prostitution (Randall, 107–8).

In a society where the natural condition of the male is to be aggressive and that of the female to be self-sacrificing, Latin-American women often see themselves primarily as nurturers. Despite extreme poverty, excessive childbearing, and abusive treatment by men, women find their lives worthwhile because they are mothers. Not too surprisingly, totalitarian governments use this deeply entrenched philosophy of *machismo* and *marianismo* to control women. For instance, feminist advances made in Chile during the Allende period were subsequently annulled by the military regime's conscious campaign to "get the women back to the home."[26] Interrogators of female prisoners in Guatemala, Argentina, and Bolivia commonly torture women by accusing them of failing as wives and mothers.[27] They are either called bad mothers or bad wives (Chungara, 27–28), or are made to feel so as they helplessly watch their children being tortured.[28] Chungara relates an instance in which Indian women were compelled to stomp on their children who had been forced by soldiers to lie on broken glass and pottery shards.[29] Rape, accompanied by the beating of female political prisoners, is a common feature of torture, which is done methodically and repeatedly by gangs of police or soldiers.[30] Therefore, *marianismo's* "glorification" of chastity and motherhood is negatively reflected in daily life by the debasement of women as human beings. Bünster-Burotto states the case succinctly: "The combination of culturally defined moral debasement and physical battering is the demented scenario whereby the prisoner is to undergo a rapid metamorphosis from madonna— 'respectable woman and/or mother'—to whore" (298).[31] While the oppression of poorer classes of women is easy to document, subtler but no less flagrant forms of discrimination have been and continue to be practiced against middle- and upper-class women.[32] "For women of the ruling class," Nicaraguan Doris Tijerino reminds us, "the choices keep you physically fed but mentally starved: [they are] the 'success' of a New York model working for charity as a social butterfly, [or] becoming the lover of a security agent . . ." (Randall, 7–8).

Despite the cultural bias, a strong feminism has been active in Latin America since the early nineteenth century. One of the first demands emerging from the feminist movement in Mexico, for example, was better educational opportunities for women.[33] Promises made as early as 1856, but not fulfilled until 1869, when the first secondary school for women was finally opened, clearly show how strong was the anti-feminine prejudice and, conversely, how determined the feminists were to achieve this goal (Macías, 9–10). Affluent families, of course, could always provide governesses for their daughters, and Victoria Ocampo and Teresa de la Parra are outstanding examples of the efficacy of this type of early education. Parra, who chose to remain single, used her successful first novel, *Ifigenia*, to expose the dilemma of her protagonist, an intelligent young woman whose sole destiny was to marry a "good" husband and to produce heirs for him. Ocampo devoted her entire life to fighting a society whose norms not only condemned her for receiving a male visitor into her parlor, but consequently forced her into an abusive marriage from which she had no recourse since divorce was illegal in Argentina.[34]

Whatever one thinks of Eva Duarte Perón's official politics and her single-minded goal to keep her husband in power, her campaign for women's rights won them the vote in 1947. She established the Feminist Party in Argentina in 1951 and persuaded her husband, Juan Perón, to name seven women to the Senate and another twenty-four as deputies. Because of her, the Argentine government turned a permissive eye on previously forbidden contraceptive use. The new Family Code of 1954 included the right to divorce for which Eva Perón had campaigned.[35] Yet this right was repealed shortly after her death (Hahner, 104). It has been argued that Eva Perón was able to benefit women only because she was married to a dictator. History, however, points to another conclusion. Juan Perón seems to have benefitted greatly from his wife's popularity among women, and his position was weakened considerably after her death in 1952. Many women participated in the massive procession in Corpus Christi to protest against him before his fall from power in 1955 (Morgan, 53). A succession of military dictatorships marked by the repression of human rights followed until 1974 when Juan Perón returned to power with his third wife, María Estela (Isabel). They were elected president and vice president, respectively. When Perón died the following year, Isabel became the first Argentine woman head of state, and in 1975 she was re-elected president of the Peronist Party. When the country faced a 330 percent inflation rate and massive labor strikes, a military junta deposed and arrested her in March 1976, ultimately sending her into exile in Spain.

The coup that deposed Isabel Perón ushered in a new wave of terror in Latin America. In the next seven years over 15,000 Argentines were jailed or simply disappeared, and between 5,000 and 30,000 people "disappeared" in Chile in a single year. One out of every 500 Uruguayans suffered the same fate.[36] Women were to be one of the strongest forces that ultimately toppled the Argentine *junta* and restored democratic rule. As early as March 1977, fourteen Argentine women began to protest the "disappearance" of their children by walking around the pyramid in the Plaza de Mayo. Although they themselves were arrested, threatened, imprisoned and "disappeared" by security forces, 2,500 other women eventually joined them. These *madres* or "Crazy Mothers," as they were called, are indicative of how the deeply entrenched philosophy of *marianismo* can be used both ways. By banding together to force the military regime to provide them with information on their missing children, the *madres* subverted the cultural system. According to the Sábato Commission, "the springboard for [the] mobilization of universal consciousness was the unsung, heroic achievement of the Mothers of the Plaza de Mayo. . . ."[37] As mothers, they were excluded from the groups officially defined as "subversives" and their maternal status gave them "a freedom and a power not available to traditional political actors, especially if they were male" (Navarro, 257–8). Their form of protest, walking silently around the pyramid in the plaza, focused attention on the repressive nature of the Argentine military regime at a time when all political opposition had been banned. These mothers, in fact, were instrumental in the fall of the dictatorship in 1983 when they exposed the torture and the disappearances to the world. *Mothers and Shadows*, written by Argentine Marta Traba, is but one testimonial to the bravery displayed by the group that constituted the biggest threat to the military regime: the mothers.

Even though Latin-American women in general have not been as involved in official organized politics as their European and North American sisters, in countries such as Ecuador, women had the vote as early as 1929, only nine years after women in the United States were finally enfranchised. Women have not participated in large numbers in the electoral process because in a society where education for women is not encouraged, many cannot pass the required literacy test (Harris, 5). On the other hand, Latin-American women have had powerful official positions. As early as 1524, Aldonza Manrique became the first female governor, ruling the Venezuelan island of Margarita for approximately sixty years (Morgan, 716). The Nobel Prize winner from Chile, Gabriela Mistral, was appointed consul to Brazil in 1939 and to the United States in 1946. Mexican Rosario Castellanos and Costa Rican Carmen Naranjo were appointed ambassadors to Israel. María Luisa Mendoza served as federal deputy for the state of Guanajuato, Mexico, and Chilean Marta Brunet served as vice consul to Argentina and later to Uruguay. Involving themselves less in corrupt political establishments, women have, rather, concentrated their activism outside the traditional political machine, taking part particularly in revolutionary struggles. Chungara records her crucial role in the history of the formation of the Housewives' Committee, which combatted the exploitation of Bolivian miners (71–9). Rigoberta Menchú and her entire family were in the revolutionary movement against Guatemala's totalitarian regime, which accounted for the near genocide of her people. Upper- and middle-class women joined their poorer sisters in the Sandinista movement in Nicaragua. Victoria Ocampo headed the Argentine Union of Women, founded in 1936 to forestall the repeal of rights won by women, including the right to their own paychecks.[38] Marta Traba, professor of art and first director of Colombia's Museum of Modern Art, risked deportation from Colombia for protesting the military invasion of the University of Bogotá in 1967.[39] Traba, who was too well known for the Colombian government to risk treating her as harshly as other dissidents, was ordered deported. The outcry against this decree was so great that it was rescinded, but Traba was subsequently forced to resign her university position and her directorship of the museum. So far as the government was concerned (although later her career demonstrated otherwise), she was "silenced" and returned to a woman's "natural" role of wife and mother. In 1982, Argentine feminists publicly denounced the Malvinas/Falklands conflict and issued a joint statement in solidarity with British feminists (Morgan, 54).

In the literary arena, women's voices have been equally prominent. Argentine authors like Griselda Gambaro, Luisa Valenzuela, Marta Traba, and Elvira Orphée repudiate military repression in their works. The surrealism of terror depicted by Uruguayan Cristina Peri Rossi; the development of young women into revolutionaries in the work of Colombian Albalucía Angel; the accounts of the oppressiveness of native Indian life in Mexico by Elena Garro and Rosario Castellanos; and the exposure of cruelty and of genocide by Guatemalan Rigoberta Menchú, Bolivian Domitila Barrios de Chungara, and Honduran Elvia Alvarado, all clearly show women's literary voices clamoring for justice and positive change in the political sphere of their respective countries.

CHAPTER 2

"To Build Bridges"

Victoria Ocampo is one of the most revered and vilified of Latin-American foremothers. A writer herself, she was unswerving in her dedication to making younger writers known thorugh her influential journal *Sur,* and to fighting "against the wind and the tide," in order "to build bridges between continents."[1] This chapter belongs to her because she constitutes an essential link in Latin American women's "matriheritage of founding discourses." Ocampo was born in Buenos Aires, Argentina on 7 April 1890, and died there on 27 January 1979. Despite her acknowledged influence on and contributions to Spanish American literature, not until 1977 was she inducted into the Argentine Academy of letters, the first woman so honored (Meyer, *Against,* 177–8). An uncoventional lifestyle and feminist beliefs ultimately generated a series of myths that made her subject "to both demonology and hagiography . . ."[2] Her life is inseparable from her work. Her extensive bibliography of books and articles written in French, Spanish, and English, plus the volume of books, interviews and articles written about her, all bear witness to the magnitude of her impact on Latin-American letters. A brief overview of *Sur,* the literary journal she founded, her ten volumes of *Testimonios,* and her six volumes of *Autobiografía* will demonstrate how far-reaching that impact was.[3]

The eldest of six daughters from a wealthy Argentine family, Ocampo discovered early the discrepancy between societal expectations for girls and for boys, regardless of class:

> Feminism was born in me when I was eight years old and I heard the nursemaids say to my male cousins: "If you cry, we're going to put skirts on you like a little girl. Men don't cry." This seemed intolerable to me . . . I knew very well that I had more endurance than those boys, that I did not cry when I was hurt . . . I wore skirts and I did not cry. . . .[4]

An extraordinarily intelligent woman, she could not be admitted to a university because she was female. Nor could she fulfill her ambition to be an actress because her parents believed that a decent young woman could not have a life on the stage (Christ, 9). Social restrictions increased as she matured. Close acquaintances with men, even efforts to converse in acceptable situations, were often thwarted:

> Sometimes . . . they carried me early from a dance because during two sets I passed the time talking, [while] sitting on a chair, with my partner [who was] sitting on another chair, in the middle of fifty spectators. My conduct was incorrect (*Autobiography* II, 33).

Ocampo contrasts her "privileged" status with the situation of the household servants, who, in her eyes, had much more freedom than she (*Autobiography* II, 14–16). She also criticizes the restrictive nature of a society that could cause her father to lament, "If only she had been a boy: she would have had a career" (*Autobiography* II, 16). In words reminiscent of Sylvia Plath, this dynamic woman describes the conditions of her youth, a time when she "lived placed inside a bell jar, deprived of all liberty which would permit someone an innocent camaraderie with young men of my age. I did not have the right to speak with whom I chose (nor anyone on the telephone), nor to write letters, nor to go out alone or with my sister or go for a walk with some girlfriend" (*Autobiography* III, 55). Argentine men she saw as ". . . those primitive, authoritarian, proud men, 'masters' of woman, [who] generally divided our sex into two categories: respectable women, mothers, wives, sisters, etc., and women who had no reason for respect, made for sex without consequences, adulteresses, crazy virgins, and simply prostitutes" (*Autobiography* III, 60). In 1912 the prevailing social norms pushed her into an undesirable match with an extreme example of Argentine manhood as she described it. The possessiveness of her husband, Luis Bernardo de Estrada, extended to threats to lock her in the house and to tell her father that she approved of adultery (*Autobiography* III, 26). Ten years later the couple, prevented by Argentine law from obtaining a divorce, legally separated (Meyer, *Against*, 42–4). The experience made Ocampo an ardent supporter of divorce, which she considered a "necessary evil,"[5] but one needed "to prevent greater evils."[6] As a result of the severe social taboos and restrictions Argentine women of her class had to endure, Ocampo acknowledges she became a "feminist since I had *l'âge de raison*" (Christ,

10). Refusing to downplay the situation in any way, Ocampo discusses it openly in all her work. While other young Argentine women, similarly restricted, escaped into the wish fulfillment of romantic novels, Ocampo rejected any identification with the heroines of the "novela rosa." Instead, she aligned herself with fictional characters like Napoleon's doomed son, the Duke of Reichstadt in Rostand's *L'Aiglon*, made famous by Sarah Bernhardt in 1900, of whom she says:

> I immediately recognized myself in the hero. Why? . . . that sick boy . . . was as much a prisoner at Schoenbrunn as I was in the house on Florida and Viamonte . . . He could not go out riding without "the sweet honor of an invisible escort." His mail was censored. He was allowed to read only those books that had been chosen for him ("El aguilucho," *Testimonios* VIII, 100).

Given this circumstance, writing became Ocampo's outlet for her frustrations.[7] In 1925 the newspaper *La Nación* published one of her articles, a significant achievement for a woman. Ocampo basked in the glory of accomplishing so worthwhile a goal, while her family worried lest she be negatively criticized (*Autobiography* III, 105).

Once freed from marital ties, Ocampo embarked upon an extended campaign to educate herself, a quest that brought her into contact with many of the best-known European and North American writers. In 1929, her American friend, Waldo Frank, suggested that she create a literary magazine. Her conversations with Frank about the focus of the prospective journal are detailed in her article, "A Letter to Waldo Frank," which appeared in the first issue of *Sur*, as the journal was named by Spaniard José Ortega y Gasset. Ocampo, the sole financial backer of *Sur* for over forty years, envisioned her journal to be international, which brought her the charge of "Europeanizing" Argentina and of attempting to deny her own culture (Adam, 135).[8] Ocampo consistently denied these allegations and insisted that she only wanted to bring France, Italy, England, the United States, and India to Argentina, and, in turn, to send Argentina to all those places (Christ, 11). She described herself as a "universalist, many-sided, many-voiced . . . But . . . also Argentine, a resident of Buenos Aires, Creole, just as much as the bread and the horses which likewise have this name" (Torres Fierro, 20). Jorge Luis Borges agreed. "She was accused of being an Anglophile and a Francophile," he said, "as if the fact of loving something were a crime. She was a hedonistic reader; she read Shakespeare or Dante with the same curiosity with which she read Valéry or Virginia Woolf."[9]

Ocampo was the product of her upper-class upbringing and her ambivalences in this regard affected both her personal and her professional attitudes. She devotes considerable space in volume one of her autobiography, for example, to her ancestors, including her Guaraní Indian grandmother, and, in so doing, seems to waver between affirming her aristocratic links while simultaneously rejecting them. Ambivalent about what constitutes "correctness" in her class, she blames herself for her lack of assertiveness in yielding to paternal opposition, that is, in neither making the theatre a career, nor ending her unhappy marriage to live with the man she loved (*Autobiography* II, 175).[10] The same ambivalence occasions her hesitation about her literary competence, a hesitation with which critics have been uncomfortable. To quote Sylvia Molloy: "It certainly accounts for the way she is so often perceived by the least kind of her critics: as a rich woman, at once fascinating and exasperating, who writes" (71). As recently as 1984, Marta Traba, a fellow Argentine and feminist literary pioneer in her own right, would scoffingly assert: "I am not an admirer of Ocampo; her literary reverences do not interest me very much and her aristocracy, still less."[11] What Ocampo wrote, however, given her time and social position, was undeniably daring. In 1937, responding to José Bergamín's published letter chiding her for not showing sufficient compassion for the Spanish Civil War, Ocampo reminded him that a still greater evil than the civil war was the continued exploitation of women.[12] In 1952, she told Ernesto Sábato that "the real proletariat of the world was that of woman, without distinction of class . . ."[13] She speaks with incredible openness in her autobiography about two of her alleged lovers, Julián Martínez and Drieu La Rochelle, and the affair with Martínez is narrated, in the words of Sylvia Molloy, "with a mixture of passion and directness rare in Spanish American autobiography, male or female" (Molloy, 65). Her opinions about the Catholic Church are unusual and outspoken. As early as 1908, she began to dissociate herself from traditional religion. Her husband's possessiveness and its attendant misery made her question the church's authority, especially where divorce was concerned: "That religion, with its dogmas, as it had been taught to me, was repugnant" (*Autobiography*, III, 55).

She was equally daring politically. Although she officially maintained that *Sur* was apolitical, in practice this was far from the case.[14] During the Spanish Civil War, for example, articles championing the republican cause appeared. Pieces favoring the Allies were published during World War II. The journal's silence about conditions in Argentina during the Perón regime was in itself a political statement.[15] *Sur* did not publish an obituary to mark Eva Perón's death, merely marking the event by placing the governmentally required black border on issues 213–214 (July–August 1952). Such an omission could hardly have escaped the notice of the government (King, "Precursor," 19). Articles published by *Sur* between 1946 and 1953 provide convincing evidence that Ocampo and her group definitely opposed the régime (King, "El peronismo," 36–38). The government never formally censored the material that appeared in *Sur*, but in 1953, at the age of sixty-three, Ocampo was inexplicably arrested by the Peronist government and detained for almost a month (Meyer, *Against*, 154–5). After Perón's downfall Ocampo dedicated a whole issue to national reconstruction.[16]

Ocampo's *Sur* is almost universally recognized as a forerunner of the literature of the eighties in its forthrightness and in its introduction of relatively unknown writers who would become internationally famous.[17] Antonin Artaud's innovative *Alchemical Theatre* (1932), for example, was translated into Spanish and first published in *Sur*. It would not appear in French until 1938 when Artaud's collection of theatre essays was published.[18] Other European writers, including D. H. Lawrence, Aldous Huxley, and Virginia Woolf, also appeared in Spanish translation in *Sur*, but equally important is the fact that many young Latin-American authors were published there: Silvina Ocampo, María Luisa Bombal, Elvira Orphée, Alicia Jurado, Olga Orozco, Octavio Paz, Alejandra Pizarnik, and José Donoso all received exposure through the pages of *Sur*.[19] Ocampo herself commented that *Sur* had recognized the greatness of Borges long before the rest of the world discovered him (Christ, 9; Bastos 2, 129). Though her penchant for favoring male authors over female writers in her literary discussions caused her to be criticized, Ocampo always insisted that her great desire was to "someday write, more or less well, but *like a woman*," for "a woman cannot unburden herself of her feelings and thoughts in a masculine style, any more than she can speak with a man's voice" ("Carta a Virginia Woolf"/"Letter to Virginia

Woolf," *Testimonios* I, 12). It is important to realize that "[w]hat might be judged Ocampo's weakness could well be, given her time and circumstance, proof of her resourcefulness. Lacking a voice of her own and a feminist system of representation, she repossesses voices of the male-authored canon . . . enunciating them from a feminine 'I' . . ." (Molloy, 75). In fact, Ocampo has been called a "chronicler of her times" because of her ten volumes of *Testimonios*.[20] Further, according to Zapata and Johnson, these *Testimonios* (which span forty years) "constitute the only comprehensive chronicle about the biggest figures of literature as a whole presented from the perspective of a woman."[21] Called "autobiographical memories," they discuss books, movies, art, friends, and nature and include transcripts of speeches, especially those concerned with feminist issues.[22] For example, her 1936 essay, "La mujer, sus derechos y responsabilidades" ("Woman, Her Rights and Her Responsibilities"), written when Ocampo was heavily involved in the Argentine Women's Union which she founded that year with María Rosa Oliver and Susana Larguía, discusses the inferior legal status of Argentine women. She employs terminology that anticipates that of the North American women's liberation movement of the 1970s: "I only wonder," Ocampo asks, "whether the word 'emancipation' is correct. Wouldn't it be more appropriate to say 'liberation'?"[23] She reprimands women for allowing their husbands to abuse them and condemns men who "enjoy allowing themselves to mistreat women" (quoted in Meyer, 228). Referring to the controversial bill before the Argentine legislature to deprive married women of the right to control their own money, Ocampo bitterly remarks: "It is incredible, and I speak now without irony, that millions of human beings have not yet understood that current demands made by women are simply limited to requiring that a man stop thinking of a woman as a colony for him to exploit and that she become instead 'the country in which he lives'" (229).

Anticipating the work of several writers in this book by almost twenty years, Ocampo explores the subjects of cruelty and torture in "The Man With the Whip." She describes scenes of governmental repression repeated almost verbatim in the works of younger women from the Southern Cone, Griselda Gambaro, Elvira Orphée, Marta Traba, Luisa Valenzuela, and Cristina Peri Rossi. Originally a speech delivered before the Women's Council in Buenos Aires on 9 November 1955, its dating is significant because

Ocampo had been jailed by the Perón regime only two years earlier,[24] and because it shows that the so-called excesses and transgressions of the Dirty War (1976–1979) were already endemic to Argentina. The speech, which begins with a reference to the day Ocampo, then a small child, saw a man cruelly beating a lame horse tied to a tree, focuses on human torture:

> . . . [T]he arrival of the two new victims of the dictatorship brought us more atrocious certainties than we had foreseen or desired. The two of them had been tortured with the famous electric needle. We only dared speak of that in whispers. A mixture of rebelliousness and terror, of pity for the victims and horror for the perpetrators, electrified the room they kept us locked in . . . As for me, it seemed that I trembled on my narrow iron bed with the same trembling as in my childhood when I had felt the brutality of the man with the whip as if he were beating me. Only now, I couldn't run to any guard or police chief, minister of justice or president of the nation. Now there existed no justice for those who thought freely or refused to adopt the dictator's doctrine (Meyer, 256).

Ocampo asks her audience to identify with those who shared the cell with the tortured victims and readily admits her constant fear of also being tortured (257).

In addition to anticipating Latin-American women writers who repudiate the totalitarian conditions of the 1970s, Ocampo shares with fellow Argentine Griselda Gambaro, Chilean Isabel Allende, Mexican writers Elena Garro, Rosario Castellanos, Elena Poniatowska, and Brazilian Nélida Piñón, the idea of female bonding across class lines.[25] Ahern, following Castellanos's self-indictment in "Herlinda Leaves" of the effects of such relationships on the humbler women, that is, their exploitation by their affluent sisters, calls the bonding between upper-class women and their female servants in Mexico "maternal colonialism" (50). Yet the depth and genuine intimacy of such relationships cannot be denied whether they are treated seriously, as in the writings of Ocampo, the Mexican writers and Brazilian Piñón, or humorously, as in Griselda Gambaro's *Lo impenetrable* (*The Impenetrable Madame X*). Ocampo's *Testimonios* feature famous personages, but few are more engaging than Fani, her maid. When Fani was hired by the Ocampo family, she was warned that she would not last long because "Miss Victoria" was hard to please. To the contrary, she stayed for forty-two years and, in Ocampo's words, "managed everything."[26] Ocampo's bonding with Fani is revealed through several anecdotes, including nights when the two women endured terrifying thunderstorms together. After Fani's death, Ocampo couched her final tribute to her in terms of the poignant friendship between the two best known and most beloved characters of Spanish literature, Don Quixote and Sancho Panza:

> Of the "give and take" there was between us, I thought that night, the *give* was hers and mine the *take*. I know of no "island" with which I could have shown her all that the "simplicity of her condition and the faithfulness of her service" meant to me, and what it deserved, unless it be this island of my heart (cited in Meyer, 208).

Ocampo's privileged position and considerable writing ability made opportunities possible for succeeding generations of Argentine women. She not only afforded young women writers a vehicle in *Sur* for making their talent known, but she also accepted whatever honors made women more visible. For example, she consented to be elected to the Argentine Academy of Letters because she concluded that her repeated refusal could prove detrimental to other women.[27] When David Rockefeller's wife told Ocampo that she was the tenth woman to receive an honorary doctorate from Harvard University, she was pleased because "this was a good sign for us women . . ." (Adam, 164). In the words of Celia Correas de Zapata, Ocampo's "well understood role as a precursor and a visionary in the field of letters and of feminism goes deep."[28] Determined not to succumb to repressive conventions, she spent her adult life fighting for what she called "justice," whether it involved driving a car, smoking a cigarette, wearing pants in public, or campaigning tirelessly for women's suffrage and the right to divorce. Ocampo opposed all kinds of oppression. No matter how unfair and cruel the criticism she received, she refused to be stifled or intimidated. Admirers deem Victoria Ocampo a "proto-feminist" (King, "Precursor," 22), "a valiant and strong woman who constructed her own destiny" (Vásquez,175). Her critics condemn her both for the privileged position into which she was born, and for rejecting that position, for daring "to break away from cultural provincialism and from the moralism and restrictions of her class" (King, "Precursor," 22). Nevertheless she was her own person and quintessentially Latin American. Her founding discourse, candidly expressed in 1975, anticipates a conviction possessed by many of the women discussed in this book. "When they try to close the mouth of a writer," she asserts, "a union between politics and culture is not possible" (Torres Fierro, 20). Luisa Valenzuela, Ocampo's younger compatriot, is but one woman who echoes this opinion. She speaks of the inseparability in the work of Latin-American women, "who are dealing more directly with political topics than their male colleagues," of politics and culture, of politics and literature.[29] "I think I have lived the experience of many Latin-American writers," Valenzuela notes, "in that you first start getting involved in politics without wanting to, because it is a matter of life and death, and little by little this involvement seeps indirectly into your literature."[30] This is the common experience of both the "rich woman," Victoria Ocampo, and of many of the women examined in this book, regardless of race or class.

CHAPTER 3

"Man's Love . . .
'Tis Woman's Whole Existence"

The early women writers discussed in this chapter, Venezuelan Teresa de la Parra, and the two Chileans, Marta Brunet and María Luisa Bombal, came from the upper middle class and were either well educated or traveled widely in Europe. Their texts describe the stultifying effects of their environment on women and the serious pitfalls of patterning themselves on the heroines of romance. Unlike the contemporary Costa Rican Carmen Naranjo, who hilariously parodies the romantic tradition in her short story *Ondina* (1983; see chapter four), these early writers instead emphasize the serious consequence of internalizing the romantic paradigm. Acutely aware of their society's oppressiveness, the protagonists of these earlier texts nevertheless remain passive and the authors remain ambivalent about the roles of their female characters. As a result, these works focus on coping mechanisms rather than on specific stratagies for change.

TERESA DE LA PARRA

Teresa de la Parra, a contemporary of Victoria Ocampo, was no less forceful than Ocampo, but unlike her, transmuted criticism of her misogynistic society into fiction rather than autobiographical memoirs or *testimonios*. Parra's *Ifigenia, diario de una señorita que escribió porque se fastidiaba* (1924; *Ifigenia, the Diary of a Young Lady Who Wrote Because She was Bored*) explores the perversions resulting from the gendered assignations of Venezuelan society. Her second novel, *Las memorias de Mamá Blanca* (1929; *Mama Blanca's Memoirs*), attempts an alternative.

Parra (Ana Teresa Parra Sanojo) was born in 1889 and died of tuberculosis at the age of forty-seven. Her two best known works, *Ifigenia* and *Mama Blanca's Memoirs,* both center on

23

issues of gender, race, and class. *Ifigenia* focuses on an immature young woman who, because of natural shyness and family pressures, surrenders to a destiny she abhors, marriage to a domineering pedant. Parra completed her second novel, *Mama Blanca's Memoirs*, in Vevey, Switzerland. The French version, *Mémoirs de Madame Blanche*, was issued in installments before the 1929 volume (translated by Francis de Miomandre), was published.[1] Miomandre would later translate the work of Lydia Cabrera, Parra's dearest friend and longtime companion. *Mama Blanca's Memoirs* is the tale of a grandmother who narrates recollections of her childhood, spent on a sugar plantation at Tazon, not far from Caracas, where Parra herself lived between the ages of two and ten. The plantation, called Piedra Azul, is described as a feminine herland. It is the bucolic home of six little girls who "formed a rising staircase stretching from seven months to seven years" (17), and of their charming twenty-four-year-old mother, fifteen years younger than their father, and whose soul "was the abode of the most delightful bad taste" (22). Also living here are Evelyn, their mulatto nanny from Trinidad, who has been hired to teach them English but instead learns a bad Spanish patois, and, finally, the foul-humored Candelaria, the cook, about whom the often-absent father frequently reiterates: "I don't care who leaves as long as it isn't Candelaria" (19). In this wonderfully unpredictable world of "pleasant and arbitrary laws" (17), referents become irrelevant: the darkest of the children is called "Snow White," the virile tomboy is nicknamed "Violeta," and the noble and loyal mulatto cochocho is dubbed "Cockroach Mustache." *Mama Blanca's Memoirs* traces the change from an agrarian feudal order to an emerging capitalist society. Parra underlines this evolution by juxtaposing, at the end of the novel, the pastoral Piedra Azul and the bustling Caracas where the children must go. There they encounter life's harsh realities, the first of which is death. Eight-year-old Aurora dies of whooping cough. They also confront discipline: "Deprived of freedoms and horizons" (105), they must now conform to the norms and discontents of civilization. They finally face the saddest truth of all—the irrevocability of change. When they return to their Eden, they find that the "bread, the fried chicken, the hard-boiled eggs [now] had the savor of sadness" (114).

Although Parra's vignettes in *Mama Blanca's Memoirs* are delightful and her characters memorable, the fact remains that the children's aristocratic herland can only be maintained at the expense of the colonial class system whereby characters like the noble emancipated slave, Vicente Cochocho, accept their inevitable destinies. Freed from slavery, Cochocho is nevertheless still black and poor in a racist and classist society.[2]

Parra also wrote short stories. The novel *Ifigenia*, written four years before *Mama Blanca's Memoirs*, is the elaborated version of a successful story previously submitted to the literary magazine, *La Lectura Semanal*, and Part II, chapter 7 of *Mama Blanca's Memoirs*, under the title "Mamá X", won a contest sponsored by the newspaper *El Luchador*.

Mama Blanca's Memoirs and *Ifigenia* are her best known works, but the latter, which won the "Grand Prix de Roman Américain Concours" in 1924, is the more interesting because of the controversy it elicited. Immediately labeled "revolutionary," it became the center of polemical discussions for and against its feminism. Today it is considered one of Latin America's early feminist works.[3] *Ifigenia* calls attention to its textuality from the outset. The central character, María Eugenia Alonso ("Ifigenia"), is dying of boredom in Caracas after returning from a four-month stay in Paris. She lives her life and structures her autobiography, the diary that forms the bulk of the novel, in terms of literary precedents. The first words of the novel, "A Long Letter Where Things Are Narrated," provide the title for Part I. Part II, in which the narrator/protagonist patterns her relationship with her lover after Shakespeare's *Romeo and Juliet*, is entitled "Juliet's Balcony." Part III, "Towards Aulis," anticipates part IV, "Ifigenia," in which María Eugenia identifies herself with Euripides' tragic heroine, the Greek princess Ifigenia whose father, Agamemnon, sacrificed her at Aulis for the benefit of the Greek army at the outset of the Trojan War.

María Eugenia encodes all her experiences in terms of romantic literature, judging her actions, for example, with references to her literary heroines. Deeming herself superior to them, she nevertheless tries to live her life through them.[4] When she writes to her lover, Gabriel Olmedo, she sees herself as the Biblical Shulamite of *The Song of Solomon*. Her meeting with Olmedo evokes the balcony scenes in Shakespeare's *Romeo and Juliet* and, alternatively, that of Rostand's Roxanne-Christian-Cyrano in *Cyrano de Bergerac*. She gauges her behavior according to fairytale *topoi*. When confident, María Eugenia compares herself to Charles Perrault's imaginary princesses; when she cannot cope, she becomes one of Perrault's imaginary shepherdesses. Moods are also patterned on literary precedents. She looks out of her window with the melancholy of "the Egyptian virgins in the temple of Isis" (260) and identifies her lover's voice with the "fatigued call of the spouse in the Canticle of Canticles" (255). The end of her love affair with Gabriel Olmedo is placed in the best tradition of romantic literature:

> This story of Gabriel and me is finished. It is a story . . . wherein lovers die as they always die in the ancient and sad stories of love . . . as Hero and Leander died, Hamlet and Ophelia, Tristan and Isolde, the lovers of Teruel, pale Werther, and . . . Romeo and Juliet (233).

Parra seems to distance herself from the heroine's romantic notions, calling into question the reliability of the narrator's perspective. María Eugenia writes to a friend, for example, that she cannot bear the provincialism in which she now lives after the sophisticated life of Europe. Yet the reader readily sees María Eugenia's own provincialism: it makes her awkward and flustered in the presence of sophisticated conversationalists like Mercedes Valdivieso. Her inability to communicate effectively causes her to lose her lover Gabriel Olmedo and to resign herself to a permanent relationship with Carlos Leal, a man she detests.[5]

Parra underlines the protagonist's adolescent narcissism, which results in exaggerated pronouncements. "All Paris" admired her beauty, intelligence, and charm (15–6). She utters naïve absolutes such as "Love does not exist" (205), and waxes eloquent about her wonderful relationship with her fiancé despite the fact that he has forbidden her to wear makeup, to have her hair cut, and even to see her beloved, sophisticated friend, Mercedes Valdivieso (Mora, 137). Parra unmasks her protagonist's affirmations of independence. María Eugenia will decry the restrictive life of a woman, claim that such "frivolities" as high heels and silk stockings do not interest her, and allege that she aspires "to be independent as a man" (69–70), yet she repudiates a feminist conference because of the women's appearance: they wear cotton stockings and unstylish shoes. She defies familial pressure, swears that she will not marry a man who is either her inferior or who tells her what to do, but she then brags that "my boyfriend and I get along wonderfully. I do everything to please him, and he, pleased, shows me his pleasure by sending me delicious perfumes . . ." (200). María Eugenia is well read and her love of reading is obvious, yet when Leal announces that women should be pious, not literate, she pretends to know little about literature. In fact, manipulation and deception seem to characterize her. A woman's power, she claims, is "that God has given us the intelligence to show the veracity of the lie" (200). Consequently, it is difficult, in the midst of so much deceit, to take seriously both María Eugenia's claim that she, like the tragic Greek heroine, Ifigenia, has been sacrificed, and that she has been forced to surrender to the sacred "Monster which is called Society, Family, Honor, Religion, Morality, Duty, Convention, Principles" (292).

Parra describes a repressive patriarchal society in *Ifigenia,* one where the protagonist's role models are indeed few. María Eugenia refuses to identify with her spinster aunt, Clara, and her grandmother tells her women are born to forgive and to sacrifice themselves. Her choice of lovers is also limited. Olmedo, an arrogant male chauvinist who has an unhappy but convenient marriage, is determined "to become someone" (231). Leal is so obnoxious that when the protagonist agrees to marry him, she openly assumes the role of the Euripidean heroine. The novel does, however, provide a contrast in the nonconventional and defiant character Mercedes, who refuses to remain trapped in an unhappy marriage and who cautions María Eugenia that societal conformity is merely another form of prostitution:

> Women who are very weak [and] sacrificing . . . know the [same] sufferings and disgust experienced by the women who sell themselves to the first passerby on the street, . . . but no one knows these things because they are hidden and kept quiet under the guise of convention and of laws (114).

But such positive role models as Mercedes are seen as outsiders. Mercedes does not fit into Venezuelan society and leaves for France after her divorce. Tío Pancho, who also warns María Eugenia against marrying Leal, is consistently tolerated as "different," as an outsider.

The message of this ambiguous novel is unclear. On the one hand, the reader witnesses the slow deterioration of a bright, charming, and unconventional young woman into a submissive, docile being who is painfully aware of the truth of Mercedes's equation of conformity with prostitution. "I am for sale," she says, "who will buy me?" (181). On the other hand, her submission elicits approval from everyone in the novel except Tío Pancho and Mercedes Valdivieso. Since Parra's authorial presence is nowhere made visible, and since Mercedes and Tío Pancho, the marginal characters who disapprove of María Eugenia's submission, are the ones most sympathetically depicted, the reader can become confused. Is María simply a weaker character than Mercedes and Tío Pancho? Does the author intend to make her appear histrionic when she equates her voluntary passivity with the sacrificial end imposed on the Greek Ifigenia? After all, Mercedes's invitation to join her in Paris does provide María Eugenia the option of leaving her provincial, stultifying environment.

Or is Parra criticizing the restrictiveness of a society that discourages serious pursuits for women? In a speech delivered at a conference in Colombia, she described *Ifigenia* as the "exposition of a typical case of our contemporary illness, that of Spanish American *Bovarisme* . . . the lack of new air in the environment."[6] She added that women need to be financially independent, that frivolity is "the real enemy of feminine virtue" and that it distracts a woman from study and a career (685). Parra, however, was always ambivalent about a woman's "proper role." Like Victoria Ocampo, she was the product of her upper-class background. Furthermore, she was deeply religious, having been educated in a convent school in Spain. Despite her comments, she made it clear that she admired female self-sacrifice. Rosario Hiriart's jarring assessment may nevertheless be correct: for Parra, Ifigenia represents "a type of modern woman whose renunciation is truly sublime, because to uphold a morality that one believes is unjust and to sacrifice one's life for an ideal that one does not hold is equivalent to being twice virtuous and seven times heroic" (Hiriart, 33–4). Parra herself once justified, without irony or disapproval, María Eugenia's possible reason for sacrificing herself, namely, "her future motherhood. And with this . . . the entire series of renunciations and sacrifices that across the centuries have always accompanied it . . . It is this that makes her succumb to the yoke of the . . . inferior man who dominates her in the absolute manner that is so typical of our countries."[7] Because of similar statements, and despite frequent disclaimers to the effect that "I made her opposite of myself," critics have repeatedly associated María Eugenia with Parra.[8] Perhaps Parra, like María Eugenia, found Venezuelan society stultifying and provincial. The fact is, however, that Parra's life choices were in stark contrast to those of her protagonist. She never married, was a well-known author, and enjoyed financial independence.

MARTA BRUNET

Like Teresa de la Parra, Marta Brunet Cásares is considered a Latin-American pioneer feminist writer. She focuses on the poor and middle classes in her exposé of the results of gendered expectations in Chilean culture: marital abuse, domestic neglect, the emphasis on women's beauty, and the consequent effects of these, loneliness, revenge, despair, murder, and anorexia.

Marta Brunet was the only child of Ambrosio Brunet and his Spanish wife, María Presentación Caraves de Cossió. Born in Chillán, Chile, on August 9, 1897, she spent most of her early childhood in the small town of Victoria where she developed an interest in the countryside, the people, their speech and habits. Since there was no school for girls in Victoria, Brunet was educated at home. In 1911 she and her parents traveled to Europe where they remained for several years. This trip brought Brunet into contact with authors who would later provide inspiration for her own texts. Her literary career continued after her return to Chile, with the publication of several poems and short stories in *La Discusión,* the local newspaper. A letter to Hernán Díaz Arrieta, who recognized her talent, made possible the publication of her first book, *Montaña adentro (Inside the Mountain).* In 1925, Brunet moved from Chillán to Santiago, where she worked on the editorial staffs of *La Nación* and *La Hora.* She was also a member of the editorial staff of *El Sur* in Concepción. Employed by the Zig-Zag publishing house, Brunet edited the magazine *Familia* from 1934–39. She began a political career in 1939, having been appointed Chilean consul in Buenos Aires. She was named third secretary for cultural affairs in the Chilean embassy to Argentina in 1948, where she was promoted to second secretary in 1950. Her diplomatic career ended temporarily in 1952 when the government of Carlos Ibañez asked her to resign. Despite loud cries of protest, she was not reappointed. From 1953–60 Brunet taught literature in the Department of Cultural Extension at the University of Chile. In 1962 she was named cultural attaché to the Chilean embassy in Rio de Janeiro, Brazil, and in 1963 in Montevideo,

Uruguay. She died of a cerebral hemorrhage in 1967 on her seventieth birthday while leading a session of the Uruguayan Academy of Letters. During her lifetime, Brunet published eight novels and more than sixty short stories, as well as several highly praised children's stories. She took an active role in the literary and civic world in which she moved, notably the Instituto de Periodistas; La Sociedad de Escritores de Chile; PEN Club; Zonta; Comité de Biblioteca del Instituto Chileno Norteamericano de Cultura; Amigos del Arte; Alianza de Intelectuales. She received many literary honors. In 1929, she was awarded first place in a short story contest sponsored by *El Mercurio* for "Tierra bravía" ("Wild Land"). In 1933 she won the Premio de la Sociedad de Escritores de Chile; in 1961, the Chilean Premio Nacional de Literatura; and in 1963, the *Atenea* Prize given by the University of Concepción for her 1943 novel, *Aguas abajo* (*Downstream*).[9]

Brunet's literary career can be divided into two parts. The first is characterized by *criollismo* or regionalism, the representation of life in the country as opposed to that of the city, the second by a focus on life in urban settings. Describing some of the poorest elements of Chilean society, her regional phase privileges female characters over male. Her first three novels, *Montaña adentro* (1923; *Inside the Mountain*), *Bestia dañina* (1925; *Treacherous Beast*), *María Rosa, flor del quillén* (1927; *María Rosa, Flower of the Quillén*), are set in the rural countryside of southern Chile, as is her trilogy of tales entitled *Aguas abajo* (1943; *Downstream*). The three stories included in *Downstream* focus on the male/female conflicts in a countryside setting seen from a woman's point of view. They subvert any romantic view of country folk as guileless or devoid of complex human passions. In "Piedra Callada" ("Silent Stone"), for example, the embittered Eufrasia, who has lost her daughter because of the brutality of the latter's husband, achieves ultimate power in a struggle with her son-in-law. In the contest over custody of the dead daughter's children, Eufrasia bides her time, engineers her son-in-law's "accidental" death, and at the end joyously exclaims, "I've won now and forever . . ." (100). In the short story "Downstream," which gives the book its name, complex emotions also poison familial relations. The author creates Harold Pinter-like vignettes dealing with incest and adultery: daughters imitate their mothers in becoming superfluous and younger half-sisters supplant older sisters in adulterous triangles. In the third story of the book, "Soledad de la sangre" ("Solitude of Blood"), the best known of Brunet's stories, an uneducated woman survives her dismal, lonely life in the isolated southern countryside by living with the memories of her once happy life as a single woman in the north. These memories are evoked by a record to which she listens to escape to a happy dream of the band she heard many years ago. Brunet's protagonist in "Solitude of Blood" endures her lonely existence only so long as she can dream. Her husband breaks the record player when (despite her desperate resistance since it is all she has) he insists on using it to entertain a guest. Wounded in the struggle, she must now decide whether to let herself die or continue to live. Dying, however, will also mean "Never more to remember . . . To die also meant giving up all that" (121). And so she decides to return home. Despite her lonely existence, living is better than not having memories of happier times. Brunet's work is similar to that of Parra, suggesting that dreams and memories are the only means by which the female protagonists can cope with their situations.[10] As little resistance as her texts seem to offer to the oppression of the female characters, in the absence of a "feminist system of representation" or of precedents for this type of criticism, Marta Brunet's dismal depictions of feminine subjugation, like those of Victoria Ocampo and of Teresa de la Parra, must be deemed extraordinarily daring.

Brunet turns to more urban settings in her later novels, *Humo hacía el sur* (1946; *Smoke Toward the South*), *La mámpara* (1946; *The Outer Door*), *María Nadie* (1957; *María Nobody*), and *Amasijo* (1962; *Lump of Dough*). Here she focuses on the subordination of middle-class women trapped in societal conventions. In the short story "Raíz del sueño" (1948; "Root of a Dream") the protagonist, Elena, learns that being a woman is not difficult provided one "learns to want nothing and to express no desire" (*Complete Works*). Brunet's young urban women become proficient in suppressing their needs in "Una mañana cualquiera" ("An Ordinary Morning"), and at becoming models of perfect obedience and self-abnegation in "Encrucijada de ausencias" ("A Crossroad of Absences"). In "La casa iluminada" ("The Illuminated House"), they learn to focus on external appearances. This motif is also found in "La niña que quiso ser estampa" ("The Child Who Wanted to Become a Picture"). Ten-year-old María Casilda, the central figure, is constantly complimented for her beauty. Led to believe that her beauty is her most important attribute, she patterns her life and gestures on the beautiful heroines of romantic novels as does Parra's María Eugenia. An eagerness to continue to be "pretty as a picture" eventually causes María Casilda to starve herself to death.

Societal expectations consistently stifle both Brunet's younger and older female protagonists. But, as Parra created Mercedes Valdivieso, Brunet also presents women who defy societal restrictions. Depicted as open-minded and self-determined, they must necessarily remain outsiders in their society.

Smoke Toward the South, considered by many to be Brunet's masterpiece, presents an array of female characters who cope as best they can within their societal restraints. They may become bitter and power-driven like the aggressive, domineering Batilde de la Riestra who, reflecting on the sweet person she once was, acknowledges that she is now "empty of all passion save that of power whose basis is money" (599). Or they may be helpless because of moral constraints, as is the case of Margarita who, pregnant with another man's child, dies. Afraid to confide in her husband, she is neglected by the midwife who fears the consequences of so "improper" a pregnancy. Her female characters may also be trapped by class constraints, as is the case of "La Moraima," the whorehouse madam, who was thrown out of her mistress's home at age seventeen because she had been seduced by the lord of the manor. The unremitting cycle of oppression is foregrounded in La Moraima's story. She sees the pregnancy resulting from the *patron's* seduction as "fulfilling her predictable destiny, as had her mother and her mother's mother and her remote ancestors, a submission that endures in the heart and makes one submit to the master . . ." (606). Some of Brunet's women figures are trapped by marriage itself. María Soledad is married to the womanizer Ernesto, who makes a distinction between his wife whom he "possesses chastely" and the women with whom he has "animal-like" adventures. María, dominated by her husband, compensates by lavishing all her love and attention on Solita, her young daughter. Solita's name, "the only one," is a felicitous word play for the loneliness (*soledad*) of her mother. "She alone" emerges to achieve a vital independence and is truly the loveliest of Brunet's protagonists, as she scoffingly pinpoints the hypocrisies she observes in the adult world. Solita is the protagonist of seven more stories entitled *Solita sola*. Free, loving, spontaneous, assertive, she is wholly herself. Brunet once said that, if asked to name her favorite character, she would unequivocally answer, "Solita" (170). Apart from the example of this child who is given immense freedom to be herself, however, Brunet's general tendency is to limit happiness for her women characters.

MARIA LUISA BOMBAL

María Luisa Bombal, unlike Marta Brunet, is not interested in the humble classes. Instead, Bombal represents the deep sense of alienation experienced by middle- and upper-class women, thereby validating Victoria Ocampo's position that "privileges of fortune do not change at all the injustices to which women [are] subjected."

Bombal, like Brunet, was Chilean. She was born 8 June 1910 at Viña del Mar. In 1922, she moved to Paris with her widowed mother. Educated at the Sorbonne, she became involved with the avant-garde movement in music, literature, and art, a movement that valorized experimental techniques, deliberate ambiguity, and the blurring of temporal and spatial categories. In 1931 Bombal returned to Chile and in 1933 became part of an Argentine literary group that included fellow Chilean Pablo Neruda as well as important Argentine figures such as Victoria Ocampo, Norah Lange, Silvina Ocampo, Jorge Luis Borges, Oliverio Girondo, Guillermo de Torres, and Pedro Henríquez Ureña.[11] Bombal's first work, *La última niebla* (1935; *The Final Mist*) was published in Victoria Ocampo's *Sur* and caused an immediate sensation because of its literary innovations. Bombal focused on the problems facing the contemporary Latin-American woman, much as Parra and Brunet had done. *The Final Mist, La amortajada* (1938; *The Shrouded Woman*), and her best known short stories, "Las islas nuevas" ("New Islands") and "El árbol" ("The Tree"), depict the deep dissatisfaction of middle- and upper-class Latin-American women. In 1940 Bombal settled with her second husband in the United States where she pursued an active literary career. She rewrote *The Final Mist* in English and sold the screenplay to Paramount Pictures, although the movie was never made. After her husband's death in 1970, she returned to Chile where she was honored for her literary achievements by the Academia Chilena de la Lengua in 1977. She died in Santiago on 6 May 1980.

Dream and reality, life and death, present and past are indistinguishable in Bombal's work. Her innovations in subject matter and technique firmly place her in the group that called itself the Generation of 1930 and that signalled the beginning of a new literary epoch in Latin-American literature. Her narrator-protagonists, primarily women, view the world through an alienated and often distorted perspective. In *The Final Mist,* the ambiguous atmosphere of "mist" makes it impossible to distinguish between the fantastic and the real. The story itself is quite simple. A man marries his cousin within a year of the death of his beloved first wife and tries to make her over into the image of the dead woman. The new wife, who remains nameless throughout the story, attempts to escape from the emptiness of her existence by conjuring up a lover. The reader of *The Final Mist* is consequently forced to piece together the inner world of the protagonist, a world which consists of psychological time, dreamlike impressions, and fantastic hallucinations.[12] The authorial position, as in Parra's *Ifigenia,* is unclear and ambivalent. Is the protagonist's alienation and suffering the result of restrictions imposed upon her by the patriarchal society within which she moves and which makes any liberating action difficult, if not impossible? Or is the protagonist's dissatisfaction in *The Final Mist* the result, instead, of her own inability or deliberate unwillingness to act? Her fantasy lover is her only reason for existing: "My lover is more to me than love—he is my reason for being, my yesterday, my today, my tomorrow" (37). Passive and inert, she waits ten years for something to happen: "I sense that within the next twenty-four hours some huge happiness will fall my way. I pass the day in a kind of exaltation, waiting" (20). The only real passion she seems to experience, apart from that one imagined night of love, is hatred for the defiant Regina, her brother-in-law's mistress who, like Mercedes in *Ifigenia,* has dared to act: to love and to suffer. The protagonist states: "And suddenly I feel hatred for Regina; feel envious of her suffering, her tragic love affair . . . she who has had everything!—love, the dizzying violence of passion, and the great deliverance that comes like a calm when the storm of sex has passed" (45).

   In similar fashion, the perspective of the protagonist of Bombal's novel *The Shrouded Woman,* is also distorted. She must die before she can realize, like T. S. Eliot's chorus in *Murder in the Cathedral,* that her life has amounted to simply "living and partly living." Bombal's technique in *The Shrouded Woman* was so innovative that Jorge Luis Borges tried to convince her it would fail.

Nevertheless, as he himself subsequently admitted, it works very well. From her casket, the dead Ana María evaluates her past, as all those whom she has loved and who have loved her pay their last respects before her burial. Among them is Ricardo, the love of her youth, with whom she had been happy, but who abandoned her in her pregnancy and subsequent miscarriage. She realizes now that he "had never remained entirely apart from her" (39). She sees Fernando, the confidant to whom she turned in her loneliness, whom she now admits "she despised . . . because he was unhappy" (94). Only in death does Ana María realize that she is the only woman her husband, Antonio, has ever loved. Seeing her surrounded with souvenirs of Ricardo, her first love, Antonio has protected himself from pain with a mask of indifference. Resenting this indifference, she responded when alive with a hatred, the intensity of which "she breathed, she slept, she laughed" (138). From the casket she views him, an old and pitiful man whose life she has ruined, and she silently cries: "I want to live! Give me back, oh give me back my hatred!" (141). She watches her unhappy brother Luis who chose the mediocrity of a "correct" wife in Luz-Margarita over the intense passion of Elena, whom he really loved. As the adulterous Regina in *The Final Mist* and the divorcée Mercedes in *Ifigenia*, Elena too, Ana María realizes, has flouted convention, convinced that "[t]he one really important thing is to save one's heart" (48). The shrouded woman realizes too late that Elena was correct, that "[t]he sin God punishes most sternly [is] the sin against life" (50).

Paying her respects to the dead is Sofía, the sophisticated wife of Ana María's first lover, considered superior to her in every way. Sofía, in fact, far from being superior to Ana María, felt so inadequate that she left Ricardo after only one year of marriage, determined she could never duplicate "the same disordered, unselfish love" Ana María and Ricardo had once enjoyed (152). As Ana María now observes her husband, children, lover, and friends from a "correct" perspective, she understands the complexities of love, of fear, of pain, in sum, the insecurity of being human, and asks, too late: "Must we die in order to know certain things?" (39). Like the nameless protagonist of *The Final Mist*, Ana María's life has been measured by tedium, by insignificant tasks: "To have to do her hair, to speak, to give orders, to smile" (133). As her spirit, separated from its lifeless body, floats freely towards its primordial union with nature, the reader becomes painfully aware that freedom for Ana María has been won only through death.

The theme of nature as the only place, besides death, where women can be "free" is recurrent in Bombal's narratives. In *The Tree* and *New Islands*, Bombal suggests that women are essentially able to intuit the mystery of nature as men cannot. The practical Luis of *The Tree* cannot understand why his wife, Brígida, leaves him as soon as the rubber tree, her only contact with nature, is cut down. The rational Juan Manuel of *New Islands* rejects the natural mystery Yolanda represents because he "feels incapable of soaring into the intricate galleries of nature in order to arrive at the mystery's origin" (111). In *The Braids*, the central character dies when the trees die because she is an integral part of nature, in close harmony with the "forest [which] had to die along with her and her hair, because they shared the same roots" (74). As we shall see, this identification of women with magic, the mysterious, and, above all, nature also pervades the novels of Bombal's fellow Chilean Isabel Allende in the 1980s and 1990s (chapter five).

La historia de María Griselda (1946; *The Story of María Griselda*), juxtaposes nature's simplicity with society's emphasis on the artificial, on its conception of female beauty. Bombal incorporated the novella, which originally appeared as an independent text in Victoria Ocampo's *Sur*, into a chapter of the English translation of *The Shrouded Woman* in 1948. Here María Griselda, the eponymous protagonist, appears only once, but she is vitally important to the lives of everyone in the family because of the havoc her beauty causes. Her husband, Alberto, becomes an alcoholic because he feels that he can never wholly possess her. Anita, her sister-in-law, suffers because her lover Rodolfo has fallen in love with María Griselda. Rodolfo, impervious to everything else, is obsessed with her beauty. Her other sister-in-law, Silvia, commits suicide because she is envious of Griselda's beauty and, further, is convinced that her husband Fred finds her less beautiful than Griselda. Finally, her brother-in-law Fred admits his fascination with her and yet must continue to live with himself after his wife Silvia's suicide. As Brunet's María Casilda starves herself to remain "pretty as a picture," so Bombal's María Griselda suffers from a "disease" ironically privileged both in society and in romantic literature: female beauty. After her sister-in-law's suicide, María Griselda confides to her mother-in-law that:

Ever since she was a small child she had had to suffer on account of her beauty. Her sister did not love her and her parents, as if to make up to her sister for all the beauty they had given her, had always kept for the other child all their affection, all their devotion (89).

The Story of María Griselda can be read either in terms of an anti-fairytale, a subversion of folklore in which the flawless beauty of the protagonist becomes a curse that is never lifted, or of women's integration with nature and subsequent alienation from the false norms of a restrictive society.[13] Either way, María Griselda finds peace only in returning to nature, where her innate beauty endears her to children, rivers, animals, and insects.

Men, unlike women, tend to dominate or destroy nature in Bombal's work. Portrayed as hunters, they seek to control, to kill the wildlife.[14] Men are recurrently associated with images of "hard, stony earth, cutting implements, cruel, shining knives."[15] They are portrayed as skeptical, repudiating any mystery, whether in nature or in women, which they cannot classify. María Griselda's husband, Alberto, wants to envelop her in "a tight net" of memory, and Juan Manuel of "New Islands" wants to classify the enigmatic Yolanda in precise categories.[16] To emphasize their relation to nature, these women are portrayed as misfits and recluses in a pragmatic, patriarchal world drained of mystery. The women In *The Final Mist* and in *The Shrouded Woman* seclude themselves in dream worlds or in memories of past happiness. In "The Tree," Brígida, resigned to a life that is "mediocre . . . and irremediable" (61), finds that only in the enclosure of her room has her "sadness vanished as if by an enchantment" (55). Yolanda, the misfit of "New Islands," secludes herself in her bathroom where she knows she will lose, for the second time, her chance at love and happiness.

Critics have noticed the "limbo" in which Bombal situates her female protagonists, a state that excludes them from historical reality and condemns them to "madness" and dreams.[17] The women are described as "retarded" ("The Tree"), "distracted" (*The Final Mist*), and "incomprehensible" ("New Islands" and *The Story of María Griselda*).[18] Silence seems to constitute their only liberating space, the need to love their only motivation, and resignation to societal norms (while dreaming of happiness) their existential condition.[19] With Byronic echoes of love as a woman's whole existence, this essentialist view of women is bemoaned by the shrouded woman. "Why, oh why, " she laments, "must a woman's *nature* be such that a man has always to be the pivot of her life?" (133; emphasis mine). Why have women no other option, she asks, but to "turn over and over in their heart some love sorrow while sitting in a neatly ordered house, facing an unfinished tapestry . . . ?" After her painful *anagnorisis*, the realization that her lover is a figment of her imagination, the nameless protagonist of *The Final Mist* also gives up. Unloved, she tries unsuccessfully to commit suicide. Deprived by her husband even of "the right to search for death," she resigns herself to following him "toward an infinity of insignificant tasks; toward a thousand trifling amusements; following him to live correctly—to cry from habit and smile out of duty; following him to die, one day, correctly" (47).

This emphasis on the futile, insignificant acts marking a woman's existence is ubiquitous in Bombal's work. The shrouded woman's life is framed in boredom, "to have to do her hair, to speak, to give orders, to smile" (133). The nameless protagonist of *The Final Mist* resigns herself "to cry from habit and smile out of duty" (47). The life of Anita in *The Story of María Griselda* becomes simply an "evasion . . . [a] losing of that real self [which] we cover up with an infinity of trifles having the appearance of essential things!" (93). The stultifying life led by these women finds expression in the pervasive theme of suicide. Both the nameless protagonist and Regina of *The Final Mist* try to kill themselves, as does Marta Brunet's central figure in *Solitude of Blood*. Bombal's Silvia in *The Story of María Griselda* and Brunet's anorexic María Casilda in *The Child Who Wanted to Become a Picture* actually succeed in their attempt. For Brunet and Bombal, their female characters appear to be happy only as children or as adolescents.[20]

Mexican Rosario Castellanos has criticized this stereotypical view of women's "essence," especially as Bombal depicts it. It is the same attitude Teresa de la Parra derogatorily termed "Spanish American *Bovarisme*."[21] Critics like Gabriela Mora, however, reject such interpretations and see, instead, the depiction of the very unhappiness of Bombal's female protagonists as an indication of the author's conscious repudiation of the essentialist view of women.[22] Nevertheless, in this regard, Bombal shows the ambivalence seen in Parra's *Ifigenia*. The female characters in both authors' work obviously suffer. But what is its cause? Is the suffering the result of their repressive patriarchal society or is it the result of the women's "natural" makeup which, as these authors see it, differs from men's and consequently alienates them? Marta Brunet thought that only children like Solita could be happy in so repressive a society but Bombal and Parra appear to internalize the *status quo.* Bombal once expressed the incredible conviction that "woman is feeling, is harmony," and that "love is the most important thing in the life of a woman." "Woman is pure heart," she said, "in contrast to man who is the grey matter and the initiator of all great undertakings."[23] Such a conviction is more dangerous than Parra's view that the desire for "motherhood" explains why women succumb to the domination of men. It is this essentialism that Rosario Castellanos criticized so strongly in Bombal's work.

In contrast with the writers who will be discussed in the succeeding pages, the feminist critique of women's oppression by the three pioneers examined in this chapter seems tame. Nevertheless it is important to remember that these works paved the way for the more radical and experimental feminist system of representation located in the texts of their literary successors. What Claudia Schaefer has said in another context applies here as well. The works of these women constitute "steps leading from images of geographical and psychological confinement to ones of rebellion . . . and freedom."[24]

CHAPTER 4

Arms and Letters: The Power of the Word

The women discussed in this chapter direct their attention less to male/female relations within patriarchal conventions and more to the difficulty of sustaining any personal relations in the circumstances of political oppression and/or societal hypocrisy. They explore other ways, proceeding from the descriptive level where force is countered with force, where power is simply transferred, to a normative level where love, compassion, and inclusiveness are the standard.

MARTA TRABA

Marta Traba, Latin America's most influential art historian and critic, was born on 25 January 1930 in Buenos Aires, Argentina. Traba received her bachelor's degree from the University of Buenos Aires in 1948, won a summer scholarship to study art in Chile, and studied art history at the Sorbonne and the Louvre. Firmly believing that Latin America had its own art heritage, which should be studied, cultivated, and appreciated, she worked tirelessly to establish a museum of modern art in Bogotá, Colombia, where she was professor of art at the university. Her dream was realized in 1962, and she was named the museum's first director. Her crusade for recognition of Latin-American art led to her appointment as director of cultural extension by the university in 1965. Traba was an outspoken critic of local and world politics. In 1967, she was ordered expelled from the country for denouncing the military invasion of the University of Bogotá. The outcry among intellectuals caused the government to rescind the order, but Traba was forced to relinquish her university appointment and to resign as director of the museum. Soon after marrying her second husband, Angel Rama, in 1969, she moved to Montevideo,

Uruguay. From that time on, the two became nomadic scholars. In 1970, Traba was a visiting professor in the Department of Hispanic Studies at the University of Puerto Rico. She was appointed professor of Latin-American art at the Instituto Pedagógico de Caracas in 1977. She lectured at several U.S. universities in 1979, and she and Rama settled in Washington, D.C. They were in constant demand as lecturers and conference speakers throughout the United States. Traba was the recipient of a Guggenheim Fellowship in 1968, and in 1983 she received two grants, one from the Organization of American States Museum of Modern Art and another from the National Endowment for the Humanities. The latter enabled her to finish a guidebook on twentieth-century Latin-American art.

Despite her fame, Traba was denied resident alien status in the United States in 1983 because she was considered "undesirable" on account of her political views. Traba, who admitted she believed in socialism but denied she advocated communism, refused to pursue the matter. She was offered Colombian citizenship by President Belisario Betancourt. In the last year of her life, Traba was living in Paris. En route to attend a conference in Colombia on 27 November 1983, she and her husband were killed in an airplane crash in Madrid, Spain.

Traba did much to popularize art and art history in Latin America. In the 1950s, television served as her medium to inform the people about their art heritage. She wrote many articles for newspapers and journals and lectured all over the world. Through her classes at the University of Bogotá, she trained a whole generation of artists. She founded a journal called *Prisma* in 1957. In 1966, she opened a bookstore that specialized in Latin-American literature. In that same year, she published seven books in various countries in a period of ten months. In all, she published twenty-three volumes on art criticism and more than twelve hundred journal and newspaper articles in fifteen countries. She opened her own art gallery in 1968.

While Traba acquired her reputation initially as an art historian and critic, she returned to writing literature in the sixties. She had already produced a volume of poetry entitled *Historia natural de la alegría* (1951; *A Natural History of Happiness*). Her first novel, *Las ceremonias del verano* (1966; *Summer Rites*), which won her the Casa de las Américas Fiction Award, features the summer experiences of a young woman in Buenos Aires, Paris,

Italy, and in some vaguely defined European city. The focus is on understanding the meaning of love and friendship. Encouraged by the success of her first novel, Traba published *Los laberintos insolados* (1967; *Sun-Drenched Labyrinths*) which explores the aimless wandering of her protagonist, Ulysses, as he searches for his identity. He returns home aware of the fact that his is "a tragedy devoid of a hero capable of representing it" (173) and that he is "a fragmented person who has been dismembered piece by piece" (170). *Pasó así* (1968; *It Happened Thus*) is a collection of sixteen short stories that deal with the dismal reality of urban life in a working-class Colombian neighborhood. One of these stories, "Los Perros" ("The Dogs") became well known and was reprinted in a volume entitled *Kinder* in Germany in 1981. Traba's themes in *La jugada del sexto día* (1969; *The Sixth-Day Game*), are similar to the work of earlier women writers in that they center on the emptiness of the lives of the upper-middle class in Latin America. This is especially true of her contemplated trilogy, of which her best-known work, *Conversación al sur* (1981; *Mothers and Shadows*), is the first. The posthumously published *En cualquier lugar* (1984; *In Any Place*) was intended as the second volume. It depicts the lives of a group of Latin-American exiles who relive their memories of Argentina.[1] The third novel, which Traba did not live to write, was to be called *Veinte años no es nada* (*Twenty Years Is Not Much*).[2]

Mothers and Shadows is narrated from a feminist perspective and has been described as a "tapestry of female voices."[3] It focuses on the effect of the repressive governments of Chile, Uruguay, and especially Argentina, on women as mothers and on the bonding resulting from such repression. The novel consists of a series of conversations between two women who have been "denied the certainty of death and the release of mourning" (Chevigny, 127). The horror of the military coup that led to Argentina's Dirty War (1976–1979), and the deep wounds that both of these occasioned in the Argentine psyche, serve as a crucial background for Traba's *Mothers and Shadows*. A brief overview of this period, therefore, is pertinent for comprehending the text.

The underlying pattern of struggle and antagonism in Argentina, which emerges violently in the late seventies and early eighties, was the subject of an essay by Domingo Faustino Sarmiento (1811–1888) as early as 1845. This former president of Argentina poignantly lamented in *Facundo* the infrastructure of the barbarism of his country and decried "the bloody struggle that tears our Argentine Republic to pieces."[4] During the Dirty War (1976–1979), some fifteen thousand citizens were "disappeared," tortured, and murdered, according to the Mothers of the Plaza de Mayo. In May 1976, the governor of Buenos Aires, General Iberico Saint Jean, stated quite clearly the goals of the Argentine military:

> First we will kill all the subversives, then we will kill their collaborators; . . . then . . . their sympathizers, then . . . those who remain indifferent; and finally we will kill the timid.[5]

In the midst of the torture, abductions and disappearances, those primarily responsible for bringing these horrors to the world's attention were the Madres de la Plaza de Mayo, who marched silently around the plaza. Perhaps safeguarded by the *marianismo* that supposedly renders Latin-American mothers invulnerable (cf. chapter one), the Madres contributed significantly to the downfall of the repressive Argentine government. They succeeded by pitting the theatricality of the oppressed against the theatricality of the oppressors. The official pomp and spectacle of the government's parades were matched by the weekly vigils of the mothers, holding up to the television cameras pictures of their disappeared loved ones. Like the televised drama of Tiananmen Square, the collapse of the Berlin Wall, the march on Washington by protestors during the Vietnam War, the Mothers too made their tragedy public and used the media to this end. In 1985 the Trial of the Century was held in Argentina, where the former commanders of the Dirty War were indicted and convicted of crimes against humanity. Five years later, however, Argentines were to see how easily dehumanization can be "forgiven." On December 29, 1990, President Carlos Menem set the criminals free "for the healing of Argentina," he claimed, and "for the rightful restoration of military prestige" (Feitlowitz, 1). A recent article by Paula L. Green on Argentine national elections, crucial to the same Peronist Carlos Menem who was intent on "reforming the constitution so he could run for another term," indicates the depth of the country's still festering wounds.[6] The 1993 report reviews incidents similar to the horrors common during the 1976–1979 period depicted in the work not only of Marta Traba, but also Griselda Gambaro, Luisa Valenzuela, Elvira Orphée, and Marta Lynch. For example, Green reports: "The journalist, Hernán López Echague, was beaten up and slashed with a razor on August 25, two days after the publication of his story that linked organized criminal gangs with high-ranking officials in the Peronist party. . . . He was told by his abductors that the next time he would be killed" (3). It is within this context, therefore, that the work of contemporary Argentine writers must be read.

The main character in *Mothers and Shadows*, Irene, is an Argentine writer who is not a political activist, although she is often jolted out of her complacency by disturbing self-imposed questions: "At what point did two deaths stop sounding [like] a lot, at what point did a hundred deaths stop sounding like a bloodbath? That's what disturbs me. Because once that point has been reached, the frontier between life and death no longer exists. The two things simply become interchangeable, identical" (29). But it is because of her son's political involvement in Salvador Allende's Chile (the novel takes place in 1973, the time of Chile's military coup), that she becomes conscious of the political repression in her own country. The other female character, twenty-eight-year-old Dolores, is a Uruguayan political activist whose husband, Enrique, has been killed by the police. She herself has been tortured and as a result has lost her unborn child. Through dialogue between the two women, and through the techniques of stream of consciousness and flashbacks, the reader learns of the experiences of two more women, Irene's college friend, Elena, and her daughter, Victoria. *Mothers and Shadows* charts both the denial and the gradual political awakening of Irene who initially insists "on believing, against all odds, in the fairytale world of wish fulfillment . . . [where] all that mattered was to stay inside the storybook with its fairy godmother and happy ending" (8–9). When Irene becomes one of the "madwomen" of the Plaza de Mayo, pleading for information about their children, she discovers that the oppression continues because others, like her, have tried to deny the horror of the political situation. No one wants to get involved. After the "madwomen's" demonstration, Irene returns alone to the Plaza de Mayo "to watch the rats slinking back once they'd sensed that danger was over. Now the whole square was full of rats loitering or scurrying around. More and more rats kept pouring in and out of the side streets" (92). Traba's visceral rage in the face of the actual situation in Argentina is quite different from the abstract existential nausea in vogue in literature some years before this novel appeared.[7] It also differs from her own protagonists' metaphysical aimlessness found in *Summer Rites* and in *Sun-Drenched Labyrinths*.[8] The younger women in *Mothers and Shadows* know that their position is a matter of life and death: "'And if we do come out of this alive,' I could hear Victoria saying in my ear, 'All that's left for us is despair, because in any case we'll be the losers. And that I know is something you've had to face'" (136).

An important theme in Traba's work is love—in all its forms. In *Sun-Drenched Labyrinths* she obliquely alludes to the incest of Ulysses and the child, Laura, who has replaced the "mother" Laura by becoming his wife. *Mothers and Shadows* emphasizes the deep bonding between women—one which can exist despite (or because of) an environment permeated with hatred and oppression. Traba describes the poignant friendship that develops between the older women, Elena and Irene, both of whom have children who are politically compromised. When Victoria, Elena's younger daughter, becomes one of the "disappeared," Irene realizes that "it was Elena, and not Victoria, that mattered to me. And the trouble is that Elena mattered to me because, in a sense, her situation mirrored my own, with a son of roughly the same age about to leave home for Chile . . ." (76). Such female bonding in *Mothers and Shadows* crosses class and generation. The graduate student Dolores, who is married, admires the beauty and elegance of the professional woman, Irene, for whom she experiences a homoerotic love while simultaneously acknowledging that she has also "fallen under [the younger] Victoria's spell" (118). Traba eschews all polarities in love. She allows Dolores the reflexivity that the serious issue of single-sex bonding warrants. Dolores loves her husband *and* her female friends. She depends on women for comfort, solace, and for a love as passionate as the one she feels for her husband, Enrique. She asks herself: "If she loved Enrique, how could she have fallen head-over-heels in love with Irene? Why was it that she couldn't bear to be parted from certain female friends, when she couldn't live without Enrique either?" (140). The nature of her love for women is not masked: "And when I think now of the passionate response she produced in me the first time we met, I can feel my cheeks burning with the same fire" (139). These honest, direct acknowledgments of bonding between women produce some of the most poignant moments in *Mothers and Shadows*. They provide the awareness, in Adrienne Rich's terms, that what has been defined as lesbian existence must be rethought as a "lesbian continuum." Within this continuum, female friendships need not be set apart from the erotic. Borrowing from Audre Lorde, and without denying the relationship of single-sex love to the physical, Rich refuses to confine it to the body, relating it, instead, "to an energy present in the sharing of joy, whether physical, emotional, psychic among women" (193). It is this sharing of joy and suffering, this "sensitive development of a sympathetic and symbiotic relationship between two protagonists whose story does not depend on their relationships with men which makes *Mothers and Shadows* a unique contribution to Latin-American literature" (Picon Garfield, *Women's Fiction*, 214).

MARTA LYNCH

The main themes in the works of the author known to the public as Marta Lynch are the debilitating effects on women of a hierarchical society in which the private sphere reflects the political barbarism of a country that formerly prided itself on its sophistication and openness. Lynch, whose real name was Marta Lía Frigerio, was born in Buenos Aires, Argentina, in 1925. She committed suicide in 1985, at the height of her career. Her thirteen novels and collections of short stories have been translated into Portuguese, French, German, Croatian, Russian, Swedish, Italian, English, and Norwegian.

Political and social views run through all her works, and they are the specific focus of her first novel, *La alfombra roja* (1962; *The Red Carpet*) which won the Fabril prize; of *Al vencedor* (1965; *To the Victor*); *El cruce del río* (1972; *Crossing the River*); and of *Un árbol lleno de manzanas* [1974; *A Tree Full of Apples*). All these novels anticipate the full-fledged violence that became an integral part of Argentine life in the late 70s. Lynch's concerns are fully developed in her novel *Informe bajo llave* (1983; *Report under Lock and Key*), where they have been incarnated in the person of the *caudillo* [the leader] Vargas and his entourage. In her short stories and novels, *Los años de fuego* (1980; *The Years of Fire*); *Los cuentos de colores* (1971; *Colorful Stories*); *Los cuentos tristes* (1967; *Sad Tales*), which won her the Primer Premio Municipal de Prosa; *La Señora Ordoñez* (1967; *Señora Ordoñez*), *La penúltima versión de la Colorada Villanueva* (1978; *Colorada Villanueva's Penultimate Version*); *Los dedos de la mano* (1976; *The Fingers of the Hand*), *Report Under Lock and Key*; and her last work, *No te duermas, no me dejes* (1985; *Don't Go to Sleep, Don't Leave Me*), she studies the relations between the sexes, exploring the themes of sexual obsession and/or the inability of her characters to love. This emphasis can best be appreciated in two of Lynch's best known works: *Señora Ordoñez* and *Colorada Villanueva's Penultimate Version*.

Señora Ordoñez was extremely well received in Argentina. Five editions were published in the first year and the novel was edited for television in 1984. The action is circular, ending as it begins, with Sra. Ordoñez's depiction of the "idiotic pantomime" of sex with her husband, or, in her words, "coitus through habit" (13–15). During this interminable sexual ritual, Sra. Ordoñez experiences feelings of "repulsion," "disgust," and "inner rebellion." The novel develops by means of flashbacks whereby the protagonist juxtaposes her repressed life as Blanca Maggi, the lower middle-class daughter of an authoritarian father for whom "his daughters' hymens were sacred and . . . [his wife's] he could vouch for . . ." (164), with her stifling life as the upper middle-class Sra. Ordoñez. From "a damn childhood, a damn father, a damn everything" (89) she sees herself going through an equally empty and meaningless existence. The protagonist's sense of futility and frustration embraces a much larger context, that of a deteriorating Argentina. The personal and the political levels become intertwined. By means of her angry acts, Sra. Ordoñez feels herself "avenged of Antonio [her lover] . . . and of a rotten society against which I rebel" (303). Lynch uses two techniques to show both the schizophrenia of her protagonist and of her country. The mirror becomes a recurrent image through which she reveals her character's distorted perspective to the reader, while the narrative itself reflects another level of schizophrenia. Half of the chapters are narrated by the self-centered protagonist whose views of the private and the political differ from the third person account that completes the story. In her bourgeois and boring life with her present husband, whose lucrative urology practice derives from "the august hemorrhoids" of the patients upon whom he operates, Sra. Ordoñez nostalgically remembers her equally sexless life with her late husband. But with him, at least, she had shared the "patriotic" and passionate allegiance to "racism, hatred of Jews, and fervent nationalism," which gave her life meaning (121). Now without a cause and obsessed with aging, she envies everyone, including her young daughter. This obsession, her schizophrenia and Argentina's, are suggested effectively through the mirrors in which Sra. Ordoñez charts her daily deterioration. The novel ends as the protagonist settles once again for the interminable boredom of the sexual ritual with which it began. The circularity effects the same malaise in the reader as does the ending of Bombal's *The Final Mist*. Sra. Ordoñez, like Bombal's unnamed protagonist, resigns herself to the tedium of insignificant tasks in her privileged existence.

There is, however, a disquieting autobiographical element in *Señora Ordoñez*. Lynch herself was as obsessed with aging as was Señora Ordoñez and lied frequently about her age. When *The Red Carpet* was published, for example, she claimed to be twenty-nine, although she was actually thirty-seven (Marting, 292). It also carries a tragic postscript: Lynch's husband commented that during the last eight years of her life, she often spoke of committing suicide. She finally did so rather than allow herself to become old (Marting, 296).

Colorada, the protagonist of Lynch's novel, *Colorada Villanueva's Penultimate Version*, possesses several of Sra. Ordoñez's traits. She is affluent and has two daughers and a son. It is Fernando, her husband, however—and not Colorada—who is here obsessed with growing old. The narrator says that any mention of "his children's ages was taboo" (74), and that the presence of his grandchild filled him with anguish: "In Fernando's eyes, as he watched the child, there was no pride, no awe, just desolation" (76). Everyone has a different view of Fernando. The reader is told he has left Argentina for political reasons, yet his daughter Agata claims he has simply taken the easy way out. His other daughter, Dolores, tries to tell her mother that Fernando is weak, lazy, and immature. Colorada's sister calls him "effeminate" and "a damn womanizer" (342). But Colorada idealizes her husband. At times, however, she admits to another "reality," sometimes fantasizing him as a "camouflaged homosexual" who disguises his real preferences by being promiscuous with women (321), while at other times imagining herself castrating him (186), or even killing him by plunging her scissors into his carotid (186–7). Themes treated in *Señora Ordoñez*, namely, the relationship between the political and the personal in the characters' lives, and that between mothers and daughters are explored here, but in a more sophisticated and detailed manner. The increased climate of fear in Argentina, where no one feels safe, is reflected in the absence of all syntactical connections between parts in Lynch's descriptions:

> Negro Jew communist homosexual Jesuit historian poet. All in a bag with a large cross facilitating their identification. Bags filled with Argentines, former Argentines, we Argentines, Argentine abortions. How can one destroy with such perfection? (102).

Lynch graphically depicts the effect of this reality on individual lives. Colorada's family eventually flees from Argentina because of the political situation. Her brother-in-law is killed "for being decent" (346–47), and her children's fellow students are being tortured and killed. At the end of the novel, Colorada is left completely alone. She refuses her husband's final written gesture of reconciliation, makes a paper boat out of his letter, and watches it glide away from her in the gutter "without giving the incident a second thought" (364). The narrator reminds the reader of her abysmal condition at the end of the text: "She will learn to drink her coffee in bars and will surely know, before long, the names of those who, like her, have their breakfast alone. She has received a letter from the faithful Dolores. Felipe is extremely irregular in his correspondence. Agata has never again called her. She has three children (one by Telephone whose existence is doubtful, two by Correspondence). Her husband has not felt the need to telephone her again" (357).

The relationship between mothers and daughters and the protagonist's condition at the novel's end are treated differently. Unlike Sra. Ordoñez, Colorada does not envy her beautiful young daughter. Her relationship with her daughter Dolores, who admires and loves her mother deeply, is beautifully described. As the two embrace, the narrator comments, "A bond unites them once more, a little dirtier perhaps, a little worn out, but so strong that, for a moment, it took their breath away" (266). The second point of difference is the protagonist's psychological state. In both novels the women realize the emptiness of their lives. But whereas Sra. Ordoñez resigns herself to a life of boredom and empty ritual, Colorada refuses her husband's offer of reconciliation, which promises a similar existence. The solitary life she chooses is preferable to that she has experienced during her marriage and that to which Sra. Ordoñez acquiesces. Nevertheless, the end of *Colorada's Penultimate Version* is disconcerting. The reader cannot help but refer to this novel when considering Lynch's suicide in

1985. Shortly before her death, Lynch finished *No te Duermas, no me dejes* (*Don't Go To Sleep, Don't Leave Me*) This novel brings to mind Alfonsina Storni, the Argentine writer whom Lynch admired and who committed suicide on 25 October 1938. Shortly before her death, Storni sent a poem entitled "Voy a dormir" ("I'm Going to Sleep") to the newspaper *La Nación.*[9] Peace and calm pervade Storni's poem as they do the fictional Colorada's soporific state at the end of the novel. It is difficult to ascertain, as Colorada lies on her bed, whether hope or the calm of death is to be found in the final lines. As she becomes increasingly relaxed, she vaguely remembers "something she's lost. But, for now, at least, her body felt good under the sheets" (365).

GRISELDA GAMBARO

While Marta Lynch's character limited herself to speaking about the "rotten society against which I rebel" (303), Griselda Gambaro's characters go to great lengths to show exactly how rotten that society actually is. Gambaro was born in Buenos Aires, Argentina in 1928. Her original career was in business. Largely self-educated, she is one of the best known playwrights in Latin America today. Her theatre relies heavily on ritual, producing real effects by means of symbolic gestures. Gambaro did not begin her literary career in theatre, but, rather, with the publication of novellas and short stories. In 1963 she received an award from the Fondo Nacional de Las Artes, which allowed her to publish her first collection of three novellas, *Madrigal en ciudad* (*Urban Madrigal*). The following year she received the Emecé Publisher's Prize for a collection of short stories and novellas entitled *El desatino* (*The Blunder*). Her novel *Una felicidad con menos pena* (1968; *Happiness with Less Suffering*) explores the same themes found in her dramatic works, cruelty and the lack of feeling in a world where human beings are expendable. Gambaro's most explicitly brutal novel, censored in Argentina the year it was published, is *Ganarse la muerte* (1976; *To Gain Death*). It is an unrelieved portrayal of a cruel world in which everyone is victimized.

The bitterness begins in the preface where Gambaro speaks of the world as divided naturally between victims and victimizers. Both "are born together," Gambaro says, "cry at the same time," and the only option, "to gain . . . death," for life is unbearable. *To*

Gain Death constitutes a mimetic representation of brutality and repression, of political savagery displaced onto the private lives of families. The novel is so bitter that its horror often results in a reification of characters reminiscent of the Grand Guignol tradition. Fifteen-year-old Cledy is raped and molested by women and sexually harassed by men in the charitable institution where she has been placed. She is "saved" by marrying Horacio Perigorde and living with his parents in an environment of horror, cruelty, and Harold Pinter-like deformation of all conventional expectations. Mr. Perigorde, Horacio's father, makes Cledy his sexual slave. Mrs. Perigorde, who resents her son's love for Cledy, welcomes her aging husband's sexual interest in his daughter-in-law and helps him confirm his virility. It is Cledy's "passivity" which is made to account for Mr. Perigorde's sexual "failures." Horacio, the son, in order to please his mother, forces his wife to pay more attention to his increasingly impotent father who, in turn, beats her mercilessly. By sleeping with Horacio, the old man claims, Cledy "cheats on him with his own son" (120). Cledy's two children also suffer from the horror of this environment. The little girl Alicia is discovered "with circular bruises on her arms and legs and her abdomen" (165). Arturo, the baby, is given a handful of sweets. As he eats the sweets, he is gleefully watched by his grandparents and his father "with the hope that he'd choke and the event would entertain them a bit" (138). Some respite from this cycle of unmitigated cruelty is made possible for Cledy when, in place of the frustrated "Mr. Perigorde [who] tied her to the foot of the bed and broke her arm" (173), she can occasionally sleep with her husband. The respite is shortlived: one day she finds her two children dead on the table. Someone has cut off their ears and put them in an envelope so the flies will not be able to get to them. No emotional reaction is registered, only the depiction of tension unresolved. Horacio becomes progressively ill-humored, "making love dressed . . . because he always fulfilled his obligations" (186). When he returns home one day, finding dinner is not ready, and smelling something burning on the stove, he kills Cledy. The novel ends as the neighborhood children chant: "The idiot is dead! The idiot is dead!" (191), and as someone remembers a refrain relevant to the condition of Cledy's body: "The illustrious corpse finally lies there with her legs together" (193).

Gambaro's 1979 novel, *Dios no nos quiere contentos* (1979; *God Does Not Want Us to Be Happy*), uses the circus as a cruel society in microcosm, but, unlike *To Gain Death*, love, hope, and friendship are now integral to Gambaro's scheme. Three characters stand out in the novel: a mute orphan boy, Tristan, whose dream is to be able to sing; La Ecuyère, the young trapeze artist who is exploited and abandoned not only by the circus owners for whom she works but also by a would-be lover who ties her up and robs her; and a lost child who is accidentally separated from his mother. Genuine camaraderie exists among the three, for, as the narrator explains, "No other destiny unites better than a shared expulsion from the same paradise: solitude fractured" (126). Tristan, the lost child, and La Ecuyère are portrayed as a triad of misfits attempting to survive in a world bent on exploiting and humiliating them, a world "which changes truth for the lie" (250). But the despair visible in Gambaro's other works is missing here. La Ecuyère accepts the fact that unhappiness is a part of life, that "God hates happiness because he is made in our image and likeness, and he does not wish us to be happy" (250). Yet, like Albert Camus's Sisyphe, who continues to push the boulder up the hill knowing it will roll down immediately, La Ecuyère is defiant to the very end. As she lifts the mute Tristan into the air, he emits a pitiful sound, finally realizing his fondest dream, the ability to sing. La Ecuyère has literally risen above her abusive, hypocritical, and exploitative world and, Gambaro says: "La Ecuyère was happy" (254).

Clearly, Gambaro is not an easy or pleasant author to read. She herself admits the pessimism of her novels but insists that they are meant to shock, to provoke readers into asking "Why?" when they have finished reading.[10] It is, however, for the dramatized versions of her novels, *The Blunder*, for example, and for her plays, that Gambaro is best known. *The Blunder* was awarded the prize of the Revista Teatro XX. *Las paredes* (1964; *The Walls*) won the Premio de La Asociación de Teatros and the Premio del Fondo Nacional de Las Artes. Her most famous play, *El campo* (1968; *The Camp*), set in Europe during the Holocaust, won her five first prizes: the Municipality of Buenos Aires, the Talia Magazine contest, the Theatrical Broadcast News, the Municipal Radio of Buenos Aires, and the Argentores Prize of the Society of Argentinian Authors. In *The Walls*, *The Blunder*, and *Los siameses*, (1957; *The Siamese Twins*), the characters' freedom is curbed either by mysterious authorities (*The Walls*), by physical obstacles such as the iron clamp (*The Blunder*), or by nature (*The Siamese*

Twins), where the twins are psychologically bound to each other. In these three, and in *La malasangre* (1984; *Bitter Blood*), Gambaro focuses on the external strategies a society uses to dominate and control its victims, and on the internal strategies to which the victims resort while collaborating in their own victimization.

Bitter Blood, whose setting is 1840, depicts a set of relationships whose domestic rituals reflect the cruelty of a totalitarian and patriarchal society at large. Gambaro offers no solution, no analysis, no options. Instead, the text simply displays the social dramas that sustain and give structure to the roles of Perpetrator, Victim, and Bystander in her society or *any* society.

The tyrannical father, ironically named Benigno, dominates his wife, his daughter Dolores, and Raphael, who is his daughter's hunchback tutor and lover. When Dolores attempts for the first time to resist and escape from her oppressive father, her effort leads to Raphael's death. Again, Gambaro creates a Pinter-like ambience of sadism and masochism within the group. Benigno, the sadistic father, takes delight in tormenting and manipulating Raphael, whose hunchback becomes a fetishistic object of derisive pleasure. He insists that Raphael take off his shirt so he can look at his deformity because "I've never seen one before" (Picon Garfield, *Women's Fiction*, 117). Gambaro nevertheless shows how complicated is the interplay of such agonistic symmetries as Persecutor/Victim, and Sadist/Masochist. Dolores and Raphael are victims of Benigno's cruelty, but each in turn is also a victimizer. Rituals are foregrounded by which they play into his much more dangerous game in order to avoid pain for themselves. Raphael strikes Dolores because she, like her father, taunts him about his hunchback, and she, in turn, cajoles her father into punishing him. The perverse cycle of ridicule and violence now results in Raphael's hump being imbued with metonymic power, as it is accorded object status separate from his totality through voyeuristic/erotic gazes, perverse touches, and the butler's sadistic mutilation of it during the brutal beating he administers. Gambaro is especially concerned with the passivity of victims. She suggests that, in order to survive, victims eroticize their experience through a masochism whose essence lies in the pleasure the victims take in anticipation of delayed gratification. In this instance, such masochism is exemplified in the destitute Raphael who must await pleasure as something bound to be late and who expects pain as the necessary condition to ensure future pleasure with Dolores.[11]

Because he is needy, Raphael stays in the household and unwittingly coopts the sadistic Benigno through a mediated masochism—his love/hate obsession for Dolores. This obsession is much more dangerous than Benigno's sadism, for it actually empowers Benigno, and objectifies Raphael into a thing of derision. In rapid succession, he is forced to be present at the betrothal of Dolores to a man who despises all "cripples . . . [since] any physical defect makes [him] cringe" (138), forced to dance with the valet who persecutes him, and beaten to death at Benigno's orders. The audience of *Bitter Blood* becomes uncomfortably aware of the rituals that constitute the play's dramatic crisis as persecutors are validated in their actions by victims who are unwittingly complicitous in their own victimization. The same vicious cycle is reflected in the relationship among Dolores's mother, Dolores, and the tyrannical Benigno. Like her father, Dolores victimizes her mother, and the mother in turn becomes her daughter's victimizer. In order to please him, she reveals to her husband that Dolores and Raphael plan to run away together. This betrayal results in Raphael's murder and Dolores's subsequent repudiation of both parents. As Dolores, bereft of lover, of father, of mother, is dragged off the stage, she screams: "No one gives me orders anymore! Now there's nothing to be afraid of! I'm not scared anymore! I'm free!" (157). Her desperate freedom alters the object formations and subject positionalities of the play. The enraged father, defied for the first time, is shaken, and this effects a change in the play's fixed structure of domination. Deprived of lover and of speech by her father, Procne-like Dolores defiantly positions herself as subject. She screams: "Silence cries out! I'll be quiet, but silence cries out!" (157).

While *Bitter Blood* examines the mechanisms of domestic violence in a society in which repression and totalitarianism are the norm, Gambaro's 1967 play, *The Camp*, becomes the microcosm of that very society. The audience is immediately struck by the absolute cleanliness of the camp, manifested by means of "a room with shiny white walls," and "well scrubbed music."[12] The three main characters are Frank, Martin, and Emma.[13] Frank, obviously the power behind the camp's operation, is "impeccably dressed" (68), his manners also impeccably correct. He does not allow the new accountant, Martin, to chew gum; nor does he permit Emma, the inmate, to act in a manner which is "unfeminine." The camp (reflecting the dual meaning of "country" and "camp" in Spanish) is described as "bucolic" and "pastoral" (59). It has an "ideal climate" (52), "happy" children, and flowers which are "perfect" in their artificiality. This fact alerts the audience to another reality behind the appearance of purity and correctness in Gambaro's *locus amoenus*. It is, to echo Mary Douglas's well-known view, the reality of a danger that Gambaro explores through agonistic symmetries.[14] Gambaro shows how the artificial, in this case the art of the theatre, can be used to attract or distract us from the crisis dividing a society. Her agonistic symmetries are couched in the binarisms of *locus amoenus*/concentration camp, happy children/attack dogs, scent of flowers/stench of charred flesh, external domination/internal submission. Though dressed in a Gestapo uniform, "there seems to be nothing about [Frank's] demeanor" which is threatening (51). Yet he provokes Martin repeatedly by dragging his coat on the floor, by refusing to give him the "accounts" he has come to manage, and by barraging him with personal questions about his religion and sexual orientation. Little by little he succeeds in making Martin submit to his will. He increases Emma's maddening itch with a salve meant to augment her torture and he orders the children's "gabble" to be silenced.

It is Emma, however, upon whom Gambaro focuses. When first presented to the audience, Emma wears a coarse grey dress, has a shaven head, a bug-infested wound on her hand and an incessant itch over her entire body. She nevertheless acts as if she were an elegant, upper class socialite, choosing her words carefully and modulating her voice appropriately. Society's "feminine" expectations for women are rigorously enforced in this camp. As soon as Emma is summoned, she looks around for her mirror, her comb, and her purse in order to touch up her makeup (63). She "raises her skirt a bit" and coos to Martin: "Oh, I wanted to meet you" (64). Shortly thereafter, she suggests seductively, "It would be so nice if I could please you" and rubs against his body (66). And Emma is equally "schooled" for her grotesque "performance" as a concert pianist. Mangy and disheveled, she nevertheless sees herself as elegant, triumphantly playing a piano that emits no sound, coquettishly praising the scent of the artificial flowers she has received for her "performance," while consciously ignoring the smell of charred flesh outside the building. She explains away her shaven head by focusing on how much easier it makes the necessity of changing into the equally grotesque wigs she uses to cover her head while "on tour." The brand on her forearm she sees as a protective and chivalrous gesture. As she explains to Martin, it was put there because "[t]hey were so afraid they'd lose me, a little child . . ." (65).

Gambaro's adjectival use heightens the tension of the already jarring contradiction between what the *locus amoenus* of this camp appears to be and what it actually is. Emma is described as filled with "enormous sadness," "desperate," "in anguish," "terrified," "trembling in a paroxysm of fear" (70–76). After reiterating the absolutely correct reactions of the other inmates to Emma's "performance" at the piano, Gambaro describes them as falling into a passive stupor, "as though they had just finished playing their role" (84). In this theatre within theatre, Emma plays whatever role she must. Even after the soldiers have mutilated Martin's face, Emma vindicates their violence by trying to give meaning to the meaningless horror that engulfs her. Martin "must have done something to deserve it" (86). The play ends as the audience hears the muffled whimpers of the terrified Emma cowering in a corner as the soldiers brand Martin, reminiscent of the end of Traba's *Mothers and Shadows*, where Dolores and Irene cringe in fear as the police bang on their door for admittance.

Gambaro's most innovative and shocking play, *Información para extranjeros (Information for Foreigners)* was written in the early seventies. It has strong affinities with American vanguard theatre, especially with Julian Beck's Living Theatre and Richard Schechner's Environmental Theatre.[15] As in Beck's *Paradise Now*, actors and audience intermingle and spectators and participants become indistinguishable in this "Chronicle in 21 Scenes" as Gambaro subtitles her exposé of the seventies.[16] *Information* is pure ritual in Schechner's sense: "The move from theater to ritual happens when the audience is transformed from a collection of separate individuals into a group or congregation of participants."[17]

Gambaro hid this strangely prophetic play in her house until she was forced to flee the country. She managed to smuggle the text out when she went into exile in Europe. So powerful is it that she refused to allow its production, fearing reprisals against family members still in Argentina (Feitlowitz, 5–6). Gambaro ruthlessly refuses here to distinguish between audience and performers in order to implicate us all in the dramatic action. The late anthropologist Victor Turner speaks of a moment in ritualized performance where the audience and the participants become a "congregation," when they share "the same set of beliefs and accept the same system of practices."[18] *Information* represents this terrifying moment. No line divides stage from auditorium, actor from spectator. The result is that the audience is transformed into participants in the reenacted horror which was Argentina in the seventies. "The work must be 'acted,' 'represented,' 'disguised,'" Gambaro cautions. "Only this will make it tolerable; otherwise no one will have the strength to watch" (Feitlowitz, 7).

Information for Foreigners: Chronicle in 21 Scenes is based on actual occurrences in Argentina. The first part of the title replicates the caption that appeared in Argentine newspapers purporting to explain to foreigners why arrests, hangings, and kidnappings had taken place. The second part suggests the chronicle of the factual record. Stage and auditorium become confused as actor-guides lead small groups of audience-participants through the dramas, the reenactments of varied Argentine newspaper accounts. In each "room" where the dramas take place, men and women are being tortured, sexually molested, raped, provoked into suicide, stripped of clothes, of dignity, and ultimately, of life.

The setting of the play is a house containing several rooms. Everything is deliberately foregrounded as theatrical. People shut doors because they are "rehearsing." The guides remind the audience to applaud at the end of the performance, the audience know they are being asked to "make believe" they are actors and voyeurs of the scenes dramatized in each room, and exaggeratedly made-up actors emphasize their theatricality. But, as Diana Taylor has said, "If the acts of terrorism Gambaro depicts are flagrantly theatrical . . . it is not simply that she is experimenting with a new kind of theatre, rather she is depicting a new kind of violence, a terrorism that is itself highly theatrical" (*Theatre of Crisis*, 136).

Entrance to *Information*, Gambaro tells us, is restricted: "No one under 18 will be admitted. Or under 35 or over 36" (71), and yet this play contains no "obscenity or strong words. The play speaks to our way of life: Argentine, Western, and Christian" (71). This play, however, does *not* "speak"—at least not in the language to which the audience is accustomed. Instead, groans and screams of victims in pain are ubiquitous. As Elaine Scarry points out, "To witness the moment when pain causes a reversion to the pre-language of cries and groans is to witness the destruction of language."[19] But Gambaro translates revolt into ritual. Just as warfare in the Papua New Guinea highlands is expressed effectively through ritualistic dancing (Schechner, *Performance Theory*, 118–23), so the pervasive symbolic, ritualistic chant of the Spanish playwright Federico García Lorca's *Blood Wedding* produces real and sinister effects in *Information* as Gambaro highlights the deep layers of xenophobia and misogyny that allow the barbarism of the military to continue. Since no distinction is made between actors and audience, all are implicated in what occurs onstage. It is a dehumanization, Gambaro suggests, which was not caused but exposed by the political situation of the seventies. As the Nazis capitalized on anti-semitism in order to mobilize a large percentage of Germans, so distrust of the "other" is seen to be endemic in Argentina. And how innocently such prejudice is perpetrated. This is the bedtime story a father tells his little girl while newspaper clippings about abductions are interspersed in the play and scenes of torture are reenacted: "Once upon a time, there was a tall man, ugly, ugly, ugly . . . (with disgust) Bolivian . . . They procreate a lot. Then they send the kids here . . . The tall man met another man. This one was a shorty . . . the short one was bad, bad. And then some men came, and since he was bad, they put him in another car to punish him. Because he was bad, bad . . . The good guys took them [both] for a ride! 'Cause they're so good!" (86–87).

Gambaro also foregrounds Argentine misogyny in the military's contempt of women. A Guide uses the formula "Ladies and Gentlemen" once in addressing the audience, then drops the "ladies" from the address because it is too long. Not only are women thereby rendered invisible but Latin-American paeans to motherhood, so-called *marianismo* (which may have assisted the Mothers in their public protests), are disclosed in the private sphere as empty cant. A mother abducted in front of her children reassures herself and them that "No one is hurting your mother" (93). She is summarily stripped and raped by her captors. As an introduction to a scene of torture about to be enacted, the audience sees a group of men over a young woman strapped to a table. Rape is seen as merely a preliminary routine, a prelude and foreplay to the real play of torture. Four times the audience is made to return with the guide to a room where a young girl is being taunted and sexually molested. She is repeatedly offered a pistol— an invitation to suicide—which she refuses four times. Her torturer grumbles as he thrusts his hand under the young victim's

skirt: "Does anyone understand women? A difficult bunch" (90).
He encourages her to pull the trigger because, after all, she is
expendable: he is convinced she is not a virgin and she has no man
to validate her existence: "And not this filth," he complains as
"(He slaps her skirt.). No way you're a virgin!" (90). He puts the
newly-cleaned pistol in her lap and invites her to use it, again
alluding to her lack of a male to validate her: "It's loaded. If you
had a boyfriend, old girl . . . But like this, Idiot, why endure so
much?" (97). When a gunshot is finally heard, the audience has
been made well aware that no one has killed the young woman.
Since it is she who has pulled the trigger, no one can be said to
have coerced her. As Elaine Scarry points out, the double bind of
the victim/victimizer relationship is that the former is doubly
dehumanized: not only is she at the mercy of the victimizer, but
she is also made to feel responsible for her own victimization. In
this way, "the one annihilated shifts to being the agent of [her]
own annihilation" (47).

Torture and sexuality are consistently intertwined in Gambaro's work: Cledy of *To Gain Death* is Mr. Perigorde's sexual
slave, the hunchback Raphael of *Bitter Blood* is a fetishized
object, the dehumanized Emma is a seductress, placating her victimizers with erotic gestures, a naked man in *Information for Foreigners* is embarrassed as he covers his genitals, and a young girl
is intimidated through obscene taunts and touches.

This equation of sexuality and cruelty is seemingly ubiquitous
in the texts of Argentine women writers who focus on oppression.
Three who come immediately to mind are Luisa Valenzuela,
Elvira Orphée, and Reina Roffé. Luisa Valenzuela will be discussed extensively later in this chapter, but a brief excursus from
Gambaro to Orphée and Roffé seems appropriate at this time.
Roffé and Orphée, like Gambaro, depict a world of unremitting
cruelty and perversion. Central to their texts is not the upper or
middle class society of Traba and Lynch, but, as with Gambaro, a
demi-monde of exploitation and prostitution.

Monte de Venus (1976; *Mons Veneris*) was Roffé's second
novel.[20] Two months after it appeared in Argentina, the book was
banned, first in Buenos Aires, then in the whole country because,
like Victoria Ocampo, Roffé was "considered immoral."[21]
Although initially interested in the novel, the newspapers refused
to discuss it or the author once they realized that *Mons Veneris*
had been censored. Roffé became a modern example of the

Roman practice of *damnatio memoriae*, whereby a person was officially "forgotten": "The newspapers silenced me; the editor not only made the remaining copies disappear, but the book and I were eliminated from the catalog . . . even friends chose not to mention the novel" (915).[22]

In *Mons Veneris* the association of cruelty and sexuality is as true of homosexual as it is of heterosexual encounters. The novel is a dismal, despairing portrait of a young lesbian, Julia Grande, who is rejected by almost everyone. She reveals her story as she tapes it for her professor, Victoria Saénz Ballesteros, who is writing a book on Julia's life. Julia's sexuality becomes all important. Whomever she trusts takes advantage of her. People steal from her, lie to her, beat her, and rape her so that "she can learn to be a woman" (101). She learns early to associate cruelty with sexuality, to do to others what they have done to her: "I would make men pay dearly," she promises, "for my few feminine attributes" (112). Julia has a child as a result of a rape, becomes a prostitute, and takes advantage of everyone she meets. She finally kills one of her lovers because she has "become tired of opening and closing my legs" (197). Her lesbian relationships are just as dismal, as she is betrayed and exploited by her female lovers. Francine Masiello has said of Roffé's first novel, *Llamado al puf* (1973), that ". . . [b]y ironizing all idealism, Roffé denies any fruitful alternatives to nostalgia."[23] In *Mons Veneris* even nostalgia ceases to be an alternative. One of the few instances of "kindness" in the novel turns out to be one more act of betrayal. Julia's teacher, Victoria Saénz Ballesteros, offers to take care of the child, Daniel, while Julia nurses her sick mother. In love with Ballesteros, Julia fears the taping sessions will end because the teacher does not believe she has enough material for a book. "Your life," she tells Julia," is not as terrible as I had imagined" (246). And so in order to appear terrible and to ensure that their sessions continue, Julia confesses that she made Alfredo's death look like the result of a drunken brawl: "I had committed the perfect crime. Had it been premeditated, it would never have been done so well" (253). After her mother's death, Julia tries to reclaim her son, but Ballesteros who has Julia's taped confession in her possession, refuses to relinquish the boy. The novel ends with Julia's lament: "They have emptied me. My mother has died and I'm left without my son, my love, my book . . . What wouldn't I give for a tiny caress? . . ." (270).

Nowhere, however, except perhaps in Luisa Valenzuela's works, is the equation of sexuality and cruelty more conspicuous than it is in Elvira Orphée's *La última conquista de el Angel* (1985; *El Angel's Last Conquest*). Orphée has remarked that hers is "one of the few novels in which one sees the issue of power from the perspective of the paid assassins of the lower hierarchy."[24] As a result, her work is more interested in the perpetrators than in the victims. Seen as ordinary, insecure men, the torturers experience a fascination and release akin to the sexual in the power they exert over their victims. While the young prostitute, Judith, is being tortured with a hooded man tied to her, the torturer/narrator describes the scene: "I hit her everywhere. First the body on top of hers, tied to hers. Then shocks to her vagina and his penis perfectly synchronized. The consummation of electric coitus" (118). Orphée's descriptions of the eroticism experienced by perpetrators of the most sadistic acts find their theoretical corollary in Georges Bataille's explanation of the connection between sexuality and the sensual desire provoked by the fascination with death. The passionate release of tension associated with the death process, what Bataille calls an "orgy of annihilation," pervades *El Angel's Last Conquest*.[25] Judith discovers, immediately before lapsing into an "incurable mental illness," that she has been tied to a corpse. Her torturer's passionate release of tension becomes a literal expression of Bataille's "orgy of annihilation." Subdued and calmed by what he has effected, the torturer comments almost poetically: "And he [the corpse] fell onto her mouth with the frozen sneer of death on his angelic face. Frost on top, somewhat gray, brown, and rotten underneath" (119). This association of cruelty with eroticism is calculated to contradict the reader's expectations. It effects the awareness that in literature as in life the association of sexuality and torture cannot be denied.

Richard Schechner theorizes that the connections between violence and sex are characteristic of Indo-European arts and literature, as witnessed by the "orgasmic even orgiastic" qualities of martyrdom depicted in Christian iconography of the Middle Ages and early Renaissance.[26] René Girard adds that "the shift from violence to sexuality and from sexuality to violence is easily effected, even by the most 'normal' of individuals, totally lacking in perversion."[27] For Roffé, Orphée, and Gambaro, the apparent normality by which the shift is effected is the most disturbing element of the equation. In effect, what has been said of Gambaro also applies to Roffé and Orphée: "The frustration, insecurity, and anxiety thematic in [their work] becomes a part of the [reader's] own experience."[28]

Gambaro's later texts, however, show a clear shift of attitude. Her novella *Lo impenetrable* (1984; *The Impenetrable Madame X*) is a refreshing change from her previous plays and novels. It is a hilarious parody of traditional motifs and genres: the quest theme, the erotic novel, as well as the conventional views of "accepted" sexual patterns of behavior. It foregrounds "the light-hearted conventions of the ribald tale," and through laughter, it dissolves themes that created tension and illustrated cruelty in Gambaro's former works.[29] Her parodies run the gamut from Aristophanes's concept of the androgyne in Plato's *Symposium* to the lesbian interludes of such male-authored erotica as John Cleland's *Fanny Hill*, the anonymous *My Secret Life*, and even Emile Zola's *Nana*. Both the erotic titillation aimed at a male audience and a macho view of sexual domination is parodied. Here is an example of Madame X's narcissistic fantasies: "[s]he regretted that her [Madame X's] body was incapable of splitting into a woman-man or a woman-woman; she'd have liked to feel her own weight and not another's, penetrate and feel herself penetrated, be both ying and yang" (18). The Gestapo-like Frank's uptight homosexuality in *The Camp* gives way now to the real, mischievous, and wholly uninhibited lesbian romp of Madame X and her maid, Marie, and to the sexual freedom of Madame X's erotic dreams where Marie becomes alternately a woman with male organs, then a woman, and ultimately, a man: "While she [Madame X] was enjoying Marie, incarnated successively in three bodies, she was even more delighted by the thought of so much accessible variety ignored by common mortals who got tied up in the knots of their own desire" (84). As erotic titillation is reduced to laughter, so sexual prowess is reduced to histrionic bathos in Gambaro's hilarious twentieth-century recontextualizing of Alexander Pope's eighteenth-century mock epic, *The Rape of the Lock*. Madame X's secret lover has to be hospitalized for exhaustion after he has had ninety-nine orgasms in the street at the sight of the lock of hair she has thrown to him from the balcony. When the interminable vicissitudes associated with the romantic quest are finally ended and the lovers are united, Madame X is sexually impenetrable because the now much older Jonathan has become impotent. How differently the theme of impotence is treated here from many of Gambaro's earlier works. In *The Camp,* for example, it was couched in recurrent allusions to Frank's possible homosexuality, and in *To Gain Death*, it produced sinister results in the form of the brutal treatment of Cledy by Mr. Perigorde. In *The Impenetrable Madame X*, however, the impotent Jonathan merely affirms with mock heroic wisdom, that "that which is impenetrable is the source of all pleasure because there is no pleasure without the unknown" (143). The novella ends as Madame X cheerfully sets forth on another sexual quest with a new lover.

LUISA VALENZUELA

Probably the most translated contemporary Latin-American woman writer, Luisa Valenzuela suffuses her work with Gambaro's parodic humor to, in her words, "break fear" and "hide death."[30]

Born in Buenos Aires, Argentina, on 26 November 1938, Valenzuela was a journalist by the age of seventeen. She has been editor of major Argentine newspapers, writer-in-residence at both Columbia University and New York University, and fellow of the Institute for the Humanities in 1981. Most of her works have been translated. *Hay que sonreír* (1966; *One must Smile*) and *Los heréticos* (1967; *The Heretics*) were published in English in 1976 as *Clara, Thirteen Stories and a Novel. Como en la guerra* (1977; *He Who Searches*) was added to the English version of her collection of stories *Aquí pasan cosas raras* (1975; *Strange things Happen Here*). The English version of *Cola de lagartija* (1983; *The Lizard's Tail*) was published in the United States several months before the Spanish version appeared in Argentina. *Cambio de armas* (1982; *Other Weapons*) was translated in 1985. *Open Door* (1988) included an English selection of three of her previous collections of short stories: *Donde viven las aguilas* (1983; *Up Among the Eagles*), *Strange Things Happen Here*, and *The Heretics*. The ironically titled *Libro que no muerde* (1980; *Book That Does Not Bite*) refers to an axiom in Spanish which encourages recalcitrant children to read. This book contains stories and essays as well as fourteen selections from *Strange Things Happen Here* and four from *The Heretics*. Valenzuela has affirmed that, contrary to its title, she hoped this book would indeed prove trenchant in its scathing depiction of sociopolitical realities (Ordoñez,

516). *Novela negra con Argentinos* (1992; *Black Novel (With Argentines)* and *Realidad nacional desde la cama* (1990; *National Reality From the Bed*) are her most recent novels.[31]

Valenzuela has received many prizes, including the National Arts Foundation Award of Argentina in 1966 and 1972, an award from the Instituto Nacional de Cinematografía in 1973, a Fulbright Fellowship for the International Writers Program at the University of Iowa in 1969, and a Guggenheim Fellowship in 1982. Her literary work, too hybrid to categorize, centers on political problems affecting Latin America, on relations between the sexes, and on metaliterary issues. Humor and irony permeate all of her work. In her collection of short stories, *Strange Things Happen Here*, for example, an erotic surrealism injects humor into such themes as terrorism, violence, pornography, and child murderers. Words become all important. In "The Verb to Kill," we know there has been a murder simply because the disturbed child conjugates the verb: "He will be killed—he is killed—he has been killed" (47). In "Neither the Most Terrifying Nor the Least Memorable" ("Neither the Most"), she goes further. Signifieds become wholly arbitrary and non-referential. Words refer only to themselves.[32] In a hilarious anticipation of the Clarence Thomas/ Anita Hill scenario, "Neither the Most" begins:

> The day he found pubic hairs in his bowl of soup wasn't the most terrifying day of his life; it was alphabet soup. The day he found an obelisk in his pubic hair the phenomenon did indeed attract his attention but not to the extent that he suddenly understood his new cartographic vocation, thanks to which all of him—his most obscure corners and smallest outward features turned into a faithful copy of the city, much warmer than the city itself and less schematic (55).

Such condensation contributes to both humor and uncertainty, forcing the reader "back to the word itself in a search for meaning" (Marting, 52). Valenzuela appropriates conventional narrative strategies to revalorize traditional meanings of words. Nothing escapes her humor in *Strange Things Happen Here*, where she freely uses intertextuality, puns, and parody. The protagonist of "Neither the Most," initially described in terms of the city's map, "suddenly stops being a city and turns into a dog, in unconscious literary homage" to Vargas Llosa's *The Time of the Hero* and to Carlos Fuentes's *Holy Places* (Marting, 53). Irreverent puns on religious and political realities are found in "Ladders to Success," where the character is ultimately converted to "the Church of Ladder-Day Saints" (69). Burlesque understatements make it possible to deal with cruelty and violence. In one story, for example, a woman shoots a man and, as he lies dying, she muses, "He doesn't interest me anymore: he's come apart like all of them, all men are alike, they don't hold up" (124). In another, a woman called Fatty allows her body to be covered with pancakes and salami. An enthusiastic crowd eats not only the pancakes but Fatty herself because it is "nice to take a bite of things and find out what's inside" (205). Cannibalism is reduced to bathos. "Eating people," the characters seriously muse, "has one danger: the irrepressible belch. It overtakes you suddenly like a mouthful coming up from the guts, and what can you do? Put on an innocent face and swallow again while puffing out your cheeks" (206).

"He Who Searches" seems as overtly traditional as Valenzuela's youthful *Clara*, in which the title of each chapter summarized its content. Yet it is the surrealistic odyssey through Europe, Mexico, and South America of a man seeking identity through metamorphosis, drugs, and sorcery. The story is divided into the four predictable phases of the search: The Discovery; The Loss; The Journey; The Encounter. The contents, however, wholly belie the conventional format. Structure and syntax are arbitrary and loose. Pages are only half filled and seemingly pointless repetitions abound. The text is reminiscent of the work of García Márquez, as trickles of blood guide the characters, and men metamorphose into animals. Language refuses to be gendered: "That's why he doesn't stop when they call him in male language, nor does he bother to stop when they call him man in female language" (198). Gambaro used the Platonic concept of the androgyne for humorous purposes, but Valenzuela adopts it for serious ends. Transsexuality, bisexuality, cross-dressing, and homosexuality in Valenzuela's works underscore her view that humans are androgynous and that sexuality is but an accident of nature.

This constant de-mythifying and toppling of moral taboos does not diminish the social impact of her work (Picon Garfield, *Women's Voices*, 146), in which political repression is central. *Other Weapons*, Valenzuela's 1985 collection of short stories, is a good example. "Fourth Version," the first story in the collection, juxtaposes love and death. The story demonstrates, however, that no refuge is safe in a country where the state has the power to make or to break laws. A young woman, Bella, uses her erotic involvement with an ambassador as a ploy to obtain asylum for political exiles. Valenzuela has described this situation as autobiographical (García Pinto, *Historias*, 232–3). Bella is shot by the military in the presence of her lover and in the "sanctuary" of a party at the embassy. "Fourth Version" concentrates on words and on metaliterary issues. It demonstrates that if "political security" is difficult to obtain, literary accuracy is no less difficult. Both narrator and reader are puzzled about the account that Bella the narrator tries to piece together from different fragments. The fluidity of the real and the unreal becomes puzzling: what really took place and what was imagined? The story becomes more complicated at the conclusion with the introduction of an imaginary (?) character, Uncle Ramon, who seems to know all about the past, including Bella's death. Is he aware of yet a fifth version of the story?

Through a bizarre late twentieth-century version of Oscar Wilde's comment from *The Ballad of Reading Gaol* that "each man kills the thing he loves," Valenzuela juxtaposes love and death in "The Word 'Killer.'" The male protagonist is a killer but, in the woman's view, "the sweetest killer of them all" (74). Through an ambiguous combination of inner thoughts and outer actions, the reader and the woman are led to realize that the man will kill the woman as coolly as he has disposed of his Korean wife, perhaps with the same strategies he learned in Vietnam: "If the victim, who's been left on the floor, can't stand the position any longer, and wants to stretch her legs, she strangles herself. It's that simple" (77). Words again are all important and are as traumatic and life-giving as birth itself. Intimidated and speechless, the woman is about to escape by jumping from the open window when she hears herself shout the word "KILLER." But the utterance is inverted, in typical Valenzuelan fashion, and juxtaposed with the metaphor of giving birth (Castillo, 130). As she screams, "[t]he voice finally manages to bolt out of her and she isn't calling out or accusing; in fact she's giving birth" (78).

The shortest story in the collection is also set in the unclear ambiance of the real and the unreal. In "I'm Your Horse in the Night," a young woman goes to jail, charged with harboring a political fugitive after spending a night with her revolutionary lover, Beto. As the story ends, however, the reader is not quite sure whether the protagonist has actually spent the night with him or whether she has dreamed it. Regardless of its reality, through the power of words she is able to make the event disappear: "Beto, now that I'm in jail I know that I dreamed you that night; it was just a dream. And if by some wild chance there's a Gal Costa record and a half-empty bottle of cachaça in my house, I hope they'll forgive me: I *decreed* them out of existence" (101).[33] "Rituals of Rejection" is the only story in *Other Weapons* where the female protagonist refuses to be victimized by the male. In love with Coyote, an unreliable lover who inexplicably abandons her for long periods, Amanda decides to leave him. She performs "cabalistic" and "domestic" rejection rituals to free herself emotionally. The story ends as Amanda looks at herself in the mirror, pained but convinced that "step by step, the mirror gives back her shape and confirms her song" (94). "Other Weapons," the last story of the collection that bears its name, is the most overtly political. Its title in Spanish can mean both "an exchange of weapons"/ "other weapons" or "I change weapons." Although the story is divided into precise sections: "the words," "the concept," "the voices," "the secret," "the revelation," and "the ending," these are even more arbitrary than were the captions in "He Who Searches." With this strategy, Valenzuela continues to invert conventional narrative techniques. Laura, the young protagonist, has been reduced to complete amnesia by the severe whipping she has received. She once tried to kill a colonel and is consequently kept imprisoned, drugged, and monitored by two guards. Her every move is watched, including her sexual domination by the colonel. Words are meaningless here but essential. "Completely devoid of recollections," with no history, no past, no future, Laura is obsessed with the "capacity to find the right word" (105). But she has neither word nor world as she is only aware of the deep scar on her back—a remnant of the torture inflicted on her. As Elaine Scarry has said, "Intense pain destroys ... self and world ... Intense pain is also language destroying: as the content of one's world disintegrates, so the content of one's language disintegrates" (35). It is the colonel who has the word and the world. It is he "who names her and names each part of her body in a doubtful attempt to reconstruct her" (129–30). As Laura once used a weapon on him, a gun, so he now uses other weapons on her, his power and his sex. Systematically and diabolically, he has forced her to depend on him "like a newborn baby" (134–35.) At the end, however, because of a change in government, he must flee. As he returns to her the gun with which she once tried to kill him, she recovers both her memory and history, and Valenzuela now inverts and subverts the expected because Laura has not been reconstructed as planned by the colonel. Oblivious of his obsessive need for revenge, she has simply accepted her condition and thereby deprived him of the satisfaction of humiliating her. Bataille explains the recurrent problem in relations of domination precisely in these terms. By accepting defeat the victim loses the very quality essential to the victimizer, namely, that she recognize his mastery over her.[34] But the drugged, amnesiac Laura has been made into a senseless thing and the only respite in her reified existense is, ironically, the colonel. Sex is all that is left to her and she begs, "No, don't leave me. Will you come back? Stay" (135). She aims the gun at him as she did once before when she tried to kill him, and the novel ends. What does the ending mean? Valenzuela has again deconstructed signifying systems and contradicted conventional expectations. Is an aware Laura mad (angry) for the years she has lost, the lover the military have killed, the humiliation she has been forced to endure and will she now kill her oppressor? Or is she just plain mad? Valenzuela uses Laura's insanity to "uncouple the narrative from its planned denouement," thus coalescing two different genres, the revolutionary tale and the sentimental novel. As Castillo has stated, the reader expects that the "revolutionary soldier would kill the enemy . . . the housewife would weep at his [the sexual companion's] defection, but only the madwoman could presume to conflate the two, pleading for love and aiming the revolver" simultaneously (135).

In her *Black Novel (with Argentines)* (*Black Novel*), Valenzuela displaces political savagery onto continents as Gambaro had displaced it onto the private lives of families in *To Gain Death*. Valenzuela illustrates two victimizers, Roberta and Agustín, Argentine writers in New York, who have simply taken abroad with them the background of Argentina's horror. They are "the offspring of someone else's crimes" (220). Agustín murders young actress Edwina for no apparent reason. He knows he must determine why he has killed her or he will never be able to write again. His search for a motive becomes his story and Roberta's effort to understand his story becomes the novel. The sociopolitical realities of Argentina envelop the protagonists in New York through recurrent and very effective intertextual reminders and sadomasochistic relationships. In indirect references to the demented child murderer of Valenzuela's story, "The Verb to 'Kill'" and to the woman of "The Word 'Killer'," Roberta shudders at "how many times the word murderer had polluted her own prose" (84). Like the protagonist of "The Word 'Killer,'" she too fears for her life in the presence of her lover-assassin, but, unlike her, does not utter the life-giving word that identifies him. Instead, she is obsessed with the terrifying question: "Would a onetime killer kill twice?" (85). The intertextual reference to "Other Weapons" is also effective. The exchange of weapons, gun for penis, foregrounded power and sexual domination in the earlier novel. The textual reference in *Black Novel* foregrounds the protagonist's impotence. The narrator tells the reader mockingly after Agustín's encounter with Baby Jane at Ava Taurel's sex parlor: "That place where all sorts of weapons were within reach, and he had not wanted to use any of them. Or had not been able to. Not even the one that that Mother-bitch Nature had provided him with . . ." (145).

The sadomasochistic relationships in *Black Novel*, as in the works of Gambaro, Roffé, and Orphée, are grotesque. Like Dostoevsky's Raskolnikov in *Crime and Punishment*, Agustín is haunted by nightmares after his crime. He sees a monstrously enlarged woman on top of him pouring molten wax on his penis, simultaneously kicking him with her heels, and forcing her huge nipples filled with a lava-like liquid into his mouth. As Agustín suffers "burning inside and outside," she snuffs out the candle on his glans (33–35). In the realm of everyday life, however, Valenzuela's characters are unable to "play" New York games. Invited to participate in the rituals of a parlor in New York City where hooded men and women live out their most violent and aberrant erotic fantasies, a shaken Roberta refuses (91–92). Agustín later remarks, "They [the sado-masochistic acts performed at Ava Taurel's place] bring back bad memories . . . How can you expect me to enjoy voluntary sexual torture when I come from a country where people were tortured for alleged political reasons, for the sheer horror of it, with desperate, not at all compliant victims? How do you expect me to enjoy it or even be interested in it? What I need is to know why someone becomes a torturer, a murderer, to know why an upright citizen can one day unawares be transformed into a monster" (103; 143). Elvira Orphée attempts to respond to the question by equating torture with the desire for "mystical experience," with the "need to seek access to the unknown through the suffering of others" (Picon Garfield,

Women's Fiction, 161). The characters of *Black Novel* attempt to explain it as the need to find "the human spirit beyond pain," the need to understand "how much the body can take" (29). Consequently, the authors and the characters of these works desperately probe a reality that has a far-reaching consequence—that of violence. Richard Schechner, as director of the Environmental Theatre, points out that the dictum of Antonin Artaud's theatre of cruelty—that violence purges—is simply not validated by experience. Schechner theorizes that "live" performances of cruelty, such as Ralph Ortiz's *The Sky is Falling*, where live mice and chickens are killed on stage in order to make the performance appear "real," and in order to sensitize us to the horror of cruelty, merely succeed in "reifying living beings into symbolic agents" (*PT*, 170). Schechner cites the work of Irenaus Eibl-Eibesfeldt, who observes that, for animals, viewing violent acts is not cathartic. "In the long run," Eibl-Eibesfeldt finds, "the possibility of discharging aggressive impulses constitutes a kind of training for aggression" (quoted in *PT*, 174). This is clear in the "Argentine" way that Valenzuela's characters Agustín and Roberta cope with their problems in New York. Agustín simply kills Edwina for no apparent reason. Roberta advises the disturbed Agustín that there is an Argentine precedent for easing his conscience. It is either to make the victim disappear or to blame the victim. "We can leave everything just as it is," she says, "dish out our typical remarks: 'Nothing has happened here,' or 'They must have done something to deserve this'" (55). But they must stay in New York. The third option, to return to Argentina, is simply out of the question. It is a question of proportion: "Too many corpses there," Agustín tells Roberta, "against only one here . . . it's a city constructed over corpses, a nation of desaparecidos. There's no possible return" (78–79).

As it was unusual for Gambaro to be funny as in *The Impenetrable Madame X*, it is also unusual for Valenzuela to be as serious as she is in *Other Weapons* and *Black Novel*. Generally she treats grave issues with a playful, Hitchcockian black humor, an approach which is clear from two of her most unconventionally defiant novels, *El gato eficaz* (1984; *The Efficient Cat*) (*Cat*) and *The Lizard's Tail*. *Cat*, like *Black Novel*, was written in New York, the city which Valenzuela claims radically transformed her art. The novel defies all conventional notions of narrative and of language. Not only does it rely on the function of the word, the word itself becomes the protagonist: "I am a trap made of paper and mere printed letters" (110).[35] The writing is playful, fluid, and open in this book Valenzuela calls her "miracle" (Picon Garfield, Women's Voices, 151). The narrator warns: "Nothing has happened here, nor will it happen, nor does it happen" (89). True to the narrator's announcement, "everything livable can be playable," everything becomes a game (67). The narrator taunts the reader: "Reading between the lines is the key" (211). Like Gambaro who used chants from García Lorca's Blood Wedding to effect foreboding, Valenzuela reduces Lorca's canonical eminence to sexual parody. The flag becomes a "fried egg" (74), and her fictional couples make passionate love to each other when they are separated, thereby practicing "telecoitus." A man falls in love with a bed and becomes a "tiny lascivious insect" so that his weight will not hurt the bed, and for the same reason, he kills anyone who makes love on the bed. Rules for fornication are "laid out" in "Let Us Play at Fornicón" (68). Valenzuela ruptures syntax and makes her work deliberately impervious to rules of structure, grammar, or logic. Questions are consistently raised about literature and women, "both of which are the products of multiple myths that the author examines, demystifies, and undermines."[36] Cat is, in Roland Barthes's sense, a "writable" (scriptible) text as opposed to a "readable" (lisible) one. Whereas a "readable" text stands for all that is traditional, systematic, analyzable, "about writable texts there may be nothing to say."[37] The only constant in Valenzuela's "writable" text is the metamorphosing feline narrator who remains the same despite her many, yet temporary, transformations. Cat embodies what Valenzuela calls elsewhere the only real search, that is, the search of a lack ["la búsqueda de una carencia"] (Ordoñez, 516). She refuses to allow the logos, the word, to cover that lack. She has explained that disguises, masks, mirrors, like humor and irony, are used purposefully in her work, specifically to "break fear" and "hide death," and that the reason for the mask is to "reveal more than it hides," that it forces her to say what, without the mask, she would be unable to articulate (Ordoñez, 512–13)

In 1982–83 Luisa Valenzuela wrote The Lizard's Tail, a book she describes as "very political . . . critical of the whole world" (García Pinto, Historias, 235). She was working on the novel at the same time that she was writing Other Weapons, and frequently employs intertextuality to foreground the link between them. Luisa Valenzuela, the narrator/character of *The Lizard's Tail*, like Bella in "The Fourth Version" of *Other Weapons* and like the author herself, is involved with helping political exiles (García Pinto, *Historias*, 222–23). The narrator Valenzuela underscores the connection between the two novels: "I can't even do my work now . . . or keep up contacts with a certain ambassador so as to get asylum for a few people at least . . . I, too, was planning a party, at the embassy, so more people could get in and request asylum" (126). Humorously and metafictionally, the narrator returns the reader to the "right" text: "And the ambassador, what an interesting fellow he is. That's another story I ought to be writing. I wonder why fiction and reality get so intertwined in me, or at least in my writing . . ." (144). Egret's whip, the lizard's tail, also serves as another intertextual link between the novels. Used as cruelly in *The Lizard's Tail* as the whip with which amnesiac Laura has been flogged in "Other Weapons," it evokes, as we have seen, the same erotic context of torture within which so much of these women's work has taken place. Egret almost has an orgasm as he lashes the young women and begins "to undress them with the Lizard's Tail, trying to catch a tipoi tunic with the long tongue of the whip, trying to snare a petticoat and pull it off" (142–43). *The Lizard's Tail* constitutes Valenzuela's response or challenge to phallic power and the phallogocentric (male centered) discourse of *Other Weapons*, where, with one exception, the men are sexually and verbally in control. Valenzuela's foreword to the Spanish version (omitted from the English) affirms: "Nuestra arma es la letra"("Our weapon is the written word"). Humor once again demythifies discourse.

The Lizard's Tail is divided into three parts. Part I introduces the Sorcerer, a caricature of López Rega, the terrible authoritarian "Sorcerer" of Argentina, whom Juan and Isabel Perón used as an advisor in occult sciences and astrology. Valenzuela admits that she wrote the novel to understand how "a supposedly intelligent and sophisticated people like the Argentines had fallen into the hands of this so-called sorcerer, a malevolent one at that."[38] The Sorcerer is bisexual. He has three testicles, the third of which is his sister, Estrella, with whom he plans to produce a son. He is his own biographer (40–41). In Part I he speaks in the first person. In Part II Luisa Valenzuela appears as one of the characters, a woman writer who is composing the Dictator/Sorcerer's life and on whose narrative his biography of macho power depends. Theirs is a fight for mastery of discourse. He struggles for power, "To rule the world is the great cosmic orgasm" (277). She battles for disclosure, "To tell his story so his existence won't go unnoticed" (126). Valenzuela the narrator concedes that his version sometimes "superimposes itself on this one and is capable of nullifying it" (125). At other times she is fascinated by his evil presence and is "tempted to go and look up the witch doc in person . . . Become his ghost writer . . . combine his knowledge and my literary talents and achieve the true work that could well be this very same book" (221). In this book, women are in charge. Estrella, the Sorcerer's testicular sister, restricts him sexually when he gets out of hand, causing him pain in the groin, and Luisa Valenzuela, the narrator/writer, restricts him textually, depriving him of the ability to produce his biography: "So you see, we're alike," she tells him. "I, too, think I have influence over others. By being silent now, I think I can make you silent. By erasing myself from the map, I intend to erase you. Without my biography, it will be as if you had never had a life. So long, Sorcerer, *felice morte*" (227). In Part III, "Three?" (deliberately posed as a question) an omniscient narrator resumes the story that Luisa Valenzuela the character/narrator has stopped writing. The account describes how the Sorcerer now transformed into the Sorcer decides to become a woman: "Freed of my male part, I shall . . . develop my other aspect, the feminine one " (234). He next plans to transcend both sexes and become a new supernatural entity: "Neither man nor woman, nothing but transition, s/he can't be classified and new genders and new pronouns have to be invented. Not neuter ones because there is nothing neuter about the Sorcer" (246). Luisa Valenzuela the author, however, ultimately castrates the Sorcerer/Sorcer. She has already deprived him of the power to produce his own text and she now deprives him of his ability to reproduce his own sex, his son (Paley Francescato, 375–82). Before he can give birth the Sorcerer explodes. The prophecy that serves as the novel's epigraph, "A river of blood will flow," has been interpreted by the Sorcerer as reflecting his ultimate and triumphant dictatorship. It is now fulfilled in Valenzuela's terms, not his. Elvira Orphée, speaking of her own hatred of torture, which prompted the writing of *El Angel's Last Conquest*, is very insightful in this regard. "Blood," she says, "is not disturbing because of its color or smell but because of its mystery. Whoever causes this channel of mystery must feel all powerful, becoming thereby a perverse sorcerer's apprentice" (García Pinto, *Historias*, 165). Like Orphée's "perverse sorcerer's apprentice," Valenzuela has caused blood to flow. It is she who has thereby become all powerful.

Just as Valenzuela de-mythifies totalitarianism and phallogo-centric discourse, so she desacralizes religious dogma. The Sorcerer is a god-like figure and the people "worship him and bring him offerings" (10). His testicular sister, like the Virgin Mary, is called Stella Matutina, "Estrella de la Mañana, Morning Star" (15). The Holy Spirit is reduced to a "flighty little bird" (213). The "great Advent" (270) of "I's" divine birth will be brought about by Egret, the "angel of the anunciation" (271). Throughout the novel, the Sorcerer is represented as a Yahweh figure, whose name is unspeakable: "Only I know how to call myself by name" (224). This irreverence is usually couched in the "sacred" number three. The three testicles become the Sorcerer's "trinity in the crotch" (141). As a result of his "Theocopulation" (255) he becomes liter-ally three persons in one: He/ Estrella/ I. His ritual incantations are triple (102). The miracles the Sorcerer performs become a tribute to his trinitarian attributes. He makes the dumb speak. The idiot Eulogio, shocked at the sight of the naked young Emmanuel (thereby recognizing one of the many names of the divine Sorcerer, "God among us"), speaks for the only time in his life to acknowledge that "Manuel's got three balls" (5). In the midst of this irreverence and irony, humor has been an effective weapon, but, as with all struggles for mastery, power in *The Lizard's Tail* has been transferred only temporarily. At the conclusion of the novel, Valenzuela admits this with horror as she foregrounds the chasm between theory and practice, between the wish fulfillment of literature and the stark reality of Latin-American politics.

> I keep on writing, with growing disillusionment and with a cer-tain disgust. Disgust even with myself for believing that litera-ture can save us, for doubting that literature can save us . . . (181)

> Tyrannies are not what they used to be. Now they have replace-ment parts. One president falls and another is ready to take over (280).

CARMEN NARANJO

The chasm between literature and reality is reiterated by Costa Rican Carmen Naranjo, who admits, "Sometimes you convince yourself that only by writing—by exposing things—as far as they let you—can you help change things; at other times you think you are in a very comfortable position writing cozily inside a room while others are dying in the streets" (Arizpe, 108–9). Her statement notwithstanding, Naranjo cannot be described as "writing cozily." Ironically and humorously she too exposes the hypocrisy of society, the harmful effects of societal conventions on women, men, and children, and focuses lovingly on, in her words, "the person who is a nobody, one belonging to an anonymous crowd" (Arizpe, 103). Naranjo was born in Cartago, Costa Rica, in 1930 and received a master's degree in Spanish philology in 1953. As a member of the social-democratic National Liberation Party, she has held several highly visible government posts: ambassador to Israel, assistant director of the Social Security Institute, minister of Culture, Youth, and Sport, Costa Rican representative of UNICEF in Guatemala and Mexico. Between 1982 and 1984 she was the director of the Museum of Costa Rican Art. Since then she has directed EDUCA, the Central American University Publishing House. During her administrative career, Naranjo published novels, short stories, and poetry. She has received many awards, beginning with the National Novel Prize "Aquileo J. Echeverría" for *Los perros no ladraron* (1966; *The Dogs Didn't Bark*) in 1966. She won the Guatemalan Floral Games literary prize for *Camino al mediodía* (1968; *Noontime Walk*) in 1967, and for *Responso por el niño Juan Manuel* (1971; *Requiem for the Boy Juan Manuel*); *Diario de una multitud* (1974; *Diary of a Multitude*), and *Sobrepunto* (1985; *Overpoint*) in 1968. In that same competition, another novel, *Memorias de un hombre palabra* (1968; *Memoirs of a Wordman*) received honorable mention. *Diary of a Multitude* also earned her the EDUCA Prize in 1974. Her short story "Hoy es un largo día" (1974; "Today Is a Long Day") won the Editorial Costa Rica Prize in 1973, and *Ondina* (1985) won the EDUCA competition in 1982. Her novels have not been translated but some of her short stories have appeared in collections.[39]

The overall theme of Naranjo's novels, like that of Thoreau's *Walden*, is that most people, under their façade of smiling faces, lead lives of quiet desperation. She seeks to shatter this façade, along with the tourist's image of Costa Rica "as a people without prejudices, a city in which there are opportunities for everyone" (*Overpoint*, 24). Her novels expose the exploitation, greed, and hypocrisy of a "hybrid system . . . always favoring the privileged, the gentlemen of opportunity, in pursuit of the business deal, the easy money" (*Diary*, 73). It is not capitalism per se, but corruption that Naranjo repudiates. In her short story, "Why Kill the Countess?," for example, it is the revolutionaries who are corrupt. The aristocratic countess, whom the townspeople love and revere, must be destroyed simply because "[s]he gave and gave without exacting anything, she's a terrible example" (Picon Garfield, *Women's Literature*, 209). In *The Dogs Didn't Bark*, Naranjo transposes her own experiences of the government bureaucracy into art. She knows only too well "what went on working in the Social Security Institute" (Arizpe, 102). *The Dogs* consists entirely of conversations with no authorial intrusions. Like a film, the meaningless private and public life of the middle-class bureaucrat/protagonist rolls tediously before the reader's eye, set forth in titles such as "The Decision," "Every Day Begins the Same," "There is Always Something To Talk About." The nameless bureaucrat, like Kafka's Gregor in *The Metamorphosis*, simply exists. He awakens, has breakfast, goes to the office, receives visitors, visits a sick friend. After work he has a few drinks with friends, visits his mistress (who reveals she is pregnant), and eventually returns home, completely inebriated, to a cool wife. The novel ends with the protagonist's somber avowal of the banality and meaninglessness of his existence. "Rather than float," he realizes, "I am sinking, and in reality I wish I could die . . . How sweet to die . . . without even the dogs barking" (208). *Diary of a Multitude*, like *The Dogs* consists "of the voices of a multitude anguished by boredom and the absence of the motivation to live, who form one voice, that of today's human being."[40] The monotony, grasping ambition, and exploitation surrounding the protagonist of *The Dogs* is shown to permeate all of contemporary society in San José. *Noontime Walk* and *Requiem for the Boy Juan Manuel* use death as their hermeneutic springboard. They are mirror images in comparison and contrast. The unnamed narrator of *Noontime Walk*, the action of which occurs between 7:30 a.m. and 12:30 p.m., reminisces after hearing about the death of his old friend, Eduardo Campos Argüello, whose grasping ambition made him a millionaire. Bankrupt, abandoned by his family, he has committed suicide. The novel centers on his burial: the funeral cortège leaves San José in the morning and arrives at the cemetery at noontime, hence the title.

As in Bombal's *The Shrouded Woman*, the past is revealed from the perspective of the present. The reader witnesses the same boredom, hypocrisy, and mediocrity in the dead man's former life as was described in the two previous novels. Space (the real/unreal), and time (past/present) become confused throughout and add to the timelessness of this Everyman's condition. The unnamed narrator of *Requiem* searches to verify the existence of a fifteen-year-old who dies in an accident. As four friends communicate, the reader realizes that the boy has actually been created by one of the speakers. Further, the fictional Juan Manuel, to alleviate his loneliness, has himself created an imaginary friend. Reality eventually prevails and when Juan Manuel can no longer invent stories, he must die. Unlike the middle-aged Eduardo of *Noontime Walk*, and before imagination loses out to reality in *Requiem*, the reader becomes aware that the young boy has nevertheless experienced love as well as loneliness and abandonment.

Overpoint, on the other hand, is an impressionistic work. Naranjo has explained in an interview that its name alludes to "the technique of *pointillisme* [which employs] words as if they were dots . . . 'Sobrepunto' [overpoint] is not a word you'll find in the dictionary, but it means dot upon dot."[41] *Overpoint* is the only one of Naranjo's longer works that has a female protagonist. Asked about this apparent "lack," Naranjo explained that women should not only explore the world of women and that "a woman has the right to think about the macroworld, to give views on it and to get into men's minds . . ." (Arizpe, 101). Just as Cuban Lydia Cabrera wrote *Cuentos negros de Cuba* (*Black Tales of Cuba*) to comfort and entertain her lifelong Venezuelan companion Teresa de la Parra, so in the same gesture of affection, Naranjo tried to comfort a friend. Speaking of *Overpoint*, she says in a letter, ". . . that work was written in San José about the life of a very dear friend who, at that moment, was very sick and I would read chapters to stimulate her and to make her see that life was transcendental" (Martínez, 219).

The world of *Overpoint* is no different from the world of Naranjo's other novels. Of San José, Olga, the protagonist says, "the best definition of this city is as a hole, with little light, no air, with all eyes upon us sticky and annoying . . ." (44–45). Olga exists only in the memory and the diary of her best male friend. The daughter of a prostitute, she is adopted by a wealthy couple who buy her. While searching for her identity, Olga experiences the societal hypocrisy already described in Naranjo's previous novels. This is coupled with the added burden of *marianismo*, the crippling idealization and objectification of women into the familiar Virgin/Whore binarism in a society wherein "women carry in them the ambiguity of a dream" (138). Olga rebels against all these conventions and in so doing contributes to her own destruction. At times the reader, sensitized by D. H. Lawrence's *Lady Chatterley's Lover*, sympathizes with the young woman who, like Lady Chatterley, has dared to kiss the gardener in her classist society. She is subsequently expelled from school, not for what she has done but with whom she has done it. She has transgressed societal conventions. Olga's self-destructiveness, however, sometimes makes the reader impatient. She does nothing about the emptiness of her life and deliberately turns to drugs and bad companions avowing, in one more rationalization, that she is but a prostitute's daughter: "I am what they so often told me I was, whether out of fear or desire to be so, the living likeness of my mother" (162). Olga never finds herself, and at the conclusion of the book she loses her children, her husband, and her life.

A brief excursus to compare Naranjo to Uruguayan Armonía Somers (Armonía Etchepare de Henestrosa, 1920–) seems appropriate at this point. Both examine the darker side of the human condition, but whereas Naranjo's criticism is humorous and benevolent, Somers's repudiation of hypocrisy in all its forms is, instead, piercing, trenchant, and disturbing. Somers demythifies values as devastatingly as Gambaro does in her most shocking works. The anonymous "little people" are no longer depicted with the compassion of Naranjo but, rather, as mean, nasty, brutish, and sexually obsessed. In "El hombre del túnel" ("The Tunnel"), for example, Somers creates a situation similar to that in Luisa Valenzuela's "The Verb to 'Kill.'" What the mind conjures up becomes the ultimate reality. The child protagonist becomes obsessed with a stranger who smiles at her as she emerges from a tunnel. The commotion her story elicits, the subsequent allegation of rape, and her lifetime obsession with the 'rapist' causes her to remark, "without anyone realizing what was happening, they taught me that in this world there is something called rape" (Picon Garfield, *Women's Fiction*, 34). As she explored mental obsession in "The Tunnel," Somers explores the scapegoat's ability to unite groups in hatred in *La mujer desnuda* (1966; *The Naked Woman*). The deep needs and sexual frustrations of an entire village emerge before a nude woman, "naked in purity and innocence," who serves as a catalyst for their unacknowledged inadequacies (60). The men awaken after years of indolence, longing for a virility they no longer have, for wives in whom they no longer see what they once loved. The women are envious of the naked woman for arousing their men. Angry and frustrated because they can no longer feel and elicit such emotions, the village joins forces to destroy the woman whose crime was to have exposed their hidden frustrations. The mental obsession of "The Tunnel," the sexual frustration and scapegoating of *The Naked Woman*, are conflated in "Derrumbamiento" (1986; "The Fall"), a short story where the Virgin Mary identifies with a runaway black slave and both are seen as victims.[42] The Virgin explains that she has been enshrined for centuries and thereby prevented from even showing her grief at the death of her son: "Since I was made marble, wax, sculpted wood, gold, ivory, I've had no tears. I had to carry on living this way, with a lie of stupid smiles painted on my face" (Manguel, 18). She persuades the frightened, reluctant slave to allow her to be human, to "melt" her by touching her. When he becomes sexually aroused, she calms his fears with an ironic response that indicates how deliberately Latin-American women unmask the *machismo* and the *marianismo* clichés that have restricted them: "You have melted a Virgin. What you now want is unimportant," she reassures him. "It is enough for a man to know how to melt a virgin. That is a man's true glory" (Manguel, 21).

   To return to Naranjo: her depiction of human foibles is as penetrating as Somers's, but seems innocent in comparison because of the humor, compassion, and irony that come to the fore, especially in her short stories. *Nunca hubo alguna vez* (1984; *There Never Was a Once Upon a Time*) is a delightful collection of vignettes narrated from the perspective of children and adolescents, but these too unmask the hypocrisy and sexism of society. Naranjo's female child narrators live in the now, unaware that a tomorrow may either efface joys or heal wounds so intensely felt at the moment, and the pre-adolescents begin to realize how complex life can be, when "behind one reality there can be another" (35). In the story from which the collection derives its name, the child narrator accidentally destroys her friend's new bicycle. Heartbroken, she feels guilty for what she has inadvertently done and pained at her friend's indifference: "I thought you would care about my torn blouse and the bump on my head that was bleeding" (13). While reminding her friend that they still share a bond of friendship, namely, a "once upon a time" that no accident can destroy, she learns how differently others valorize experiences. The adults rejoice at the child's miraculous survival, but her friend's reaction is painful: "Piece by piece you picked up all the useless fragments of your bicycle, and you turned around like an indignant, furious goose to tell me I never want to see you again in my whole life and forget that there ever was a once upon a time, because there never was" (16). The child narrator in "It Happened One Day" learns how easily reality and truth can be confused. She finds out that her friend is a liar, the culprit who has torn pages from a school text and then denied it to the teacher and the students. Crushed that her trusted friend has done this, the narrator at first struggles alone with the realization: "Now I know you steal, lie, and make everyone else look bad with no consideration at all for any living creature" (35). Then she decides to share this burden with her father, who, instead of sharing her chagrin, actually finds her friend's album of cut out pages very funny. Her friend too is angry with her but "not from shame but from rage because I didn't know enough to respect your privacy, your secrets, and you made me feel ashamed, like a worm" (35–36). The experience has possibly taught the child/narrator the proverbial wisdom, to "cultiver son jardin," to mind her own business, but it has also confused her: "That was also how I, too, fell from the pedestal and was shattered into little pieces. But now I think maybe I need to make my own album of cut-outs to see what I want to be like from now on" (36). The narrator in "Everybody Loves Clowns" learns how to survive in a sexist society. She wants to be a clown: "But daddy explains that there's no such thing as a girl clown, nobody hires women to be clowns because they're clowns to begin with, they paint themselves and they always wear costumes, no one will pay to see them because they can be seen for free out on the streets and in the parks" (48). Initially alienated after deciding to be a male clown since she cannot be a female clown, the child learns how to get along in society. She learns that the ubiquitous adult query about what she wants to be when she grows up is purely rhetorical. What adults really expect is conformity and she conforms: "Now they talk to me again and grandma didn't forget me after all, they laugh and smile with me. And when they ask me what I'm going to be when I grow up, I answer that

I'll be whatever they want" (50; emphasis mine). She has learned to dissimulate, to satisfy her needs in a way that is inaccessible to adults and, consequently, to their disapproval: "And to make sure they'll really love me, I have settled for being a clown disguised as someone who doesn't realize that's what she is" (50).

Women are also the center of Naranjo's fiction in two other collections of short stories, *Ondina* and *Today Is a Long Day*. The female child of *There Never Was a Once Upon a Time* has become a woman in these stories but the conventions and norms of her society remain the same. Naranjo's "Las sonrientes tías de la calle veinte" ("The Smiling Aunts of Twentieth Street") describes what happens to women who grow up to be "whatever 'they' want." Alicia and her sister Julia, "the smiling aunts," dedicate their lives to caring for their elderly mother. Although Alicia had opportunities for a personal life "many years before" (27), she has now dedicated herself to her mother lest "people consider her ungrateful." Immaculate housekeepers, obedient daughters, exhausted hostesses, the women take care of their mother's numerous ills. Naranjo gives the reader a glimpse into the wages of self-sacrifice. At times, it is humorous. Sexually lonely, the women blush at the books they read but leave dog-eared those pages that describe "the terrible things people engage in" (31). At other times, the women's desperation at the intransigeance of their mother is seen through interior monologues: "Everything for an old woman who if she did give something also had the capacity of sucking their blood, a vampire." They live with the guilt of their hidden thoughts: "I can't go on, I hate her and she will never die" (32). But the mother survives everyone. Aware of her last child's death simply because the daughter has not responded to her daily summons, the mother goes to the kitchen and fries her own eggs. But a lifetime of being cared for has left its mark. She laments, not her children's deaths, but the absence of their unstinting dedication as she repeats: "Mamita is hungry, very hungry and no one to take care of her. Poor mamita" (33).

In "Simbiosis del encuentro" ("Symbiotic Encounter"), Naranjo hilariously inverts roles to show how women's so-called natural functions affect their image. Ana and Miguel have a passionate love affair. Eventually Miguel becomes ill. He vomits and has strange cravings. His breasts swell and his abdomen grows. Ana sadly remarks, "The orgasm was a thing of the past" (38). Miguel is pregnant. They consider an abortion, but he runs away carrying Ana's unborn child. In her chagrin "as a wronged father" (40), Ana's abandonment becomes as hard to bear as her complexion which, in its prolific hirsuteness, now requires her to shave her face twice a day (41). The humor of the reversal does not, however, eliminate the seriousness of the story. By de-familiarizing the normal, Naranjo distances the reader into an objective stance from which the reality of pregnancy in a woman's experience can be appreciated. First, sexual desire is diminished ("Orgasm was a thing of the past"). Second, the pregnant Miguel is seen, and sees himself, as a monster: "At six months . . . [Miguel had] the most horrible body one can imagine in a man: a pointed belly, huge sagging breasts, a slow exhausted walk, a hunch back. The nausea continued to interrupt breakfasts, lunches, dinners, conversations" (39).

Even more compelling is the wonderfully evocative story, "Ondina," whose heroine's name has for centuries been associated with fairy tales and folklore. Paracelsus's tale of the water sprite who could obtain a human soul only if she bore a child to a human husband is best known through the eighteenth-century romance, *Undine*, by the German Friedrich de la Motte Fouqué, and through the 1939 play, *Ondine,* by Frenchman Jean Giraudoux. In Naranjo's story, the equally mysterious Ondina also lives in the interstices of two worlds. Taken from the collection of the same title, the short story "Ondina" is a humorously understated, ambiguous tale which is narrated with a sexual frankness bordering on the grotesque. An older bachelor visits the home of a virtuous woman in her forties. Merceditas, whose reputation is impeccable, lives with her parents. In the living room, the visitor sees the portrait of "a very beautiful young lady with piercing, light green eyes" identified as Ondina (Picon Garfield, *Women's Fiction*, 192–93). Obsessed with her, he has graphic sexual fantasies and tries to learn more about her. But Ondina remains a mystery. Merceditas's mother hangs up the telephone when he calls. Merceditas does not respond to his certified letter of inquiry. Her father merely "listened to me, smiled and answered that I should forget it; it was impossible" (194). When Merceditas's parents are killed in an accident, the bachelor goes to offer his condolences. He opens a door and accidentally witnesses a bizarre sexual encounter between a cat and a female dwarf, who, it turns out, is Ondina. This, however, is no story of the pitiable deformity of a beautiful young woman, for Ondina is a woman in every way except size, just as the mythical Ondine was human in every way except soul, which she acquired by marrying a mortal and bearing a child. Naranjo's Ondina has not been subjected to the restrictions placed on "normal" women in her society and is totally uninhibited, sensual, and erotic. After midnight, when the bereaved have been sedated, the man finds the "most beautiful dwarf I had ever seen" sitting on his lap showing him "everything she'd learned in her solitude." After the jealous cat, her tutor, scratches the man's penis brutally, the man makes a decision. But what does he decide? Does he marry the conventional Merceditas or the mysterious Ondina? The story concludes with this ambiguous sentence: "The betrothal was set for a month after the mourning period. Ondina attended the wedding; the cat stayed home" (197). With *Ondina,* the romantic tradition is reduced to parody.

It is interesting to note in passing that when female characters are represented ahistorically, as they are in the works of Parra, Bombal, and to a degree, Brunet (chapter three), the writers resort to dream worlds and escape mechanisms. On the other hand, in the works focusing on political realities, the romantic element is almost non-existent. Love and hate become concepts suffused with political urgency and with the accompanying reflexivity we have found in the texts of Gambaro, Valenzuela, and Naranjo.

CHAPTER 5

"To Build New Worlds"

Two interesting issues emerge in the multitude of critical discourses on modernism and postmodernism. The first concerns the shift in emphasis from the literary work as product to the literary work as process, whereby the activity itself, and not the completed action, becomes the primary issue. The second centers on whether the allegation is true that experimental authors subvert fictional norms. Regarding the first issue, it is true that the reader of postmodernist works is less interested in *mimesis*, an illusory sense of representation, and more in *poesis*, participating in the making of the text at hand. The second issue, the supposed subversion of norms in experimental fiction, is dismissed by the postmodernist writer as another modernist illusion. As Roland Barthes pointed out almost thirty years ago: "Far from being a copy of reality, literature is, on the contrary, the very consciousness of the unreality of language: literature that is the most 'true' is the one that knows itself to be most unreal insofar as it knows itself to be essentially language. . . ."[1] Ann Jefferson's more recent focus on radical forms of contemporary literature reiterates Barthes's position. For Jefferson, experimental writing, because of the awareness of its distance from so-called reality, is genuinely "realistic." It lays bare the systems through which reality is constructed, not only in fiction, but in everyday life,[2] and it foregrounds the postmodernist conviction that ultimately, all is conditioned by textuality.[3]

It seems appropriate at this point to distinguish among three types of postmodernism discussed in this book. The first is a ludic postmodernism that plays on its own fictive processes, the "opera aperta" of an Umberto Eco, the novels of an Italo Calvino. It exposes the systems through which the author constructs reality. Cuban/Mexican Julieta Campos is postmodernist in this sense, as is Brazilian Helena Parente Cunha. The second type of postmodernism, also ludic, centers on serious political issues while playing with language and conventional literary forms. This type found expression in the works of Luisa Valenzuela discussed in chapter four. Valenzuela approaches serious issues in playful ways, fore-grounding techniques of ironic banter, sardonic humor, and black comedy. Valenzuela, in fact, has emphasized that humor for her is "as important as breathing [and] must also be used as a weapon" (Ordoñez, 516), and that it is a weapon that both hurts and heals, analgesic in the sense that it forces us "to laugh at what ultimately is not at all funny."[4] The third kind, resistance postmodernism, will be discussed more fully in chapter six. Whereas ludic types of postmodernism lay bare the systems through which reality in fic-tion is constructed, resistance postmodernism exposes the fiction-ality of reality itself. It belies the "made up" versions of events and questions the veracity of official claims. Resistance postmoder-mism is experimental in the sense Elaine Scarry has pointed out, that the intense pain experienced by these women is language-destroying (35). Even when it can be articulated, it fits uncomfort-ably in the sanctioned narrative modes of storytelling.

JULIETA CAMPOS

Julieta Campos's approach to fiction is unconcerned with political issues and consequently is ludic in the first sense. She treats litera-ture as if it were a verbal, intertextual, and linguistic game. In the opinion of some, Campos's work has not received the attention it deserves precisely because of its non-political, ludic quality.[5]

Born in Havana, Cuba, in 1932, Campos received her B.A. from the University of Havana, studied at the Sorbonne in Paris, and later earned a doctorate from the University of Havana. She became a journalist in 1956, writing for various magazines and newspaper supplements. She is a novelist, short story writer, critic, and translator of numerous English and French books. A resident of Mexico, where she does all her writing, she has also taught lit-erature at the National Institute of Public Education, Acatlán, and the National Autonomous University of Mexico. Campos has been on the editorial board of such important journals as *Vuelta* and has been editor of the *Revista de la Universidad de México*. She has been awarded grants from the Alliance Française and the Center for Mexican Writers (1967). In 1974, she won the Xavier Villaurrutia Prize for *Tiene los cabellos rojizos y se llama Sabina* (1974; *She Has Reddish Hair and Her name Is Sabina*). She served as president of the P.E.N. Club of Mexico in 1978. Campos is well known for her novels: *Muerte por agua* (1965; *Death By Water*), *She has Reddish Hair and Her Name is Sabina* (*Sabina*), *El miedo de perder a Eurídice* (1979; *The Fear of Losing Euridice*), and for her collection of short stories, *Celina o los gatos* (1968; *Celina or the Cats*). Other short stories have also been favorably received: "Historia de un naufragio" (1976; "Story of Shipwreck"), and "Jardín de invierno" (1978; "Winter Garden").[6] Her critical works include: *La imagen en el espejo* (1965; *Image in the Mirror*), *Oficio de leer* in 1971 (1971; *The Business of Reading*), *Función de la novela* (1973; *The Function of the Novel*), and the hybrid critique/narrative, *La herencia obstinada: análisis de cuentos Nahuas* (1982; *The Die-Hard Heritage: An Analysis of the Story of the Nahuas*), in which she explores the indigenous oral tradition of the Nahuas from the perspective of Freudian psychoanalysis, Lévi-Strauss's structuralism, and Propp's morphology of folklore.[7]

Julieta Campos is prominent among today's writers of ludic postmodernist literature in Latin America. Her work, especially *Sabina,* has been described as "one of the best examples in Latin-American literature today of what Umberto Eco defined as an 'open work,' replete with ambiguities, contradictions, plural meanings, and disjointed and fragmented structuring of characters and scenes in constant metamorphosis" (Picon Garfield, *Women's Fiction,* 241.) Her first novel, *Death by Water* (*Death*), written when Campos was suffering from the absence and the imminent death of her mother who was afflicted with cancer, focuses on the concept of time. Here time is not chronological, as both past and future coalesce in the present, and things themselves, not their "meaning" or symbolic value, become all important. In her collection of critical essays, *Image in the Mirror*, written at approximately the same time as *Death*, Campos describes writing as an immediate communication with elemental things, with a "reality that is for itself, beyond any symbol" (36). *Death* amply illustrates her critical theory. Campos reifies the falling rain whose ubiquity permeates the novel, falling incessantly, corroding and rotting vegetation, and enveloping the novel in an "almost sexual" atmosphere of humidity (44). Because time combines past and future, neither youth nor old age remains constant or distinguishable. A case in point involves the elderly Eloísa and the younger characters, Laura and Andrés, who are seen "at the same time and [are] not distinct" (118). Narrative accounts of the past result in "a magical experience of transforming that time into another time without allowing any subtle anguish to intervene . . ." (47). The narrator fights a losing battle against time, for even in her novel time flows irrevocably, and "cannot be recovered" (108). This conviction is emphasized through to the novel's conclusion, when the narrator observes the wet spot her drinking glass has made on the tablecloth as it is slowly drying. Before her eyes the spot is becoming a thing of the past, a testament to the novel's aborted attempt at recapturing past time: "It will dry soon," the narrator realizes. "There will be no trace, not even a vestige of the place where the glass was . . . even I, though I might try to prevent it, will also forget" (142).

Campos attempts a straightforward narrative in her second book, the collection of stories entitled *Celina or the Cats*, the most traditional of her works. The short story for which the collection is named, provides a good example of Campos's style. It is a psychological thriller about a couple who have been married for thirteen years. As Bombal emphasized women's association with and men's alienation from nature, so Campos uses cats rather than nature to achieve a similar effect. The husband resents the mysterious world Celina shares with the cats, a world her doctor-husband is too pragmatic to understand. Empty, desperate for Celina's recognition, he sends her anonymous notes in which he invents extramarital affairs involving himself. The resulting tension replaces Celina's indifference to him. When she commits suicide, thereby putting an end to the torture he has inflicted on her, he is destroyed. In her discussion of relationships of domination, Jessica Benjamin explains that resistance, tension, and defiance are essential if control is to be effective. The victimizer's satisfaction comes from the challenge of conquering the resistance. With Celina's death, the husband's life is empty. In Benjamin's words, "The exhaustion of satisfaction that occurs when all resistance is vanquished, all tension is lost, means that the relationship has come full circle, returned to the emptiness from which it was an effort to escape. Total loss of tension, de-differentiation, means death of the self."[8] The novel ends as Celina's husband forces himself to "believe that it was I who destroyed Celina or at least believe I precipitated things . . . because if not, Celina's death would be as if she destroyed me" (34).

Campos's later novel, *The Fear of Losing Euridice* (*Euridice*), is a *Genesis* of fiction, the genesis of the love story which, for

Campos's narrator, is the genesis of all discourse. Narrative is described as dream fulfillment, as the quest for an imaginary object of desire—the word that will become text. And so Campos's novel of the Golden Age, of Utopia, of the Happy Isles, begins: "In the beginning was Desire. Desire engendered the Word which engendered the couple, which engendered the Island" (7). The novel is "the story of a dream" (11). Ubiquitous literary, artistic, and cinematographic intertextual allusions within the text and in the margins of the text, together with well-known topoi of enchanted islands and of the traditional couples of romance, foreground the literariness of *Euridice*. Chiastic parallels reinforce the absence of contours between the real and the unreal in the novel: "The island . . . was then the site of the dreamed meeting or the site dreamed of the meeting" (13). The parallels foreground the narrator's perplexities. Concerning the lovers, she says: "I still do not know if they love because they dream or they dream because they love" (14). She also has doubts about the text itself, wondering whether "I write as if I were dreaming. Or dream as if I were writing" (74)? A deliberate play of micro- against macro-narrative takes place as the protagonists become authors of works entitled "The Fear of Losing Euridice" within the novel itself. All this emphasizes what Campos has called elsewhere the condition of a text as simply "a work of art," and not, as conventionally assumed, a reflection of reality (*Image In the Mirror*, 6). Ultimately, *Euridice* ends as it has begun. One of the protagonists/potential authors, Monsieur N., foregrounds its circularity. At the end of the novel he reads a sign that says: THE FEAR OF LOSING EURIDICE. The narrator emphasizes that we are, ipso facto, back to our original position: "Anyone would say that he [Monsieur N.] has begun to dream the story of someone who, dreaming his own desire as if he were dreaming of an Island, dreams that he wants to narrate a story of love" (168).

It is in her best known novel, *Sabina*, that Campos's unabashedly playful treatment of literature as a pure artistic construct can be most fully appreciated. The auto-referential *Sabina* revels in its self-reflexivity. It begins and ends by exposing both the fictionality of fiction and the textuality of reality. The narrator tells us at the outset: "I am a character who looks out on the sea at four o'clock in the afternoon. But *I am also someone who imagines I myself am that character*" (11; emphasis mine). As it begins, so *Sabina* ends with the same playful foregrounding of its fictionality. One of the narrative voices informs the reader that the novel which may be written, and which might still be read, has nothing to do with her: "When I was a little girl I used to see the ocean at all the street crossings, but that has nothing to do with the novel that you are writing as if I were thinking about it, while I refuse to continue being your character . . ." (178). She also says that the time has come for *Sabina* to end: "They advise me that at least the appearance of an ending, the fiction of a period, is indispensable. And I do put one here" (179). The entire novel of 179 pages consists of one moment, when the narrator, Sabina, looks out to sea at four o'clock in the afternoon on the last day of her vacation in Acapulco. Consistent metafictional questions and intertextual allusions within the narrative baffle the reader schooled in traditional criticism. The narrator is, as Campos herself comments, "a composite figure, the embodiment of many characters who split and develop into a multitude of possible characters" (Picon Garfield, *Women's Voices*, 87.) Five characters/narrators, four women and a man, are recognizable. Each of them questions the nature of time in the novel, its character, its theme. They ask at different times which of the five is speaking. They even question whether the novel *Sabina* can be written: "I ought to have written a novel," one of the narrators remarks, "but novels, they say, are written with things that happen and nothing has ever happened to me. I have done nothing more than sit here . . ." (12–13).

Despite its playful teasing, however, some things do happen in *Sabina*. They are couched in the conventions of the detective fiction dear to the postmodernist writer/reader. There is a suicide or a murder and the reader seeks a hermeneutic springboard from which to interpret it. Is *Sabina* a detective story disguised by the familiar experimental techniques known to readers of Italo Calvino, Cabrera Infante, Luisa Valenzuela, or Julio Cortazar, for example? The reader seems to be encouraged in this regard by the author or one of her narrators to persist in searching for clues since s/he has been conditioned by the conventions of order and logic in detective fiction. In Hutcheon's words, "The reader expects them and needs them in order to read the work, in order to participate in the case."[9] Campos avails herself of these conventions in order to tease the reader: "How can you leave precisely now when all is about to be disclosed?" (32). The reader is led to believe that close reading of the novel will produce promising results. Consequently s/he carefully observes the narrator who on

8 May, 1971, tries to warn a young woman "of the danger" of "slipping in between the ropes that separate the cement floor . . . [t]he girl is completely alone and in her game there is a kind of defiance of the surf's violence" (247). The reader follows the supposed sequence of events in the 9 May 1971 morning edition of the newspaper which reports that "[a] woman of uncertain age died yesterday upon falling into a ravine some fifteen meters from her room in an Acapulco hotel . . ." (249). Such apparently sequential association, however, is soon belied by one of the narrators who knows "the character better than anyone because I invented her, independent of the facts and even of her will . . ." (250), and who knows that the circumstances surrounding the woman's death are simply wrong. It is clear that *Sabina* is not in the tradition of Valenzuela's or Calvino's detective fiction, and so the reader searches for another hermeneutic springboard. Could *Sabina* be a parodic variation on Pirandello's characters in search of an author? But Campos's characters do not lack a potential author. They lack a novel in which to exist. Hovering between what is fictionally real and what can become really fictional, *Sabina* may be seen in the tradition of such Spanish novels as Miguel de Unamuno's *Niebla* (1914; *Mist*), wherein the author confronts his fictional character precisely on the issue of the latter's freedom to go his own way. In *Sabina*, an array of possible fictional protagonists is available: "the very slender girl" on the beach whom the narrator/author observes as material for her novel; her boyfriend; the "solitary woman who in a Fellini movie . . . would listlessly cross the naturally symbolic and somewhat melodramatic vestibule of a luxury hotel in an Austrian spa." There is the "other slightly chubby" woman and her Japanese companion, the "old German woman and her grandson" and the Polish grandfather. But even this possibility is nullified. The narrator/author seals the potential characters' literary fate. They cannot find a home in her fictional world for they belong in a traditional novel, one composed of "ties and origins and endings," which hers is not. The narrators/authors finally "give up" offering clues to *Sabina*'s genre. The reader is simply unequal to the task and so they spell out the answer: "The only *datum* the reader can rely upon without fear of being deceived," they say, "that which constitutes the key to this book and consequently to the identity of said character, appears on page 111 where one ought to have already discovered it . . . and everything else [is] a mirage or a dream" (177). On page

111, however, what the eager reader actually finds is but a repetition of, not a solution to, the puzzle. Here, in a French version is a sentence that simply repeats the title of Campos's book: "Elle a les cheveux roux et s'appelle Sabine."

Critics have pursued this authorial/narratorial clue. For Bruce-Novoa the intertextual reference is clear: Campos is actually alluding to Anaïs Nin's pentalogy of works and paying Nin a sincere tribute while "correcting her focus." From this perspective, Campos is performing on Nin what Harold Bloom calls "an act of *Tessera*, a 'completion and antithesis,'" and in so doing, makes of the character Sabina "a direct challenge to male figures," and of the novel itself "a feminist deconstruction of male logocentrism."[10] Alicia Rivero Potter also sees *Sabina* in a feminist context, as an embryonic feminine novel that contrasts the mode of writing of the male narrator in "the labyrinth" with the feminine mode of the four female narrators who write in different places throughout the novel.[11] The gender question is certainly an interesting one to raise vis-à-vis *Sabina*. Julieta Campos herself has vacillated about it. When queried about *Sabina* during an interview, she asserted that the fact that one of the narrators was a man was "purely accidental. He could have been a woman." Yet she also conceded that perhaps "unconsciously" the woman writer was made to prevail in the novel (Picon Garfield, *Women's Voices*, 88). My interpretation of *Sabina* is, rather, closer to those critics who remind the reader that the only certainty in *Sabina* is that a woman looks out to sea at four o'clock in the afternoon on her last day in Acapulco.[12] Given that fact, *Sabina* becomes a wonderful linguistic game, a novel without origin or development whose only reality, in Barthes's terms, is language itself.[13] In this context the playfully untrustworthy clues become the very *raison d'être* of the novel. As with life itself, Campos's literature is made up of moments frozen in words that cannot be depended upon to provide meaning but which, instead, constitute "a defiant challenge" to conventional chronology and "to the inexorable flow of time" in the novel.[14] Julieta Campos once described *Sabina* as an effort "to rescue time from its flux, from its journey into death, by trying to detain a portion of that time that eludes us" (Picon Garfield, *Women's Voices*, 83).[15] In this way, Campos's *Sabina* becomes a world unto itself unrestricted by any effort to re-present another reality. It pinpoints itself as nothing but art. Such a deliberate artificial world, in Hutcheon's words, simply "reflects the human imagination, instead of telling a secondhand tale about what might be real in quite another world" (47).

CRISTINA PERI ROSSI

Christina Peri Rossi, unlike Julieta Campos but similar to Luisa Valenzuela, approaches serious issues in a playful manner. A native of Uruguay, Peri Rossi (1941–) is known primarily for her novels, short stories, and poetry. She has also been a journalist, teacher, and political activist. For ten years she taught literature in Montevideo, and contributed to various newspapers and magazines, *Marcha*, among others. She won the *Marcha* Prize for *El libro de mis primos* (1969; *My Cousins' Book*) and the Narrative Prize awarded by Arca Publishers for *Los museos abandonados* (1969; *The Abandoned Museums*). She received the Palma de Mallorca Award for *Indicios pánicos*, (*Signs of Panic*), the Benito Pérez Galdós Prize for *La rebelión de los niños* (1980; *The Children's Rebellion*) and the Inventarios Provisionales Prize in 1973 in Spain for a book of poetry named *Diáspora*. Contemporary Uruguayan writing has developed under unique historical conditions, reflecting the country's social turbulence, severe political repression, and violent change. Many of Uruguay's best known writers exhibit an acute critical awareness of the oppressive social reality within which and often against which they write. This is especially true of Cristina Peri Rossi, whose resistance to the increasing oppression of the Uruguayan government caused her to become a member of a coalition of leftist parties whose goal was to overthrow the government. She was forced into exile and has lived in Barcelona, Spain, since 1972.

Critics have equated Peri Rossi's systematic subversion of traditional forms with the deliberate displacement of a social context in crisis onto the imaginative plane.[16] She tries to naturalize all that is human, including the erotic. Children often serve as her vehicles for returning to a world free from oppressive norms and bourgeois structures. The books written before her exile, *Viviendo* (*Living*), *The Abandoned Museums*, *My Cousins' Book*, and *Signs of Panic*, all reflect "an almost apocalyptic vision of the world in the process of disintegration."[17] Peri Rossi deliberately breaks with traditional generic modes and patterns of discourse, explaining her procedure thus: "I proceed through images . . . I never pose an argument, theme, story . . . and so the digressions emerge naturally . . ." (Deredita, 140). In another context, she calls her work "clearly symbolic," and her literary objective the effort "to establish an allegorical universe."[18] Consequently, it is nearly impossible to summarize her works, although recurrent themes are found in her novels and in her poetry. As is to be expected, one theme is the debunking of societal myths and norms. In *My Cousins' Book* and *El museo de los esfuerzos inútiles*, (1983; *The Museum of Useless Intentions*), Peri Rossi satirizes capitalism, patriarchal institutions, psychoanalysis, militarism, and political repression. She breaks through sexual taboos, refusing to privilege or denigrate any form of eroticism. She discusses incest in *My Cousins' Book* and in *La tarde del dinosaurio*, (1976; *The Dinosaur's Afternoon*) as an innocent, childlike experience. She describes children as wiser than adults because of their lack of inhibitions. She depicts, with equal naturalness, the barrenness or possibility of all loves: heterosexual love in *The Abandoned Museums,* and homosexual love in her books of poetry: *Evohé,* 1971; *Diáspora,* 1976; *Lingüística general,* (1979; *General Linguistics*), and in her novel *Living.*[19] Homoeroticism is treated poignantly and naturally throughout.

   La nave de los locos (1984; *Ship of Fools*) is possibly Peri Rossi's most important novel. While previous themes are present, the emphasis is different. The author handles eroticism with a new tenderness and approaches humankind's ship of fools with genuine compassion. Sebastian Brant's fifteenth century metaphor of the *narrenschiff,* best known through Katherine Anne Porter's *Ship of Fools,* Pío Baroja's *La nave de los locos* (*Ship of Fools*), and Michel Foucault's *Madness and Civilization,* provides the impetus for the text. The original comprehensive attitude toward her characters can best be grasped in her reiteration of the phrase "hell is not being able to love" (153). Peri Rossi plays with the Shakespearean idea of the world as a stage and describes all of her characters with compassion and understanding: the old woman who insists that her dying husband is simply seasick; the fat man whose lower lip is split by a bullet and who keeps his bar open all night for a teenager and her black child, "in the hope that the young mother and her daughter, sleepy and tired, would return" (40); the powerless Vercingetorix, who, unlike his heroic predecessor, is simply another victim of political oppression. He is "brutally pushed into the back of a car without license plates"

(53), and put in a prison camp for two years. He simply accepts the fact that, like so many others, he too "would be thrown from a plane to the bottom of the sea" (55). The characters of Peri Rossi's ship of fools are displayed before the reader as the narrator, Equis—a letter of the alphabet (X), an anybody, and an anti-epic hero—implements the oneiric command he has received to describe the city.[20] We see the young midwesterner who cannot fend for herself in New York. For a while she carries a sign: "I'm very lonely. Please someone talk to me" (67). She has now become one more casualty of city life: "The papers report that Kate killed herself around midnight on a bench in the square—an overdose of barbiturates" (69). There are the other victims, the pregnant women who, "weighed down by their loneliness and their anxiety" (178), are being driven to abortion clinics. There are also the would-be victims who are quite capable of taking care of themselves. The blonde female dwarf, a supposedly easy prey of bullies, allows no one to humiliate her: "She scratched his face with her fingers, childlike, but with nails as sharp as claws" (54). And love, in all its forms, is made to survive this would be inhuman world. The narrator makes love to an "aging cherub" and lovingly describes the fat, naked body of the sixty-eight-year old woman (74). Morris, the older author, unlike the guarded and obsessed Gustave von Aschenbach in Thomas Mann's *Death in Venice*, spends much of his time writing "androgynous" books and acknowledging openly and enthusiastically that he has "fallen madly in love with a nine-year-old boy. His name is Percival" (150).

Peri Rossi unmasks the love that lies in relationships unsung by society, as evidenced by Percival, who stays out late at night to protect the ducks from someone who is poisoning them. The wonder of so simple an act in a deteriorating world is pinpointed as remarkable and "Morris knew that he was in the presence of a knight of the Holy Grail, that there was no way of dissuading him from his noble decision" (148). With tender compassion, Peri Rossi describes the encounter between a prostitute and an impotent man. One poor creature, whom "someone had beaten . . . up the night before" (189), undresses mechanically, no longer pretending "to act out happiness or pleasure" (193). The other poor creature has sought her out because he does not fear to reveal his impotence to one rendered as powerless as he.[21] Then there is the lesbian couple who impersonate Marlene Dietrich and Dolores

Del Rio in a theatrical act. It is of such ordinary human scenes that
Peri Rossi makes extraordinary Joycean epiphanies. It is during
the "barren" scene with the prostitute that the narrator's mind
begins to clear and after the scene with the lesbian couple the
answer to his fundamental question about love is answered. Peri
Rossi's modernizations of traditional myths (the ship of fools,
Vercingetorix, Percival) do not constitute a form of wish fulfillment. At times she unveils fairytales and romance with sardonic
humor. She dismisses the quest motif by attributing to it an inces-
tuous motivation. "Princes and knights lost their lives," she comments, "in the foolish attempt to answer the obscure question,
which kept the daughters only for their fathers' hands and eyes"
(188). She inverts the courtly love tradition by giving it a homosexual emphasis: Dante wandered the streets before his exile, she
tells us, "as much in love with Beatrice as with his fellow poet
Guido Guinizelli" (76); and for all his devotion to Guinevere, her
character muses, "I think that deep down Lancelot loved Percival"
(148). Literary characters are parodied humorously. Echs, for
example, would like to be named Ulysses but "he would have felt
obliged to re-write the *Odyssey* in modern terms: any excuse to
keep one away from a self-sacrificing wife" (919). Neither Ivan
nor Humbert would be suitable names. If he called himself Ivan
"somebody would think of him as a refugee from behind the iron
curtain" and "as for Humbert, it was impossible after the publication of *Lolita*" (19). Nor can cities be named without jeopardy.
After all, "Vergil and Dante . . . paid dear for their lack of discre-
tion on this point" (32).

Her allegories, however, are often serious. The oppression in
Uruguay that forced her into exile in Spain is often evoked in the
background of her work. *Signs of Panic*, for example, depicts people—babies and mothers—trapped in water jars and children
eaten by ever-lurking cats. One story from her collection *Una
pasión prohibida* (1986; *A Forbidden Passion*) is especially pertinent in this regard. It is the story of "El angel caído" ("The Fallen
Angel"), which becomes a metaphor for the way everyday existence can make us indifferent to the suffering of others. Breughel
used the theme in his painting of Icarus, who fell to his death
because he had flown too close to the sun and his wings, sealed
with wax, melted. W. H. Auden, in his poem "Musée des Beaux
Arts," glosses Breughel's depiction of human indifference in the
midst of suffering. Auden writes: "About suffering they were

never wrong, / The Old Masters:how well they understood . . . how it takes place . . . / In Breughel's *Icarus*, for instance: how everything turns away / Quite leisurely from the disaster; the ploughman may / Have heard the splash, the forsaken cry, / But for him it was not an important failure. . . ."[22] Peri Rossi too depicts a fall from heaven. It is an angel this time and he falls as the result of a pre-*glasnost* war between Russia and the United States, which has effected a nuclear catastrophe. An apathetic people, benumbed by the frequency of such nuclear disasters, simply ignores the fallen angel. One kind woman pities him, thinking he has fallen from a monument nearby. She counsels him not to get back on his pedestal, since he might be killed: "Because politics in our country is constantly changing, today's hero is yesterday's traitor" (14). A band of soldiers appears and treats her brutally. She falls while being pushed violently into an armored car, and the angel muses whether anyone "would miss this fallen woman" in a world where even fallen angels are ignored (15). So natural is Peri Rossi's style that her allegories can be understood by readers who do not know the original sources she so brilliantly "de-familiarizes." But her works, given her erudition, are much more rewarding when read against the myths with which she plays.

In the context of Peri Rossi's innovative use of myths and legends, a brief excursus seems pertinent to the different treatment that Argentine Alejandra Pizarnik, born in Buenos Aires on 29 April 1936, gives to de-familiarizing myths and folklore, Pizarnik died after consuming an overdose of seconal on 25 September 1972, while on leave from the psychiatric hospital where she had been interned.[23] Like Peri Rossi's, Pizarnik's work is also allegorical and self-contained, but closer to poetry than to prose by virtue of its absence of story and the absorption of the reader into the narrator's inner world. In *Extracción de la piedra de locura* (1968; *Extraction of the Stone of Folly*) Pizarnik employs a widely held medieval concept that posits insanity (folly) as the result of growths (stones) in the brain, which have to be removed surgically. The concept was still current in the sixteenth-century Dutch paintings of artists like Bosch and Breughel, and it is this metaphor that Pizarnik uses (Graziano, 50). Also motivated by an oneiric impulse to speak of what she sees, Pizarnik, like Peri Rossi's narrator reworks myth and recontextualizes literary *topoi*. The differences between Peri Rossi and Pizarnik, however, far outweigh the similarities. Whereas Peri Rossi sees love as transformative in a world of indifference and loneliness, in Pizarnik's world love is one more illusion. To use her words, "I have had many loves . . . but the most beautiful was my love for mirrors" (*Extraction*, "A Dream Where Silence is Made of Gold," 56). Pizarnik's world is permeated with mirrors, death, and silence. It is a world where "Death has restored to silence its bewitching prestige" (*Extraction*: "Fragments for Dominating Silence," 52), where the metaphor for humankind is not Peri Rossi's ship of fools, but a wagon of dead bodies: "in my dream a circus wagon full of dead corsairs in their coffins . . . [and] silence, always silence, the golden coins of the dream" (*Extraction*, 59, 57).

Peri Rossi's penchant is to focus on the extraordinary in the ordinary, whether in the figure of a modern Percival protecting defenseless ducks, or in that of a modern Vercingetorix accepting his inevitable fate. Pizarnik, on the other hand, finds it extraordinary merely to continue living. The narrator in "Arbol de Diana" (1962; "Diana's Tree"), for example, laments: "With our eyes closed and a suffering truly too great to bear we play the mirrors until forgotten words sound out magically" (Graziano, 40). The effort involved in living is also reflected in her reworking of myths. She evokes the Hansel and Gretel tale simply to regain "a silence like the little hut lost children find in the forest" (*Extraction*, 58). Hesiod's *Works and Days* is remade into Pizarnik's somber *Works and Nights* wherein she becomes "nothing but an offering/ a pure wolf's roaming in the forest . . ." (46), and even the Greek soothsayer Teiresias becomes mute in her text as she sees "[t]he dolls gutted by my ancient doll hands, the disillusion upon finding pure stuffing (pure steppes, your memory): the father who had to be Teiresias, floats in the river" (*El infierno musical*, 1971; [*The Musical Hell*] 68).

All forms of love are found wanting in Pizarnik's works. Incest, is reduced to near bathos in her posthumous Alice-in-Wonderland-like *Textos de sombra y últimos poemas* (1982; *Texts of Shadows*): "The crazy queen sighed. 'I have slept with my mother. I have slept with my father. I have slept with my son. I have slept with my horse,' she said. And added. 'So what? Death spit out another petal and yawned'" (82). In *La condesa sangrienta* (1971; *The Bloody Countess*), which is based on Valentine Penrose's *Erzébet Bathory: la comtesse sanglante* (1963), Pizarnik allies homosexual love with the medieval malady of melancholia, illustrated in the perverted dementia of the countess who tortures and murders more than six hundred young women. In the "exclusively feminine universe"

(100) of *The Bloody Countess*, Pizarnik emphasizes the grotesque-ness of homosexuality: "No one was ever able to confirm the truth of the rumors about the countess's homosexuality," the narrator says, although "[c]ertain details are obviously revealing" (100). The countess's sadistic acts with young women are described, her "less solitary lecheries" are alluded to, her scandalous trial is recorded: "A servant swore during the trial that a mysterious aristocratic lady disguised as a boy would visit the countess. On one occasion she found them together torturing a girl. But she couldn't say whether they shared other less sadistic pleasures" (100). And Pizarnik's view of heterosexual love is equally bleak. It constitutes a kind of fossilized memory:

> Where a boy and a girl once made love, there are ashes and spots of blood and pieces of fingernails and pubic curls and a bent candle which they used for obscure ends and spots of sperm on the mud and rooster heads and a ruined house drawn in the sand and pieces of perfumed papers which were love letters . . . (*The Musical Hell*, 74).

Pizarnik never rises above her world of mirrors, death, and silence. The Mexican Rosario Castellanos repudiates such literary stereotypes of women in her "Meditación en el umbral" ("Meditation on the Threshold") as virgins, whores, madwomen, or suicides, and demands "another way to be human and free./Another way to be." In her play, *El Eterno Femenino* (*The Eternal Feminine*), she equates this "other way" with the creative imagination: "It's not good enough to imitate the models proposed for us that are answers to circumstances other than our own," she explains. "It isn't even enough to discover who we are. We have to invent ourselves" (Ahern, 356). Alejandra Pizarnik desperately tried to invent herself but failed. Her journal entry for 15 April 1961 records that failure. She describes her life as "lost for literature by fault of literature. By making myself a literary character in real life I fail in my intent to make literature with my real life, since the latter doesn't exist: it's literature" (Graziano, 113).

ISABEL ALLENDE

Isabel Allende's use of the romantic tradition is different from that of the women discussed so far. The addiction to romance has had tragic results in the dreamy novelistic worlds of Parra, Bombal, and Brunet. It has been humorously parodied in the novels of the politically centered Gambaro, Valenzuela, and Naranjo, and has been the object of sardonic and black humor in the poetic prose of Alejandra Pizarnik. In Allende's works, however, no matter how closely the serious political situation of Latin America is represented, the romantic element takes precedence. If the female characters in the texts of Parra, Bombal, and Brunet can be said to be constructed by the discourse of romance and the "novela rosa," Allende's are produced, instead, by melodrama.

Allende was born in Lima, Perú, in 1942. Her father served as a Chilean diplomat. Her uncle and godfather was Salvador Allende, the socialist president of Chile from 1970 to 1973. On 11 September 1973, his government was toppled in a military coup that led to his assassination. After her parents' divorce, Allende spent her childhood in Santiago, Chile with her maternal grandparents. This childhood experience would be transmuted years later into the fictional background and characters of her 1982 novel *La casa de los espíritus* (*The House of the Spirits*). Allende passed her adolescence in Bolivia, Europe, and the Middle East with her mother and diplomat stepfather. Some of her experiences are reflected in her 1987 novel, *Eva Luna*. A journalist for television and newsreels until 1973, Allende stayed in Chile for several months after the coup, often transporting to safe asylums *personae non gratae* to the new government. Her political activities jeopardized her own safety and in 1974 she fled with her family to Caracas, Venezuela. Although her exile was lonely and traumatic, she concedes that: "If there had been no exile, no pain, no rage built over all those years far from my country, most likely I would not have written ... [*The House of the Spirits*]."[24]

To date Allende has written four novels: *La casa de los espíritus* in 1982 (1985, *The House of the Spirits*), *De amor y sombra* in 1984 (1987, *Of Love and Shadows*), *Eva Luna* in 1987 (1988, *Eva Luna*), *El plan infinito* in 1991 (1993, *The Infinite Plan*), and a compilation of stories, *Cuentos de Eva Luna* in 1989 (1991, *The Stories of Eva Luna*).

The House of the Spirits (*The House*) and *Of Love and Shadows* (*Of Love*) describe political events clearly identifiable with the political history of contemporary Chile. The climax of *The House* is a coup similar to the one that brought down the socialist government of Salvador Allende in 1973 and imposed the ensuing dictatorship. *Of Love* focuses on the discovery in 1978 of the remains of fifteen peasants who were buried alive in the Longuén Mine, Chile, in 1973. *Eva Luna*, although primarily fictional, includes sporadic allusions to political situations. This novel, like *Of Love*, features a massacre, this time in one of the Army Operations Centers (233). Guerrillas and military personnel form part of the book's action, and the protagonist Eva Luna alludes to the fact that after "a brief interval of republican freedom, we once again had a dictator" (62). The story of Eva Luna is, however, primarily a novel of the storyteller's development. *The Infinite Plan*, Allende's latest novel, takes place in the United States. Here she captures the Latino culture and the problems experienced by Latinos in a North American setting.

Isabel Allende is first and foremost a storyteller. Her novels and her characters are the "stuff" of romance. Even in the midst of political horror, the characters construct their interpretations according to soap operas and popular song. Eva Luna calls her televised script of the guerrilla/military bloody warfare, for example, "Bolero, as a homage to the songs that had nurtured my girlhood hours and served as a basis for so many of my stories" (263). She lives her life "like a novel" (268). Allende refers to *Of Love* as "the story of a woman and a man who loved one another so deeply that they saved themselves from a banal existence" (Preface). And Gregory Reeves, a character in *The Infinite Plan*, concedes that "Carmen had become the protagonist of her own novel" (242). Most of Allende's novels have a proleptic structure since they are told in retrospect. Alba recounts the events of *The House*, Eva narrates *Eva Luna*, and Gregory Reeves's lover in *The Infinite Plan* tells us the story Reeves has told her "of his earliest memory" (5). Consequently, the sense of destiny as being already written, which gives *The Infinite Plan* its title, is indicative of all Allende's novels.

None of her novels has received international attention equal to that devoted to *The House of the Spirits* even though it, like the 1994 movie version, has met with very mixed reviews. It is upon *The House of the Spirits*, therefore, that I will focus. The novel has consistently been compared to the Nobel Peace laureate Gabriel García Márquez's *One Hundred Years of Solitude* and, in the process, has been labeled derivative. Allende's literary reputation has been termed a Euro-American construct, "invented" so that a woman writer can be made to represent the Boom and post-Boom generation.[25] It has been heralded for its androgyny, for its femino-centric world where the women propel the narrative.[26] Regardless of critical opinion, it is a fact that *The House of the Spirits* was powerful enough to be censored by the Chilean government when it was first published by Plaza y Janés in Barcelona, and popular enough to have been translated into over fifteen languages.[27]

The House of the Spirits centers on four generations of the Trueba-del Valle family and spans six decades from the early twentieth century to the military coup of Augusto Pinochet in 1973. Its genesis was an unsent letter written by the exiled Allende to her grandfather dying in Chile (the model for Esteban Trueba in the novel), reassuring him that memory survives mortality. The letter grew into the present novel, a fictional compilation of familial and political recollections.[28]

The narrative is composed of different voices. The reader learns in the epilogue that the third-person narrator of the story is actually the last Trueba-del Valle offspring, the granddaughter, Alba. The sources of Alba's narration, and consequently of *The House*, are her grandmother Clara's notebooks and Alba's own recollections. Those who are responsible for Alba's narration are Clara's ghost, which urges her to write in order to survive her prison ordeal, the political prisoner Ana Díaz, who gives her paper and pencil with which to carry out the project, and eventually her grandfather, Esteban Trueba, "who had the idea that we should write this story" (430). The story entails, then, recollections of the pre-coup period (the child and adult Clara's notebooks), the coup and post-coup terror (while Alba is in prison), and the time of her release and of the death of her ninety-year-old grandfather. Interspersed with Alba's third-person account is the first-person version of Esteban Trueba, the axis of the family saga. At times the third and the first person versions contradict each other.[29] As a result, the validity of Clara's and of Alba's interpretations of events is sometimes contested by Trueba's narrative. Other narrative strategies, especially those concerning agency and tone, have troubling effects as I will show shortly. But first a brief synopsis of the novel is in order.

The first two chapters introduce the principal characters. Nivea is the activist-suffragist matriarch who has given birth to fifteen del Valle children, of whom eleven have survived. Her politically minded husband is Severo del Valle. Ten-year-old Clara is a clairvoyant who foretells events and has uncanny telekinetic powers. Rosa, the eldest daughter, is an unreal beauty with green hair and yellow eyes. She is engaged to Esteban Trueba. Rosa is killed early in the novel by poison intended for her father, del Valle. The young Esteban Trueba is determined to get rich in order to marry the beautiful Rosa. His unhappy childhood of "privations, fear and guilt" results in an adulthood full of "fury and his outsized pride" (46). This fury characterizes Trueba's iron rule over the family country house, *Tres Marías*, a rule manifested by violence toward the men and subjection of the women: "Not a girl passed from puberty to adulthood that he did not subject to the woods, the riverbank, or the wrought-iron bed" (63).[30] The reader is also introduced to several other characters, notable among whom is Férula, a self-sacrificing spinster, whose appearance reflects "the ugliness of resignation," and who has woven for her young brother Esteban an "invisible net of guilt and unrepayable debts of gratitude" (42). The peasant girl, Pancha García, is Trueba's first rape victim at *Tres Marías*. Her progeny is central to the novel's cycle of cruelty and revenge. Her grandson, Esteban García, tortures and rapes Esteban Trueba's granddaughter, Alba, the third-person narrator of the story. Finally, there is Pancha García's brother, Pedro Segundo García, who is Trueba's foreman. He is the father of Pedro Tercero García, who becomes the lover of Trueba's daughter Blanca, the political comrade of Trueba's son Jaime, and Esteban Trueba's enemy.

The plot of *The House* is uncomplicated. Nine years after her sister Rosa dies, Clara, the clairvoyant and the youngest del Valle daughter, breaks her self-imposed nine-year silence in order to announce her marriage to Rosa's fiancé, Esteban Trueba. The novel describes their ensuing turbulent marriage, Trueba's unscrupulousness, the political vicissitudes and the military coup's aftermath of terror in a Latin-American country easily identifiable with contemporary Chile. It is, then, not the plot but the way in which Allende constructs it that warrants critical analysis. Political events are at the center of both *The House* and *Of Love*, but even critics who dismiss Allende as derivative, and those who acknowledge that little originality can be ascribed to one who "has left the novel genre about where she found it," nevertheless concede that her writing has struck "a blow for freedom and love against the tyranny that still grips her beautiful country."[31] The seriousness of political events, however, so central to at least two of her novels is undermined by two recurrent literary strategies. The first, which applies in varying degrees to all her novels, is what John Krich calls "a conspicuously mechanical fatalism."[32] In this novel where the possibility of negotiation, agency, and resistance is critical, a sense of resignation, of irrevocability, prevails. The second distracting literary strategy is what I see as a prurience, and out-of-place eroticism, that suffuses serious scenes with a shock element, undermining their impact.

A sense of "the writing finger writes and having writ moves on" pervades the novel. The peasant girl, Pancha García, for example, makes no attempt to defend herself from Esteban Trueba's violent rape, for, "Before her, her mother—and before her, her grandmother—had suffered the same animal fate" (57). This relentlessness characterizes places and persons: Trueba's daughter Blanca makes love to Pedro Tercero García, the nephew of the rape victim, "where years earlier, Esteban Trueba had stolen Pancha García's humble virginity" (156). Alba is born with the same green hair her Aunt Rosa had (202), and she invents exotic animals "much like those Rosa had embroidered on her tablecloth" (270).

A novel that is narrated in retrospect allows for intrusive narratorial anticipations and interpretations that are already conditioned by the narrator's knowledge. The narrator of *The House*, consequently, highlights his omniscience. He begins and ends the novel with exactly the same lines, reminds us that, as Esteban Trueba had cut off Alba's father's fingers, so Alba's will also be cut off, informs us that Amanda will die for her brother Miguel "[f]ulfilling a promise she had made him many years before" (425), and reveals that Pedro García's clay images "would later be her [Blanca's] only means of survival" (173). Even the intricate relationships participate in the complicated web of fate that binds the characters in *The House*. I will point out but two related examples. Pedro Segundo García, Trueba's right-hand man and Clara's friend, is also the father of Trueba's worst enemy, Pedro Tercero, and the brother of Trueba's first rape victim, Pancha García. As a result, the grandson born of the rape, Esteban García, "instrument of a tragedy that would befall her [Alba's] family" (190), is related to Alba, *his* rape victim, on both sides: his grandmother, Pancha García, is the sister of Pedro Segundo García, who is Alba's paternal grandfather. Esteban García's grandfather, Esteban Trueba, is also Alba's grandfather, the father of Alba's mother, Blanca. The fatalism is so marked that the reader is surprised to learn that it took an entire novel for the narrator to "suspect" at the end of it that "nothing that happens is fortuitous, that it all corresponds to a fate laid down before my birth" (431).[33]

Allende's second strategy, equally distracting from the seriousness of events, is to use scenes with contrived and misplaced humor. Uncle Marcos has died of a mysterious African plague and his body is stored on board a ship, alongside the vegetables of the Chinese cook (18). Another, presumably funny, incident occurs with young Rosa's corpse. Her autopsy is performed on "the slab of marble where Nana [the cook] kneaded pastry and chopped vegetables" (27). The decapitated head of Clara's mother, violently severed in an automobile accident, has been abandoned in a hatbox in the basement. When Clara dies, Trueba orders her body buried and adds, "While you're at it . . . you might as well bury my mother-in-law's head. It's been gathering dust down in the basement" (293). At times a prurience, a misplaced eroticism, makes the scene disturbing. For example, the grief-stricken Trueba cannot leave his beloved Rosa's tomb. A scene of genuine sorrow is perverted as Trueba surmises that the caretaker sees him as "one of those crazed necrophiliacs who sometimes haunt cemeteries" (35). The incident is permeated with a bizarre eroticism, wholly out of place with young Rosa's tragic death: "The strongest feeling I remember having," Trueba tells us, "was frustrated desire, because I would never be able to . . . run my hands over Rosa's body, to penetrate her secrets . . ." (37).[34] One particularly grotesque example involves the unwitting voyeurism of the ten-year-old Clara who watches her sister's autopsy. Clara sees the young mortician's "shirt stained with blood and his eyes drunk with love" while Rosa's "intestines [lie] beside her [Rosa] on the salad platter" (38). After the autopsy Clara watches as he "kissed Rosa on the lips, the neck, the breasts, and between the legs . . . panting . . ." (39). Is it any wonder that Clara does not speak until nine years later? These scenes seem wholly out of place and contrived in order to shock. Disturbing as Allende's misplaced humor and her "conspicuously mechanical fatalism" (to use John Krich's words) are, most disturbing is the peace and reconciliation posited at the conclusion of *The House*. It is a reconciliation achieved, as Gabriela Mora has shown, through recourse to conventional stereotypes and, in my view, to age-old conservative *topoi*. The story of the good-hearted prostitute, Tránsito Soto, who "was indefatigable and never complained" (69), for example, ends happily. She has become the successful madam of a hetero-/homosexual bordello and is on excellent terms with the new military government. The revolutionary Pedro Tercero García chooses love over politics. He is the only one, besides the conservative Esteban Trueba, who seems bent on changing the political picture. Yet Pedro Tercero goes, instead, into exile, happily making love, not war. The immoral and violent Trueba does not "die like a dog" (132) as Férula foretells, but rather, peacefully in his granddaughter Alba's arms (Mora, 55). And Alba, after the horror of her torture and repeated rapes, is released pregnant by an unknown man. A contrived peace permeates her conviction that, as with everything else in *The House*, she is simply part of a "terrible chain," "an unending tale of sorrow, blood and love" (432).

Alba's acceptance of rape as a given, a mere link in an essential and natural "chain of events," is most disturbing of all (431). "The day my grandfather tumbled his [Esteban García's] grandmother Pancha García . . . he added another link to the chain of events that had to complete itself," she explains. "Afterward the grandson of the woman who was raped repeats the gesture with the granddaughter of the rapist, and perhaps forty years from now my grandson will knock García's granddaughter down among the rushes . . ." (431). Once the inevitability of violence toward women is posited, Alba attempts to transcend hatred by pardoning, loving, and waiting "for better times to come" (432).[35] Allende falls, at the end, into the masculinist *topos* of "rape for a good cause." From Verginia and Lucretia in Roman antiquity to the Virgin Mary in Christian tradition, the violation of a woman's will has often been justified by its transcendental consequences. Whether these be the founding of new governments, the birth of a divine being, or, as in Allende's case, the cosmic and circular vindication of past rapes or the anticipation of future peace, woman's body has been made systematically subservient to the body politic.[36] It is with this dangerously contrived resolution that Allende attempts to build a new world at the conclusion of *The House of the Spirits*.

ALBALUCÍA ANGEL

Colombian Albalucía Angel succeeds where both Pizarnik and Allende fail. She invents a "herland" where women can be truly "human and free." Like Pizarnik, her narrative is often closer to poetry than to prose, whether she is re-gendering the traditionally male genre of the *Bildungsroman,* which she does in *Estaba la pájara pinta sentada en el verde limón* (1975; *The Painted Bird Was Sitting in the Green Lemon Tree*), or inventing a totally new feminine reality such as that found in *Las andariegas* (1984; *The Wanderers*). Born in Pereira, Colombia in 1939, Angel pursued her collegiate education in literature and the history of art at the Universidad de los Andes. She studied art history with Marta Traba at the University of Bogotá, continuing her studies in Paris and Rome where she performed as a folk singer. In the late 1960s she began to write seriously. Besides literature, Angel has published articles on art and been involved in filmmaking. Her several documentaries about Colombia constitute an important subject in her literary corpus.

Colombia and the Colombian experience form the basis for *The Painted Bird Was Sitting in the Green Lemon Tree* (*The Painted Bird*), which won her the Vivencias National Novel Prize, and *¡O gloria inmarcesible!* (1979; *Oh, Unfading Glory!*), a collection of short stories. The political context of *The Painted Bird* is the civil war period in Colombia in the 1940s and 1950s, appropriately called La Violencia. The novel is partly autobiographical. "I have lived 'La Violencia' as the story of *The Painted Bird* since I was seven," Angel once revealed, explaining that her resultant nightmares did not cease until she wrote her novel (García Pinto, *Historias,* 49). Divided into twenty-two segments with no chapter numbers or headings, and composed of the reminiscences of the female narrator's youth and adolescence, the narrative seems disorderly. Its chronology is often difficult to follow. The epigraph nevertheless provides the reader with a clue to the novel's organizing principle. Taken from the work of Dylan Thomas, it reads: "The memories of childhood have no order, and no end." The frontispiece, a selection from Joaquín Estrada Monsalve, provides a second clue, this one about the subject matter. The quote, from Monsalve's *April 9 in the Palace,* speaks of the "dark night" of Colombia's soul but, at the same time, encourages Colombian youth to "rise from the ruins" (8). The third possible clue occurs on the first page of the narrative as Ana, the narrator/protagonist, says of the events to which she has been an eyewitness: "I don't believe the story they tell, let the fools fall for it" (9). The reader is thereby prepared for a story which will not be linear since the events are the reminiscences of a child, a story which acknowledges the "dark night" of La Violencia in Colombia, and one in which the narrator will give the lie to the official version by recounting the "true" one. Only the first two clues are borne out by the text.

As the novel begins, the narrator holds an imaginary dialogue with a lover about to be tortured. It ends with his actual torture. Angel's narrative is, above all, an explanation for the reason average children join guerilla groups when they reach adulthood. The reader witnesses the experiences of the narrator/protagonist and her little friends as their carefree world is violently invaded by the most crucial event of the novel, the assassination of the liberal presidential candidate, Jorge Eliecer Gaitán, in 1948. The gaiety of the children's existence is continually contrasted with the country's violence. Authentic historical documentation in the form of radio reports and actual photocopies of newspaper accounts of Gaitán's assassination are interspersed through the child's narration. Intertextual discussions of testimonials of real assassinations permeate the novel: those of revolutionaries like Malcolm X, Lumumba, and Camilo Torres. Besides interweaving different media, the novel blurs boundaries. This is made especially clear in Angel's use of three binarisms: fact and fiction, bathos and pathos, and the juxtaposition of traditional and revisionist history. Their effect is to undermine the omniscience of the narrator and to force the reader's careful attention.

The fact/fiction violation of boundaries whereby "real" events and fictive events are given equal importance confuses reality with fiction. Ironically, this device makes the narrator's "true" story seem just as subjective as the official version she disclaims. The juxtaposition of bathos and pathos suggests that tragedy is a fact in the children's world as well as in that of the adults. It belies any possible sentimental view of childhood on the part of the reader vis à vis the child's narration. For example, mischief becomes poignant when Julieta, a little schoolmate, wins the medal that Ana wants. Ana taunts, teases, and provokes Julieta with typical childhood mischief. Her punishment is to write one hundred times: "I am sorry I was mean to Julieta." This scene of the repetition of the one hundred lines is duplicated after Julieta is tragically killed by a bus. Ana tearfully conjures up a litany of "100 lines" to the dying Julieta, this time through fervent promises that she will be good, she will lie no more, she will never be mean again, if only

Julieta lives. At times, the juxtaposition is genuinely humorous. In the aftermath of Gaitán's assassination when increasing violence is announced hourly over the radio, little Ana sadly announces that on the day of his murder she had "lost all innocence forever" (32). The shocked adults soon learn that Ana is actually speaking about the tooth she lost that day. In the panic, no one had remembered to put money under her pillow, and consequently Ana no longer believes in the tooth fairy (Pérez Mouse) of Latin-American folklore.

The opposition of the traditional and the revisionist views of history strikes at the very heart of Latin America's historical reality, not merely at the official version of the state's terrorist tactics during La Violencia. Ana's aunt contrasts the official Spanish version of the glorious colonization of the Latin-American world, which Ana and the children still learn in school, with what today would be called the postcolonial perspective. For the child who believes the aunt's version over the school's official version, this simply translates into the fact that "the native indians were the gifted ones and that the Spaniards were the beasts" (87). The reader is thereby subtly reminded that inter- and intra-textually, the narrator's caveat at the beginning admits multiple perspectives: "I don't believe the story they tell, let the fools fall for it" (9).

Angel's writing in the eighties is no longer concerned with the grand scale of Colombia's politics, but is more interested in male/female relations in her society. Her feminist novel, *Misiá señora* (1982; *The Missus*), is structured in a series of three "imágenes" (images). The first, "I have a doll dressed in blue," deals with protagonist Mariana's childhood and adolescence. The second, "Antigone without a shadow," is concerned with her courtship and marriage, the birth of her two children, and her mental deterioration, which results in her internment in a mental institution. The last "imagen," "The masters of silence," focuses on the painful memories the protagonist associates with her mother and her grandmother. *The Missus* centers on Mariana's struggle to be herself in a patriarchal society. An upper class "lovely child," she is encouraged to be submissive, passive, and, above all, thoughtless. The novel is infused with societal views derogatory to scholarly women. Mariana is warned, for example: "Be careful of thinking that you're a scholar. Men are bored [with a scholar] and find one [a woman] who is less presumptuous" (101), and in a diatribe against Virginia Woolf whose "nonsense" her husband was supposed to have published, all women writers are simply discounted because "Women who write are dirty . . ." (205). The reader is, consequently, not surprised with the comments following little Mariana's announcement that she wishes to be an airline pilot. "You are a girl," comes the swift response, "in other words that is taboo, understand that" (146). Constantly informed that motherhood is "the noble work of woman" (149), and that women must know how to sew and how to cook, Mariana accepts as irrevocable a pattern that "has always been written thus . . . to break down that structure would result in destroying the norm, in subversion, chaos . . ." (144).

Angel sketches "a new way" for women to be in *The Wanderers*. She plays with structure and language, eschewing patriarchal order, logic, and unified plot. The narrative consists of the absence or the unorthodox use of punctuation, of fragments and of phrases rather than sentences. Angel's background in art history is apparent in *The Wanderers* (García Pinto, *Historias*, 36–40). A combination of drawings and of verbal images of women is highlighted on separate pages as she interweaves women's history across continents, beginning with indigenous Colombian creation myths. Though it owes much to Monique Wittig's *Les Guérillères* (*The Female Warriors*) for its origin, the author makes clear from the outset of the work that it is also a search for Latin-American roots.[37] *The Wanderers* focuses on the re-creation and the re-valorization of indigenous myths in the manner of writers like the Mexican Carlos Fuentes or the Guatemalan Miguel Angel Asturias. Circular in structure, it begins and ends with references to both Wittig's *The Female Warriors* and to Latin-American myths. It is primarily a feminist odyssey. Critics have, in fact, described the book as "a self-conscious attempt at fictionalizing postmodern feminist theory into a novel" (Marting, 37). Angel herself has said that she wanted to demythify, desacralize, reinvent the version of those who participated in history diferently from men, that is, women (García Pinto, *Historias*, 57). The female wanderers' sojourn is "from nowhere toward history" (11). The preface suggests that this will be accomplished through images and the imagination. Guided by childhood stories that she transforms into visions, Angel does not attempt to analyze or explain them. Instead, she tells the reader, she "dreamed the reality and constructed chapters of pure longing for what women have preserved in time almost without our realizing it, for stories in other voices, for a vision in which they did not participate historically in the same way [as men did]" (11). If in the process, Angel comments, she has destroyed some of the reader's treasured views, and abandoned enchanted woods and myths of sleeping beauties, the reason "has not been to provide an answer. I do it rather as a mode of inquiry" (11).

This lovely poetic work begins with the indigenous creation myth of the Kogui Indians of Colombia, wherein the sea is the mother of creation, a creatrix who is also thought and memory. The narrative ends with Latin-American lore, the well-known women of its history and legends. Women's history is thereby created in *The Wanderers* through the four semicircular and circular arrangements of famous women. The arrangement is not hierarchical from top to bottom. Because of its circularity it privileges no one and, because of its visual and literal unconventionality, the names stand out and demand to be remembered. The narrative deals successively with Egyptian women, the ancient cultures of Greece, Rome, and ultimately the culture of Latin America. The novel's oneiric ambiance permits the women varied experiences that are articulated not through traditional totalized narratives but through cryptic fables. The women make no effort to encode themselves in either old or new scripts. They simply are. Angel focuses lovingly on the parable-like fragments of these incessant wanderers who, like their author, seek no answers. Rather, they explore other ways. In one of its initial quotes, *The Missus* poses a question that is taken from *The New Portuguese Letters* of the three Marías of Brazil: "How can one reinvent gesture or word, if everything has been invaded by the old meanings . . . ?" (11). Angel addresses herself to this query with her playful invention in *The Wanderers*. She answers by bypassing old meanings and exploring new ways. The novel ends hopefully with a significant quote from Wittig's *The Female Warriors*, auguring a new beginning: "They say that all those forms indicate an antiquated language. They say that everything has to begin again. They say that a great wind sweeps over the earth. They say that the sun will rise."

HELENA PARENTE CUNHA

Helena Parente Cunha, like Julieta Campos, is to be numbered among Latin America's writers of ludic postmodernist literature.

A Professor in the College of Letters at the Federal University of Rio de Janeiro, Cunha was born in Salvador, Brazil, in 1929. She has published a considerable body of short stories, such as *Cem mentiras de verdade* (1985; *One Hundred Lies of Truth*); *As doze cores do vermelho* (1988; *The Twelve Colors of Red*); *O grito do silêncio* (1983; *The Shout of Silence*). Her poetic works include *Corpo no cerco* (1978; *Body Besieged*); *Jeremias, a palavra poética* (1979; *Jeremiah, The Poetic Word*); and *Maramar* (1980; *Maramar*). Cunha's already established literary reputation was internationalized with the publication of her novel *Mulher no espejo* (1983; *Woman Between Mirrors*), her only work translated into English.

The protagonist in *Woman Between Mirrors* is a middle-aged wife who studies her many reflections in a three-way mirror. At the outset of the narrative, she plays the metaliterary games Julieta Campos plays, but whereas Campos plays with the notion of author/narrator, Parente Cunha plays with the notion of character: "Now, when my faces come into alignment, one over another, and the dates come together, I'm going to begin my story . . . No, I'm not going to write my memoirs, or my biography or paint my portrait. I'm a made-up character. I exist only in my imagination and in the imagination of my reader" (1). Like Campos, she scoffs at the role of the author/narrator: "We need to keep it straight who's character, narrator, and author. I'm the character here. The narrator is herself, the woman who writes me. The author has nothing to do with the story. The authoress, that is. These are three entities which, as it so happens, have come together. Here, the narrator, that is, the woman who writes me, is a character of the character. My character. Which doesn't cancel out the basic difference. As I've often said, she's who she is, I'm who I am. As for the authoress, I don't know who she is. She doesn't come into the story. Or does she? Could we be projections of her fantasies?" (52). Cunha also plays with the notion of a unified perspective. In the manner of the "novela rosa," the protagonist tells the reader that her husband "likes to have me near him . . . waiting for him, sweet-smelling, keeping my voice low, or in one of my silent moments . . ." The "woman who writes me," on the other hand, with the brutality of an Alejandra Pizarnik, strips this romantic fiction of all illusion as she counters—in script:

When your husband arrives, you keep hoping he will take the glass of ice water, instead of that damned rum with lime you're supposed to make strong enough, and enough of it, to last the approximately two hours before the dinner ceremonial, when he comes to the table high or dead drunk and then anything can happen, like the time when he forced the housemaid to sit at the table to eat and then simply went to bed with her. And you? Where did you hide to pretend you couldn't see this depravity? How many times did he come home drunk and smash up the glasses and the china? How many times did he beat you up? Enough of pretending and fantasizing happiness that isn't there" (21).[38]

As with *Sabina, Woman Between Mirrors* plays with the notion of closure in conventional fiction: "As long as I don't hand my story over to her," the character muses, "my slender story of subjection and revolt, she, my authoress, will be left with the disagreeable sensation of not knowing how to bring the job she has underway to a successful finish" (82). The woman between mirrors, however, ultimately comes to terms with the nature of mirrors: "Reverse is the same as the opposite side. Reverse is different from the same side" (6). As with the mirror images, the women become reversed. The "woman who writes me," formerly the rebellious one, marries a biology teacher and settles down to a colorless life with him. The formerly conventional housewife becomes "an unprincipled hussy" who fills her nights with wild dancing and sexual escapades in the black section of Bahía. At the conclusion of the novel, the woman between mirrors who earlier defiantly affirmed, "I have to fight to exist," now exists (51). Her identity is no longer dual nor fragmented into fictional doubling. She sees herself, instead, as "an entire face in a shard of glass. A single face . . . The face. Me . . ." (132). It is clear that Cunha plays metaliterary games while also exploring the issue of female identity. The reader is left with the question: is the woman between mirrors the conventional housewife, is she the lascivious "woman who writes me," or is she perhaps both?

ROSARIO FERRÉ

The Puerto Rican Rosario Ferré (1942–) also plays with the notion of female identity and she too uses Cunha's double imaging. In one of her short stories, "Cuando las mujeres quieren a los hombres" ("When Women Love Men"), taken from *Papeles de Pandora* (1976; *Pandora's Papers*), Ferré explores the situation of two women, both named Isabel, who love the same man. The first, his black mistress, Isabel La Negra, (based on a legendary Puerto Rican madam), is a prostitute. Financially secure, she is stereotypically depicted as sensual and uninhibited. Her use of language reinforces the image. It is vulgar, even obscene, as she describes what she does to and for the "rich boys" in the brothel. Rosario Ferré has explained her deliberate use of obscenity: "If obscenity has been traditionally used to degrade and humiliate woman, I said to myself, it should be doubly effective in redeeming her."[39] Isabel Luberza, the wife, on the other hand, is also a stereotype. Blonde, green-eyed, pure and conventional, she tries everything to bring her husband back. First, she does everything to please him in bed, allowing him to do whatever he wishes. She sets the table correctly; she washes his clothes correctly; she makes his bed correctly. When living correctly does not bring her husband back, however, Isabel Luberza tries suffering correctly. She mortifies her flesh in order to make Isabel La Negra "get back on the right path" (42). In the midst of her travail, her husband dies, leaving half of his estate to her and half to his mistress. They are equal now.

The title of Ferré's story is a shortened form of a Puerto Rican refrain that refers to a woman's votive offerings to win or to retain the man she loves: "When women love men/they take four candles and light them/in every corner" ("Cuando las mujeres quieren a los hombres,/Cogen cuatro velas y se las prenden/por los rincones"). Ferré uses refrains like this, posited as universal assumptions, in the same way that she sets up situations, traditionally accepted as "natural" in the story. After the man's death the dual narrator (both women's voices are juxtaposed), referring to the refrain, accepts the significance of the refrain. They merely wonder whose votive offering was ultimately successful and whether the man so divided his inheritance in order "to see who would win" (26). The scenario is a set piece: a proverbially accepted Latin-American *ménage à trois*—a man, a wife, and a mistress; two female rivals whose rivalry is exacerbated by differences in class and race, and the predictable contest to determine who will prevail—the fair, pure, legitimate wife or the dark, raunchy prostitute. Given the stock rules of the game Ferré has established, it is predictable that the wealthy prostitute should usurp the role of the now publicly humiliated wife. As charitable matron and philanthropist, she deprives the wife of her home, and converts it into a brothel in one of the island's best neighborhoods. But Ferré sub-

verts all readerly expectations as well as the game she has created
in the process. The two abused women do not hate each other. In
fact, they unite in a deep and loving relationship. Like Cunha's
woman between mirrors whose "faces come into alignment, one
over another," the two Isabels see their images in the mirror "one
upon the other as with an old photograph lovingly placed under
its negative" (27). Their distinct identities become blurred as they
"purify [themselves] of all that used to define us, one as a prostitute, the other as a society matron" (27). When the two pool the
man's inheritance and make their brothel the best in San Juan, the
reader is made privy to Ferré's systematic blurring of such binarisms as black/white, mistress/wife. A loving confusion between the
two women, "between her and her, or between her and me, or
between me and me" (29), is used to describe their new identification. At the end of the story, the two women, like Cunha's mirror
images where "Reverse is the same as the opposite side . . . different from the same side," are literally reversed. The white woman's
skin has become "naked and dyed black" (31), while the black
woman's hair has become soft and pliable, and her skin "no
longer black but white" (44).

ANGELES MASTRETTA

What is of particular interest in the works of Peri Rossi, Angel,
Cunha, and Ferré is the issue of agency in the women characters.
Their protagonists appropriate myths, clichés, and proverbs previously used to objectify females and make them serve their own
purposes. In the same way, Angeles Mastretta (1949–) reappropri-
ates the bolero in her best known work, *Arráncame la vida* (1989;
Mexican Bolero). The novel centers on Catalina, not yet fifteen,
who marries a middle-aged, corrupt politician and womanizer.[40]
Their story develops against the backdrop of Mexican history and
politics of the 1930s and the 1940s. Whereas the traditional hero's
process of development ends with marriage and tranquility, Catalina's begins, instead, with marriage and widowhood. The goal
of her quest for self-identity is not integration into, but repudiation of, that society whose restrictive norms have curbed her freedom. Bored and frustrated as is Bombal's protagonist in *The Final
Mist*, Catalina too is "always waiting for something to happen,
whatever, except the sameness of each morning" (27). She must

put up with the general's commonly known corruption, his "eight hundred crimes and the fifty mistresses" (54), and his incessant demands. She has to raise five of his illegitimate children as well as the two they have in common.

Catalina's awareness of the political assassinations her husband Andrés has ordered marks the first step in her development as an independent woman. Upon learning what he has done, she vomits, locks the door of her room, and informs the children that they will now be cared for by the maid. She tells Andrés that she knows all. She refuses to make love with him, stays out until midnight, and when he asks her who has authorized her to do so, she simply answers: "I authorized myself" (84). Catalina falls in love, for the first and only time in the novel, with the talented director of the National Symphony, Carlos Vives, and they become lovers. Politically astute, Vives sees through and repudiates Andrés, his political party, and the stratagems they use to govern. Andrés orchestrates Vives's assassination. Vives's brutal murder, combined with the death of her father, marks a crucial step in Catalina's development. The thirty-year-old adolescent rebels for the first time in her life. Like the desperate Dolores in Gambaro's *Bitter Blood* who also has nothing to lose once her lover has been assassinated, Catalina becomes openly defiant. She stays out one night with a new lover, Alonso Quijano, with whom she merely fills her tedium, and asserts her independence. The defiant act is wasted on Andrés, who has also stayed out all night. This becomes a turning point. "Without deciding it," Catalina realizes, "I became a different person" (201). She forces Andrés to buy her a Ferrari and to open a personal checking account for her. She installs a door between their rooms which he can enter only when opened, and she is audacious enough to kiss her lover Quijano in public. The novel ends as Andrés is buried, a moment that proves cathartic for Catalina. She is finally free of a husband she has ceased to love and is free to cry for the only man she had ever loved, Carlos Vives. In a reiterated and inverted version of the behavior of the protagonists of Parra, Brunet, Bombal, and Ferré, who did everything "correctly," Mastretta's Catalina, who had to repress her tears at her lover's burial, is finally able to cry for him at her husband's funeral: "I thought of Carlos, that I had gone to his burial with the tears forcibly repressed, and then, *as was correct* in a widow, I cried more than my children did" (226; emphasis mine).

Mastretta's delightful novel transgresses with consistent humor, ideas, genres, and norms traditionally accepted as universal and correct. Like Peri Rossi, Mastretta treats incest as natural, whether it is overt, as in the case of the siblings, Octavio and Marcela, or whether it is simply suggested, as intimated between Andrés and his mother, both of whom Catalina leaves alone "so as not to disturb the romance" (47). Sexual awakening is treated frankly and naturally. *Machista* views of virility are humorously debunked in the scene at the brothel. The men, who "resembled children at recess time," gather to compare the size of their penises, "a game between them," Mastretta's character says. They only tolerate "the women there so no one will think they are gay" (197). The taboo against masturbation is humorously and frankly burlesqued as Catalina's sister Teresa tells everyone she has been awakened by the strangest noise coming from Catalina's bed "as if . . . [Catalina] were drowning. My mother became very worried and even wanted to take me to the doctor. [For] in that way had the tuberculosis of [Alexandre Dumas's] Camille begun" (13–14). The novel's most interesting aspect, however, is Mastretta's use of the Mexican popular song, the *bolero*, as the title indicates. Something so beloved to Mexicans as the bolero form, so "natural" in depicting "universal" pain and sorrow, is subtly debunked. Its sentimentality is made to serve as contrasting background to crucial, non-sentimental events in the novel: while Catalina cuts her hair, in the background two intertextual references, music and art, reinforce her sadness as the lyrics from the same bolero that Frida Kahlo used in one of her paintings are sung: "If I loved you because of your hair, now that you're shorn I love you no more" (57). When Catalina is attracted to the homosexual Fernando, a sentimental bolero serves as backdrop to a love that can never be. Tender, romantic lyrics are played during a violent scene when General Gómez Soto almost strangles his mistress Bibi. In the midst of a tense *ménage-à-trois* meeting of Carlos, Andrés, and Catalina, the innocuous, sentimental ballad prepares a now-sensitized reader for tragic events to come. Three boleros are sung in sequence as the love affair of Catalina and Carlos begins to unfold, and as the singer Toña asks, "And the two of you, what? . . . Do you love each other or are you about to do so?" (142). The reader is not surprised when this scene is soon followed by Carlos's assassination. The final use of the bolero in the novel simply serves to highlight the unhappy marriage of Lilia, Andrés's daughter, to the middle-aged Emilio. As the sentimental lyrics promise joy, the reader is aware that the vibrant Lilia has been used by her father "as a bargaining chip for [his] political alliances" (Schaefer, 103). With incredible temerity Mastretta unmasks both Mexican machismo and the corruption of the 1930s and 1940s that provided the foundation for the "new" Mexico (Schaefer, 88–103).

In *Mexican Bolero*, Mastretta has succeeded in restructuring the classical male-centered *Bildungsroman* to make it work for the female hero. Franco Moretti's discussion of the *Bildungsroman* focuses on two of Yuri Lotman's principles of textual organization, which become especially helpful in appreciating Mastretta's appropriation of the genre. These are the principles of "classification" and of "transformation."[41] According to Moretti, when classification is stronger, as in the classical *Bildungsroman*, events are meaningful because they lead to a specific ending, namely the hero's integration into society. In the classificatory text, marriage acquires great value. The hero's necessary, arduous trials, because they are primarily external, do not seriously endanger his equilibrium. The text's organization is consequently clear and stable. When Lotman's other principle of textual organization, that of transformation, becomes stronger, however, the opposite is true. No specific ending is predetermined. Not marriage but adultery and its consequent instability become integral to the text's organization. Freedom rather than marital happiness becomes the hero's goal, and in the midst of these conflicting values, compromise is a recurrent theme. In Moretti's words, the focus of the story is in "its narrativity, [in] its being an open-ended process ... [its] meaning resides precisely in the impossibility of 'fixing' it" (Moretti, 7, 6–10). This is the case in *Mexican Bolero*. It is not possible to "classify" Mastretta's novel. She coalesces the historical novel and the love story, juxtaposes oficial and dominant versions of Mexican history with other versions "representing individual dissent" (Schaefer, 88–89), and subverts the *Bildungsroman*. Her novel concludes where the traditional *Bildungsroman* usually begins. Only at the end of the novel, when she is widowed, is the protagonist, Catalina Ascencio, finally free to embark on the quest of self-discovery. Free, she tells the reader, "of so many things I would no longer have to do." And, the narrator tells us, at last Catalina feels "almost happy" (226).

CHAPTER 6

Indigenista and Testimonio Literature: "Let Me Speak"

With the exception of Marta Brunet and Griselda Gambaro, the writers discussed in the book have either come from the upper and middle classes or focused on them in their works. The writers examined in this chapter, on the other hand, come from vastly contrasting backgrounds. Their commonality is that they focus on the humble classes and are united in their exploration of the condition of oppression.[1]

LYDIA CABRERA

Born into an affluent family in Havana, Cuba, in 1900, and reared by devoted domestic servants, Lydia Cabrera makes the stories and folklore that her black nannies recounted in her youth the basis for her creative work. From 1922–1939 Cabrera lived in Paris. It was a fortuitous time, for France had just "discovered" the esthetic importance of the African world. Picasso, Braque, Derain, and Vlaminck had revived "primitivism" in painting. Apollinaire published the first album of black sculpture in 1917. As early as 1914, the North American Louis Mitchell exposed Europe to African music through his introduction of jazz. In the field of literature, African culture and mores became focal in Blaise Cendrars' *Antologie nègre* (1921); Paul Morand's *Magie noire* (1928); André Gide's *Retour de Tchad* (1920); and Philippe Soupault's two works, *Voyages au Congo* (1929) and *Le nègre* (1929).[2] As the Guatemalan Miguel Angel Asturias would discover his native Maya culture in Europe, so Lydia Cabrera turned to her Afro-Cuban folkloric tradition during her residence in Paris. The early contact with her nanny's oral African myths, the emergence of *négritude* in Paris and of *negrismo* in Cuba during the twenties, and the anthropological studies of her brother-in-law, Fernando Ortíz, all contributed to her serious interest in Afro-Cuban folklore.[3]

In 1936 Francis de Miomandre, Teresa de la Parra's translator and friend, translated Cabrera's *Cuentos negros de Cuba* (*Black Tales of Cuba*) which she had written to entertain her lifelong and now tubercular friend, Parra. They were published as *Contes nègres de Cuba* by Gallimard who had also produced Asturias's *Legends of Guatemala*. Four years later, at the insistence of Gabriela Mistral, Cabrera published the stories in their original Spanish version.[4] When Cabrera returned to Cuba in 1939, she discovered that interest in Afro-Cuban culture had intensified there. Her brother-in-law, who would write the prologue for her 1940 *Black Tales of Cuba*, had published his work. In addition, Rómulo Lachatañeré had published his study of Yoruba mythology, ¡O mío Yemayá! (*Oh My Yemaya!*) in 1938; and Ramón Guirao was preparing his *Cuentos y leyendas negras de Cuba* (*Black Stories and Legends of Cuba*) published in 1942. Cabrera regularly produced collections of short stories based on Cuban folklore over the next forty years: *Porque . . . cuentos negros en Cuba* (1948; *Because . . . Black Tales in Cuba*) and *El monte* (1954; *The Mountain*), which Guillermo Cabrera Infante has described as "perhaps the best book written in Cuba of all time."[5] Other volumes include *Refranes de negros viejos* (1955; *Proverbs of Old Black People*); *Anagó: vocabulario Lucumí* (1957; *Anagó. The Vocabulary of the Lucumí*); *La sociedad secreta Abakúa narrada por viejos adeptos* (1958; *The Secret Society of the Abakúa Narrated by Its Ancient Practitioners*); *Otán Lyebiyé: Las piedras preciosas* (1970; *Otán Lyebiyé: The Precious Stones*); *Ayapá: cuentos de Jicotea* (1971; *Ayapá: Stories of Jicotea*). The last concerns the antics of the tortoise Jicotea, the favorite character of Afro-Cuban folklore and myth.

It is important to note that Cuba's attitude towards its black population has always been unique. From the colonial period to 1886, over a million and a half blacks were brought to Cuba. As a result, they outnumbered the whites by more than one hundred thousand people, constituting fifty-eight percent of the population. Rather than being subsumed, however, black culture significantly influenced white culture. Afro-Cuban domestic servants outnumbered their owners in any given household, and the resultant interracial camaraderie ensured that customs, food preferences, religious festivities, etc., were kept intact (Valdés-Cruz, 16).

In *Ayapá: Stories of Jicotea (Ayapá)* Cabrera explains that, aside from the obligatory rites of Christian baptism and required attendance at certain liturgical ceremonies, Afro-Cubans continued their African religious practices in the *cabildos de nación*, which were meeting places where blacks from the same African nations elected kings and queens as part of their religious ceremonies (265). Cabrera describes the *cabildo* as "a temple, a school of languages and traditions of each African group and effective societies of mutual assistance, for the members of each *cabildo* bound themselves by a religious vow to help one another in all the adverse circumstances of their lives" (*The Mountain*, 24). African Americans, Cabrera points out, employed a modified form of mainstream Protestantism in their religious practices and thereby lost much in the process. Her view in this regard is harsh: "[I]n the US there is nothing left of Africa, while the African culture remains vital in Cuba and Brazil."[6] Afro-Cubans kept their hymns, sang in their languages, and formed secret communities. Cabrera claimed that she was able to compile a Yoruba and an inedited Bantú vocabulary, as well as a work on the sacred language of the Abakúa precisely because "beneath a Catholic façade" Cuba and Brazil have always kept the language and religion of Africa intact (Guzmán, 36). Cabrera makes much of Catholic-African transcultural influences in the Afro-Cuban Creation and the Great Flood stories in *Ayapá* and in the myth of the miraculous birth of the hero in *Because . . .* (233). In 1971 she presented a paper titled "The Orishas in Exile" at the Thirtieth Congress of Applied Anthropology in Miami, where she explained how the Afro-Cubans retained their deities, while cloaking them with different names: the African goddess *Obatalá* and Our Lady of Mercy simply exchanged places; *Yemayá*, goddess of the sea, assimilated with the Virgin in her role as patroness of Havana and of sailors; *Changó*, the African overseer of thunder and fire, became a double for Saint Barbara; and *Ogún*, the blacksmith, became associated with Saint Peter because of his iron keys. Consequently, "the sixteen *orishas* [deities] of the Yoruba pantheon were Catholicized and adored separately by the blacks, in the way the whites did in the churches [but] . . . in their African way and in the *ilé-Orishas* or temple-dwellings" (cited in Valdés-Cruz, 18). At times Cabrera humorously allies the two religious traditions, de-hierarchizing Christian dogma in the process: "Olafi made the world . . . Olafi, Obatalá, Ibaibo . . . who were three and basically one . . . the Pineapple, the Mammee, the Sapodilla: three names, three forms, three colors, three different tastes, but all three the same: Fruit. Like the Father, the Son, and the Holy Spirit" (*Because* . . . , 95).

Cabrera does not simply "collect" African mythology in her narratives. She "recreates" it while remaining faithful to its origin and culture. Such "treachery," according to Jean Franco, can be "enabling and emancipatory,"[7] and for Matías Montes Huidobro, fictional reconstruction is the most authentic way to point out the social, political, and historical reality of a culture (*Homenaje*, 49). Such artistic reconstruction can be seen in Cabrera's *The Secret Society of the Abakúa* in which she literally "translates" stories told by illiterate elderly Cubans whose language is a mixture of fragmented Spanish and African dialects. Cabrera admitted to an interviewer that her work was based very loosely on Afro-Cuban legends or songs, that they simply gave her themes for stories which "are always completely recreated" (Levine, 14). In her etiological tales, Cabrera does what Jonathan Culler and Malcolm X also attempted to do, though in different ways. Culler tried to read patriarchal texts as a woman in order to understand a woman's perspective. Malcolm X read Gregor Mendel's *Findings in Genetics* as a black reader in order to undermine the notion of originary whiteness: "If you started with a black man," Malcolm X pointed out, "a white man could be produced; but starting with a white man you never could produce a black man—because the white chromosome is recessive."[8] In a similar way, Cabrera writes "Hay hombres blancos, pardos y negros" ("There are White, Brown, and Black people") from the Afro-Cuban perspective in order to explain the Afro-Cuban's internalization of the racial categories imposed on them. Cabrera's tale, like Malcolm X's conclusion, posits the first human being as black, formed from the clay residue that followed the first deluge. In this story, three blacks discover a body of miraculous water that can make them white. The youngest enters first and emerges as a white person. The second enters, but because the water is no longer clean, he becomes a mulatto. The third finds only mud and, consequently, can only wash the bottom of his feet and the palms of his hands, which turn white. Cabrera's tale thus explains colonial reality: "The young man, filled with pride . . . said within himself: 'I am much superior to my brothers! They will be my slaves! The color of my skin is the color of Olofi. God is white—as I am, and in his name I will make them submit to my will'—and in a loud voice—: 'I will be called Eléyibbó.' He broke a branch from a tree and in the name of God he ground their bones with blows. The second, humiliated . . . conceived then an unremitting hatred, a secret envy . . . for his white brother. He held his black brother in contempt and becoming just like his white brother [*arrendajo*] took his rage out on him with kicks . . . 'I am worth more than you because of the vestiges of white in my skin . . . My name . . . Kucundukú.' The broken black man merely said: 'I was Black. Black I am. My name is Erú . . . '" (*Because* . . . , 11–13). The problem with Cabrera's unreflecting version is that the cause of black oppression is thereby shifted from the white person onto the blacks themselves. Color prejudice in its different degrees, mulatto, quadroon, etc. (cf. chapter one), is a creation of white colonialism, internalized, not initiated, by blacks.

The etiological tale of Eleíjibbó, Kucundukú, and Erú is pivotal to Cabrera's literary output. She never romanticizes blacks. Like Jicotea, the tortoise of Afro-Cuban fables, who can be benevolent and malevolent simultaneously, so are all blacks in Cabrera's work. An earlier Cuban author, Gertrudis Gómez de Avellaneda (1814–1873), also focused on the Afro-Cuban in her novel *Sab*. In Avellaneda's work the black slave, Sab, became the object of the Euro-American need to see the black as benevolent, as the "noble savage," a foil for the corrupt industrialized society Avellaneda described. Sab also became the object of Avellaneda's need to provide what, for her, constituted real slavery, namely, the institution of marriage: "The slave, at least, can change masters," Sab writes his lover, "can expect to buy his freedom with gold someday; but woman, when she raises her emaciated hands and offended brow to plead for liberty, hears the sepulchral voice of the monster cry: 'In the tomb'."[9] Cabrera's treatment of the black as a human being, despite her occasional lapses into the old chestnut of "victimizing the victim" as in *There Are White, Brown, and Black People,* concurs with Franz Fanon's salutary view. "The man who adores the Negro," Fanon warns, "is as sick as the man [and woman] who abominates him."[10] Cabrera does not distort history in her work as blacks become co-conspirators with whites in the oppression of their own brothers and sisters. Her tales may evoke a mythical African past replete with magical incantations and rhythmic dances side by side with a past overshadowed by the Spanish presence in Cuba, but she never falls into romantic primitivism.[11] She depicts the contemporary reality of black oppression, shows how the oppressed often duplicate the attitudes and behavior of the oppressor, and shows that victims are capable of any action that will ensure survival. The stories of the shrewd, androgynous tortoise Jicotea, whom we have mentioned, provide a microcosmic representation of the black reality. In *Black Tales*, Jicotea, worn out "like a black slave," torn and broken by beatings, nevertheless emerges as a survivor. She simply accepts that God "had created the day for suffering and labor," and awaits the night which is made "for love and dance" (*Ayapá*, 133). Through artistic wish fulfillment, these literary myths are designed to give the victory to the underdog. The guinea hen of *Black Tales*, like Jicotea and like the monkey in *Because . . .*, for example, cheats, lies, and ultimately outsmarts a stronger adversary (258). Valdés-Cruz's remark about the guinea hen in *Black Tales* can be used to summarize most of Cabrera's animal fables: "Cabrera recreates with this story Cuban colonial society with all its hierarchical structures and shows us . . . how this tiny hen who comes from Guinea, . . . like the blacks she symbolizes, can outsmart them all with her ability" (56).

What Lydia Cabrera tries to do for the Afro-Cuban, the Mexicans Rosario Castellanos and Elena Garro try to do for the Indian, and Nélida Piñón for the Brazilian black. All try to understand the deep-seated historical prejudices emanating from colonialism and their internalization by the oppressed. They present postcolonial resistances which destabilize power relations formerly constructed in stable binarisms of white power versus ethnic powerlessness.

ROSARIO CASTELLANOS

Born in Mexico City on 25 May 1925, Rosario Castellanos was heavily influenced by Indian culture during her childhood, living first on the family ranch near the Guatemalan border and later at Chiapas. After receiving an education at the National University of Mexico and the University of Madrid, she became director of the Chiapas Cultural Program where she worked with Indians for several years. She was also press and information director for the National University of Mexico. Her first publication was a collection of poems in 1948, but her fame as a writer was assured when

Balún Canán (1957; *The Nine Guardians*) and *El oficio de tinie-blas* (1962; *Rites of Darkness*) were published. Castellanos was named Mexican ambassador to Israel in 1971, and simultaneously appointed lecturer at Hebrew University. She was accidentally electrocuted on 7 August 1974 when she turned on a lamp in her apartment in Tel Aviv after stepping out of the shower. Castellanos was the recipient of many literary prizes. In 1953 the Mexican Writers Center awarded her a grant for research on women in Mexican culture. In 1957 she won the Mexican Critics Award, and in 1958 the Chiapas Prize for *The Nine Guardians*. In 1960, she received the Xavier Villarrutia Prize for her collection of poems *Lívida luz* (*Livid Light*). Other awards included the Sor Juana Inés de la Cruz prize for *Rites of Darkness* in 1962; the Carlos Trouyet Prize for literature, 1967; the Elias Souraski Prize for *Poesía no eres tú* (*You Are not Poetry*), the last a feminist reversal of the well-known lines by the nineteenth century Spanish poet, G. A. Bécquer.

Castellanos's early life in Chiapas, the site of historical conflicts between the Tzotzil Indians and the landholding families, is transposed into two of her best known novels. *Rites of Darkness* describes a Chamula Indian uprising, actually a modernization of a revolt that occurred in 1867. *The Nine Guardians*, her most famous work, deals with the changing relations between whites and Indians as a result of President Lázaro Cardenas's 1941 land and education reforms, which mandated that Indians have access to the Spanish language and to property. The narrator of *The Nine Guardians* is a seven-year-old girl whose nanny is an Indian. The child is consequently made privy to two worlds, that of her parents, the masters, and to that of her beloved nanny, an oppressed Tzotzil Indian. The novel examines the fragility of victimizer/victim relationships through the perspective of the child who narrates the events. Castellanos always warned that it was an error to schematize Indian-white relationships: "At first glance, one has the impression that the role of victim corresponds to the Indian, and that of victimizer to the other. But human relations are never so schematic, and social ones even less so. The masks sometimes change, the roles alternate."[12] It is this alternation of roles that *The Nine Guardians* records. The novel begins with a sense of irretrievable loss as the child's nanny sadly repeats the refrain the child has heard so often from her lips: "And then in anger they dispossessed us, they confiscated what we had treasured: the word, which is memory's strong-box" (13). The narrative describes how the Indians reappropriate the word and the right to the property of which they have been deprived. The landowning child is the first to give the word back to the Indians, since she narrates their situation. The reader sees the landowners' fear of dispossession and their deep contempt of the Indian in the angry reaction of the child's mother to Cardenas's reforms: "The Indians. He [Cardenas] doesn't know them; he's never been near them and found out how they stink of filth and drink . . . He's never given them a job to do and taken the measure of their laziness. And they're so hypocritical, so underhanded, so deceitful" (46). The Indian women are not abused, as a stranger to their culture might suppose. Raping or seducing them, the child hears, is "doing them a favour, really, because after that the Indian women were more sought after and could marry where they liked," and even the Indian male "always recognized this virtue in his woman, that the *patrón* had found pleasure in her" (79).

This stable perspective with its accepted attitude on the part of the whites, however, begins to be destabilized in the novel, confusing the child-narrator and explaining what is happening to the reader. The implementation of Cardenas's reforms, that is, the Indians' new access to the primary source of white power, to their language, and to their land, has caused a division among the Indians, turning them against one another. The nanny's explanations are of no help. The Indian worker has been killed by his own people, she explains, "because your father trusted him" (34). She herself has been wounded because "I was brought up in your house. Because I love your parents, and Mario and you" (19). The girl understands her parents even less. They fire the beloved nanny because she, an Indian woman, has dared suggest that the Indians have power to harm a child of the landowning class, that Mario, the younger child, is ill as a result of the Indians' revenge. Her warning falls on deaf and angry ears and the boy dies. This discounting of the nanny, at once racial, sexual, linguistic, and social, this "inattention to the communicative aspect of a supposedly powerless figure brings about the redistribution of power in formerly stable power relations that is central to the text."[13] The increasing redistribution of power relations culminates in the confrontation between the white landowner, the *patrón*, and the Indian leader, Felipe. Until this point, the child narrator has given language and history to the Indians by telling their story. It is her father, the landowner, who must now give them back their land. It is the indian leader himself who retrieves both. Castellanos indicates this in one of the most powerful scenes in the novel as the father and the servant confront each other. The father addresses the lowly Indian in the latter's Tzotzil dialect, itself the language of the powerless, but Felipe answers him in the forbidden language, Spanish, the tongue of the powerful. Having appropriated the word, the Indian Felipe now appropriates the land. "The landowner," he now informs the *patrón*, "is an institution of the past" (223). But Castellanos knows, as Teresa de la Parra knew, that like the liberated black slave Vicente Cochocho of Parra's *Mama Blanca's Memoirs*, the Indian Felipe in *The Nine Guardians* must still exist in a racist and classist society. The Indians may have obtained their rights, but the book's conclusion shows that rights do not change attitudes. Castellanos underscores this reality in the child's final words. Returning to the ranch and searching for her nanny in the crowd, she remarks: "Even if I see her, I'll never recognize her now. It's so long since we've been parted. Besides, all Indians look alike" (271).

ELENA GARRO

Elena Garro, Castellanos's contemporary, also emphasizes in her work the fragility of roles between victimizer and victim, as well as the consequences of "inattention to the communicative aspect of supposedly powerless figure[s]." Born in Puebla, Mexico, on 15 December 1920, she attended the National University of Mexico where she was involved with the theatre. She married Octavio Paz—the recipient of the Nobel Prize for Literature in 1990—before she was twenty-one. The couple, who have one daughter, Helena, divorced in 1959. In 1963 Garro returned from Paris, where the family had resided, to Mexico and in 1968 she was jailed for nine days for possible involvement in instigating the student protest that resulted in the massacre in the Plaza de Tlatelolco. After her release, and in the midst of virulent criticism, she fled the country, living at various times in Spain, the United States, France, and Japan. Garro's texts reflect her concern for the poor and the oppressed, particularly the indigenous Mexican.

In *El árbol* (1967; *The Tree*), possibly her most gripping tale, Garro makes the reader aware of both the power of language and the consequences of what Sandra Cypess has called "the inattention to the communicative aspect of a supposedly powerless figure." The story consists of a dialogue between two women, Marta, the wealthy mistress of the house who lives alone, and Luisa, an Indian who comes to her one Saturday evening because she has no one else to whom she can turn. Her Indian husband has beaten her and she arrives with "bruised nose and ear from which a stream of half-coagulated black blood was oozing" (Picon Garfield, *Women's Fiction*, 71). Marta refuses to listen to the Indian's story. Through an omniscient narrator, the reader is made aware of issues of class and race relations: Marta "would have liked to tell the Indian she was odious and that if Julian had hit her she deserved it . . ." (71); her reaction to the battered Luisa is annoyance, for Luisa's "misery inspired nausea" in her (71). She is contemptuous of Luisa with the "old creole repugnance toward everything indigenous" (78), and she finally cries: "Shut up, already, you're the one who's possessed" (75). At the moment that Marta issues this order, the relationship between the two women is reversed and the story moves inexorably to its tragic climax. Garro wrote to Emmanuel Carballo that "memories of the future" actually predict what is to come. She even added that she would often change the end of her novels "in order to change [her] future."[14] The cyclical concept of time permeates all her work, and in *the Tree* her premise that the past is a projection of the future begins to unfold the moment Marta "provoked her [Luisa's] confidence by saying she was possessed. She had wanted to scare her and the only thing she achieved was to open the floodgates for her devils to escape" (81). Luisa appropriates the word, refusing to allow Marta to "read" her. No longer the object of Marta's Euro-American script of the Indian, Luisa becomes the subject of her own script, one for which Marta's racial stereotypes are inadequate. The reader learns that Luisa killed a woman long ago and spent over ten years in prison. There she experienced a new world, namely, friends, abundant food, bathrooms, telephones, medical care. As a result of her prison experience, she acquired a dignity unknown to her as an Indian. She shows Marta the knife she used to commit the murder. It is her talisman, "the key that had opened her door to equality, dancing and happiness" (85–86). As the mood changes, so the power relations shift. Marta is uneasy, afraid, silent. Luisa, on the other hand, is "amused," her previously lowered eyes now have "malicious sparks" (78). She ignores Marta's commands to cease speaking and to leave the knife with her. Still silent, her silences are no longer subservient but "premeditated" (79). A fearful Marta is taunted by Luisa: "Fear is very noisy," she tells her (77), and reiterates, "How very alone we are" (84). Luisa is returned to her beloved Tacubaya prison at the end of the story after she has killed Marta. But she is now a stranger there. She finds that the intervening ten years have changed everything in the prison. Caught in the impasse of Garro's cyclical time, she realizes that the past may constitute recollections of things to come, but time, as she once knew it, is "never to be recovered" (86).

In 1964, Garro published her collection of short stories, *La semana de colores* (*The Week of Colors*). Within these narratives she again explores the idea of the circularity of time. Her preoccupation with the marginalized becomes more centralized as she bases many of her stories on Indian folklore and superstition, even employing Indian modes of speech in her narration. In "El anillo" ("The Ring"), a young Indian woman, Severina, finds a ring. The villagers believe that the ring is cursed and that Severina is a victim of the evil eye embedded in the ring. She is temporarily cured when she vomits an "animal which held in its paws pieces of her heart" (167). In order to secure a permanent cure, Severina's superstitious mother kills her daughter's lover, because, in refusing to return the "cursed" ring, he is to blame for the evil eye. Too late, the superstitious villagers discover that Severina has actually had an abortion and further, that the ring, far from being cursed, has the lovers' names engraved upon it. "La culpa es de los Tlaxcaltecas" ("The Tlaxcalans Are to Blame") is one of Garro's most widely read stories from this collection. Past and present again coexist on the same plane. Laura, an Aztec Indian reincarnated into a twentieth-century descendant of the Spanish conquerors, must choose between two men and two time periods: the defeated Inca husband of her sixteenth-century past or the affluent westernized white husband of her twentieth-century present. Once again the focus is on female bonding between classes. As Victoria Ocampo described her bonds with Fani, so Garro portrays the relationship between Laura and her servant Nacha, who also "manage[s] everything." Nacha watches her mistress's gradual transformation, and eventually helps Laura to return to her former existence. Nacha literally wipes out all trace of Laura's twentieth century present: "She washed the coffee cup . . . turned the light off, and left no trace of her missus having been there" (457–58). Her mission accomplished, Nacha simply disappears: "When Laura had left forever . . . Nacha left without waiting for her wages" (458)[15]

Garro's recurring theme of the past as a projection of the future becomes the very title of her novel, *Los recuerdos del porvenir* (1966; *Recollections of Things to Come*). Not as successful as her short stories, it was written in the 1950s and stored for over ten years. Garro uses stock fairy-tale *topoi* but, unlike Rosario Ferré and Angeles Mastretta, she does not treat them ironically. In the first part of *Recollections*, Julia, General Rosas's mistress, is the most beautiful woman in Ixtepec. It is the search for this beauty that brings young Felipe Hurtado to the village. Julia is a damsel in distress, victim of the cruel Rosas who beats her mercilessly. She escapes with the "hero" Hurtado during the night, aided by a miracle that makes time stand still, and on the proverbial white horse of romantic lore. The second part of the novel deals with the cruelty of Rosas and his army toward the ethnic population during the Cristero War, which ensued when President Calles tried to replace the Catholic Church with a national one.

There is an interesting reversal—though it is not as forceful or as functional as is Ferré's or Parente Cunha's—in the technique of doubling in *Recollections*. It is Julia the prostitute who refuses to be "seduced" by the general's power, while the respectable, upperclass woman Isabel "prostitutes" herself for power, becoming a substitute for Julia with whom alone Rosas is obsessed. Isabel's betrayal makes her a symbolic figure. She becomes a latter-day Malinche, the Indian interpreter and mistress of the Conquistador Cortéz who "betrayed" her people by aiding him in the conquest of Mexico. The same circularity of "The Tlaxcalans Are to Blame" where past and future intersect, and of "The Tree," where the sixteenth and the twentieth centuries converge, occurs at the end of *Recollections*. Isabel, turned to stone because she "preferred the love of the man who ruined me and my family," is also caught within Garro's view of the cyclical nature of time. She is forever to remain an icon, "a memory of the future forever and ever" (289).[16]

Feminist analyses of Garro's *Recollections* vary widely. Jean Franco sees the women in *Recollections* as passive victims, either romantic "legends like Julia, the elusive phantom of male desire, or like Isabel . . . undesired surrogates who are not objects of desire but who allow themselves to be seduced by power" (138). Sandra Cypess, on the other hand, sees these women as agents of their own actions. Trapped by the confines of a patriarchal society, they nevertheless choose to escape, as Julia does, or to exercise power and control deliberately as does Isabel over Rosas "instead of being controlled by him" ("Figure of Malinche," 127).

NÉLIDA PIÑÓN

The Brazilian Nélida Piñón also explores the subject of female bonding between class and race. Born in Rio de Janeiro, Brazil, in 1937, of a Spanish father and a Brazilian mother, Piñón maintains that she did not consider herself Brazilian until she became an adult and began to write in Portuguese.[17] She has been a university professor in Brazil, at Columbia University, Johns Hopkins University, and the University of Miami. She is one of only four women elected to the Brazilian Academy of Letters. Her career began when she worked for the newspaper *O Globo* and the journal *Cadernos Brasileiros,* for which she was assistant editor. She has been a full-time fiction writer since 1955 and has published eight novels and three collections of short stories, several of which have earned her literary prizes. Her fiction has been translated into Spanish, French, and Polish. Her novels *A república dos sonhos* (1984; *Republic of Dreams*) and *A doce cancâo de Caetana* (1987; *Caetana's Sweet Song*) have been translated into English, as have some of her short stories. A reviewer of Piñón's "Big-Bellied Cow" calls it "one of the great short stories to come from Latin America in recent years."[18] Convinced that "woman doesn't have a language of herself,"[19] Piñón omits verbs, and creates jarring and oftentimes shocking juxtapositions, ellipses, and shifts (Picon Garfield, *Women's Fiction,* 267). As Luisa Valenzuela has suggested that women inject logocentric writing with estrogen,[20] so Piñón theorizes that women must "contaminate" patriarchal culture: "The contamination is happening at the heart of culture, in the articulation of realities . . ." (Castro-Klarén, 79). Her themes can be spiritual, (*Guía-mapa de Gabriel Arcanjo* (1961; *Guide-Map of the Archangel Gabriel*); erotic, (*A casa da paixado* (1972; *The House of Passion*); political/historical, *Caetana's Sweet Song. The Republic of Dreams,* a semi-autobiographical presentation of four generations of a family whose roots are both

Spanish and Brazilian, is her best known work. One of the poignant features of the novel is the friendship between the matriarch Eulália, and her black servant Odete, which offers an interesting portrait of female bonding in Brazilian literature. Odete and Eulália have lived together for fifty years. Like Ocampo's maid Fani and Garro's Nacha, Odete "manages everything." Odete "gradually took over the running of the household . . . Discreetly, giving orders as though it were really the mistress of the house issuing them" (47). Eulália frequently gives Odete her clothes. In order to look like her beloved mistress, Odete vainly tries to gain weight. An orphan, she even goes so far as to invent a family she visits on her day off in an attempt to create a genealogy for herself in imitation of her mistress. Eulália, says the omniscient narrator, "was aware that Odete copied her life even though she lacked the means to reproduce it. Thus it was she who provided Odete's constricted imagination with bits of life" (59). As Eulália prepares to die, it is significant that she thinks of Odete first when she is disposing of her material goods. After inspecting her jewelry box, Eulália consigns its entire contents to Odete. The novel addresses complicated questions of class, which become most interesting in the context of Lydia Cabrera's comment that it is only in Cuba and in Brazil that the African slaves retained their language and culture. The mistress Eulália stereotypes all blacks as "gentle" as a result of her friendship with the maid, Odete. Eulália's husband pinpoints another reality, however, namely, that "[s]lavery had so deeply wounded their souls that, for decades to come, they would be forced to subject themselves passively to the dominating, racist impulses of the white man" (49). It is the new generation, Breta, Eulália's granddaughter, who underlines Lydia Cabrera's view of the effect of the African presence in Brazil as well as in Cuba. Without the Africans, she explains, "we would be incurable despots and a bloodthirsty people . . . And we would not have at our disposal words that enhanced new feelings. If we owed to the Portuguese our robust idiom, . . . it was to the Africans that we owed the softness that had seeped into all the strata of the language, thereby teaching us a verbal intonation welling up directly from the soul" (49).

In the *indigenista* fiction of Rosario Castellanos and Elena Garro, and the *negrismo* of Lydia Cabrera, and even Nélida Piñón, it is white women who attempt to re-create the lives and the conditions of Indians and Blacks. Recent Latin-American writing, however, has felt the impact of a new narrative mode by which marginalized people take over their own narrative, albeit sometimes through the use of an interlocutor. Such literature is not written from the margin, as is so often supposed, but actually in the interstices of two cultures, that of the oppressors and that of the oppressed.[21] It is produced, in Richard Schechner's description of experimental theatre, in the "creases" of society (*Performance Theory*, 142). Critics have defined the *testimonio* or testimonial narrative as that of personal witness and involvement geared to disclosing the continuing struggles of a group or nation, designed to make an outside world join the cause for which the group is fighting and writing. Testimonial narrative is primarily "resistance literature."[22] Less interested in the aesthetic/literary than in the political, the *testimonio* makes claims to the truth of its matter. Its manner frequently becomes rhetorical because its objective is to persuade the reader to take immediate political action. The testimonial narrative of Latin-American women constitutes, in the words of Jean Franco, an "entirely original concept of feminist 'intellectuals'": "Among these one would count the Mothers of Plaza de Mayo and the Chilean women's movement, and the Guatemalan Rigoberta Menchú. What distinguishes these women from either Anglo-American or French critics is that they have found ways of aligning gender politics with other forms of struggle without subordinating gender issues and without sacrificing politics" (Franco, xxii–xxiii).

Testimonial narrative, as is well known from the works of African-American and Native American writers in this country, has been the privileged form of both male and female authors who wish to describe their experiences as marginalized members of a racial or ethnic group. The same is true of the Latin-American *testimonio*. Rodolfo Walsh's *Operación massacre* (1969; *Operation Massacre*); Hernán Valdes's *Tejas verdes: diario de un campo de concentración* (1974; *The Diary of a Chilean Concentration Camp*); Miguel Barnet's *Biografía de un cimarrón* (1966; *The Autobiography of a Runaway Slave*) and his *Canción de Rachel* (1970; *Song of Rachel*) are some of the best known examples of testimonial narrative written by men in Latin America.[23] Since this book deals with women writers, I will restrict my discussion to the most prominent female exemplars of this type of narrative: Domitila Barrios de Chungara, Rigoberta Menchú, Carolina María de Jesús, Elvia Alvarado, and Elena Poniatowska. Before discussing testimonial narrative in critical/theoretical terms, a brief summary of the *testimonios* of these writers is necessary.

DOMITILA BARRIOS DE CHUNGARA

The *testimonio* of Domitila Barrios de Chungara, *"Si me permiten hablar . . ."*: *Testimonio de Domitila una mujer de las minas de Bolivia (Let Me speak! Testimony of Domitila, A Woman of the Bolivian Mines)*, edited by Moema Viezzer, recounts the political process that transformed her from a passive, reticent Bolivian miner's wife into the leader of the Housewives' Committee, which pressed for higher wages and improved living and working conditions for the miners. It is interesting to note, in passing, that the meek request in the Spanish title reads *If You will Allow Me to Speak. . . .* In translation, Chungara's request becomes the English imperative, *Let Me Speak!* Moments like these are humbling reminders of the truth that, when "translating" the language and the literary texts of diverse cultures, classes, and races, the *traduttore* becomes (alas!) in some form a *traditore*.

Bolivia stands out as one of the few cases in Latin America of an organized political experience involving women. [24] Chandra Mohanty has criticized the ubiquitous assumption of the so-called helplessness of the Third World woman who is viewed as enduring a double oppression. Supposedly oppressed both by gender and by being "Third World," she is automatically presumed to be poor, uneducated, tradition-bound, and family oriented.[25] The accounts of women like Chungara provide proof that even in the poorest ethnic groups of Latin America such presumptions, when true, do not necessarily render women helpless. These women are powerful both in their resistance and in the impact they occasion because of that resistance. Throughout her *testimonio*, Chungara refuses to be emplotted either in stereotypical cultural scripts or totalizing paradigms. When she is jailed for her political activity in the Housewives' Committee, she repudiates, to use Edward Saïd's terminology, all Euro-American "redemptive paradigms."[26] The women from the Popular Christian Movement attempt to make "the savage" Chungara sign a false document, supposedly to "save" her children. She consciously opts for her role as her people's leader over the role of mother. "My children," she tells her oppressors, "are my property, not the state's. And so if the state has now decided to murder my children in the underground room where you say they are, well then let them murder them. I think that will weigh on their consciences, because I won't be guilty of their crime" (127–28).

RIGOBERTA MENCHÚ

The testimony of the illiterate Maya-Quiché Indian of Guatemala who became a national leader in the struggle for human rights provides one of the most impressive examples of human agency in Latin-American writing today. Rigoberta Menchú was the recipient of the Nobel Peace Prize in 1992, joining such internationally known winners as Daw Aung San Suu Kyi, Henry Kissinger, and Anwar Sadat. *Me llamo Rigoberta Menchú y así me nació la conciencia* (1984; *I, Rigoberta Menchú: An Indian Woman in Guatemala*) describes her political odyssey. In order to break down the language barriers between herself and her fellow Mayans, she learned to speak Cakchiquel and Tuzutuhil. She learned Spanish, the language of the oppressor, and, through the Venezuelan/ French interlocutor Elisabeth Burgos-Debray, reported her people's struggle. The reader of this *testimonio* learns about the genocide of Menchú's family and of her people and the slow and painful disintegration of traditional Maya-Quiché culture as it is transformed through the violence of the sociopolitical system. Menchú's brothers and sisters died of malnutrition and pesticides. Her father was burned to death by the military during the occupation of the Spanish embassy in Guatemala in 1979. Her mother was raped, tortured, and left to die in the most horrible fashion. Another brother was tortured to death by the Guatemalan army while the family watched without daring to utter a word. Menchu's family, a sacred unit for the Maya-Quiché, breaks up and separates for security reasons and in order to mobilize politically. Menchú herself is forced to violate her people's customs to struggle for the survival of their culture. Like Chungara, she is forced to subordinate what is crucial for a woman in her culture and in the dominant culture, namely, marriage and children. Leadership takes precedence over personal feelings. "When I became a revolutionary," Menchú tells us, "I had to choose between two things—the struggle or my *compañero* . . . there I was between these two things—choosing him or my people's struggle. And that's what I chose, and I left my *compañero* with much sadness and a heavy heart" (225–26). Her renunciation of marriage and children is a deliberate decison. She and her woman friend agree never to get married, "because marriage meant children and if she had a child she couldn't bear to see him die of starvation or pain or illness" (88).

ELVIA ALVARADO

Don't Be Afraid Gringo is the account of Honduran Elvia Alvarado, a *campesina* (peasant) organizer with the National Congress of Rural Workers (CNTC). Medea Benjamin compiled this book based on approximately thirty hours of taped interviews with Alvarado, who focused on the increased climate of fear in Honduras as it became the unwitting middle ground between the Sandinistas in Nicaragua and the growing strength of the Farabundo Martí National Liberation Front (FMLN) in El Salvador, which threatened to topple the U.S.-backed Salvadoran government. Honduras served as the base for the Nicaraguan rebels, the Contras. Alvarado was imprisoned and tortured twice because of her activities. She was already on the military's blacklist because of her organizing work with the peasants when she agreed to tell her story and she increased the peril to her own life by having her *testimonio* published. Alvarado's is a story of poverty, suffering, and abandonment on the part of her government, her church, and her men. Like Chungara and Menchú, this undereducated woman unmasks her society's totalizing and redemptive paradigms. Of the church she says: "They wanted us to give food out to malnourished mothers and children, but they didn't want us to question why we were malnourished to begin with" (16). Of the myth of marriage: "When men and women start living together, there's a tremendous double standard. Because the women have to be faithful to the men, but the men don't have to be faithful to the women . . . Men kill their wives for sleeping with another man" (46). Imprisoned, tortured, threatened with death, she subordinates all to her people's cause. "Every time I leave my house," she remarks, "I'm not sure whether I'll come back or not. I'm ready for everything, and I'm not afraid to die. Because I know the *campesinos* will continue the struggle, and that my death will be part of that struggle" (137). Alvarado's account is not meant to be a heroic story, a *Bildungsroman* that ends when the heroine successfully overcomes all odds. Alvarado admits: ". . . sometimes I get so overwhelmed by the odds against us that I break down and cry . . . I see us being persecuted, jailed, tortured. I get exhausted by all the internal problems between the *campesino* organizations. And I see all of Central America going up in flames. I start to wonder if it's worth it. I start to think maybe I should just stay home making tortillas" (142–43).

Despite such momentary pessimism, Alvarado, in concert with Chungara and Menchú, refuses to be overcome by the violence of the society, and she encourages the reader to join in the struggle: "We are used to planting seeds and waiting to see if the seeds bear fruit," Alvarado tells the reader. "We're used to working on harsh soil. And when our crops don't grow, we're used to planting again and again until they take hold. Like us, you must learn to persist" (144).

CAROLINA MARÍA DE JESÚS

Quarto de despejo: diario de uma favelada (1962; *Child of the Dark*) records the life of the black woman, Carolina María de Jesús, in the *favelas*, slum settlements on unwanted swamplands in São Paulo and on high hills in Rio de Janeiro. Jesús's text, whose title literally means "Room of Garbage," was edited and published by Audalio Dantas, a newspaper reporter. As a teenager, Jesús worked as a maid for a white family in São Paolo. She hated the work but loved a good time. "I was too independent and didn't like to clean up their messes," she says. Like Lydia Cabrera's Jicotea in *Ayapá: Stories of Jicotea*, Jesús "used to slip out of the house at night and make love" (10). After four months they fired her. Pregnant, jobless, and alone she had no place to go but to the *favela* where she built a shack. Three children later, she and they were trapped in a cycle of poverty and hunger. "How horrible," she says, "to see your children eat and then ask: 'Is there more?'" (110). Jesús does not speak of unique experiences in her *testimonio*, but is, rather, the mouthpiece for all the *favelanos*. "Here in the *favela*," she explains, "almost everyone has a difficult fight to live. But I am the only one who writes of what suffering is" (43). She describes the poverty, degradation, and cynicism that a life of poverty in the "*favela*, branch of Hell, if not Hell itself" effects (166), and the bigotry and racial hatreds that societally sanctioned inequality and class structures inevitably breed. As Chungara grew up hearing people call her a "dirty Indian child" (49–50) and a "savage" (128), and as the twelve-year-old Menchú was contemptuously referred to as an "Indian whore" (100), so six-year-old children, reflecting their parents' attitudes, taunt Jesús: "You're writing again, stinking nigger!" (34).

The diary became an instant and academic success, internationally read and discussed, even retextualized. Françoise Ega, from Martinique, makes Carolina de Jesús a literary figure in her *Lettre à une noire* (*Letter to a Black Woman*). Here Jesús becomes the recipient of letters sent to her from France by Mamega, a young black Antillean woman. Written between May 1962 and June 1964, the letters describe the suffering of young women from the Antilles who go to France hoping to find a better life and who are treated little better than slaves. Carolina de Jesús acts as Mamega's mentor. Separated by both country and by language, for Mamega speaks French and Jesús speaks Portuguese, Mamega, nevertheless, feels closer to Jesús than to her country's middle-class blacks. They do not share her experience, while, conversely, Jesús lives it: "They read you out of curiosity," she tells Jesús. "I will never read all that you have written . . . I *know* it" (24; emphasis mine).[27]

ELENA PONIATOWSKA

A somewhat different kind of *testimonio* is the testimonial novel, of which genre Elena Poniatowska is most representative author. Poniatowska, born in France on 19 May 1933 to a Mexican mother and a Polish father, moved to Mexico at the outset of World War II. She became a journalist and secured her reputation as a writer when she published *La noche de Tlatelolco* (1971; *Massacre in Mexico*), her collection of seemingly random interviews and reports on the events of 2 October 1968 that resulted in the deaths of several hundred student protestors during a peaceful meeting in the Plaza de las Tres Culturas (Tlatelolco) in Mexico City. Although other works have appeared in response to the events occurring at Tlatelolco, notably the essays of Octavio Paz, Carlos Fuentes, and the journalistic work of María Luisa Mendoza, Poniatowska's version is probably the most widely read.[28] Despite its initial impression, it is scrupulously literary in expression (Young, 17), consisting of a polyphony of sometimes contrary views of Tlatelolco by different participants in the tragedy (Beverley, *MC*, 16). Extracts of the comments made by students and faculty give "an uncanny experience of the simultaneous spontaneity and inevitablility of events" (Chevigny, "Transformation of Privilege," 57). The text possesses much of the immediacy found in a newspaper account of a catastrophe still taking place. It is an image best compared to the black and white canvas of Picasso's *Guernica*, in which the paint appears still to flow from the screaming horse's mouth before the tragedy he witnesses. Octavio Paz, in his introduction to the English translation of Poniatowska's book, pinpoints what makes this text distinctive. Poniatowska's urgency suffuses *Massacre in Mexico* with "the same burning ideal that inspired the students' demonstration and protest."[29]

Hasta no verte Jesús mío (1969; *Until I See You Again, My Jesus*) is probably the best known example of the testimonial novel. Poniatowska presents the events surrounding the Mexican Revolution of 1910 from the perspective of a firsthand witness, an elderly laundry woman, Josefina Bórquez, whom she renames Jesusa Palancares. The elderly woman speaks of her womanizing father, numerous stepmothers, and her own loveless marriage to an abusive captain during the revolution. A widow at seventeen, Palancares has never remarried and prides herself on her fierce independence: "That is why I am alone, because I want no one to have control over me" (153). She too is wary of all redemptive paradigms: unions, the Catholic Church, the government. She gives the lie to all grand narratives, subverting sacred myths and legends alike. She parodies the indigenous *nahual*, sacred to Menchú (20): "The nahual is a Christian disguised as an animal so he can steal" (123). She debunks popular legends of revolutionary heroes, which have since become official history: "The revolutionaries are pure bandits, thieves . . . protected by the law . . . that's why they all fight to be general . . . in a year or two they're already rich" (78). And of the Revolution that had promised so much and effected so little in the lives of ordinary people, she says, "it has not changed anything. We're only more hungry now" (126). Much of the power of this book has been attributed directly to its revisioning of official history by one "who watched from the margin as it was being created" (Chevigny, "Transformation of Privilege," 55).

But what is testimonial narrative, and from where does it derive its powerful impact?

TESTIMONIAL NARRATIVE

Testimonial narrative, as I have suggested, exists in the "creases" of society. It locates itself between the cultures of the oppressors and of the oppressed, between the discourses of the factual and the fictive. Far from eradicating the borders between the two discourses, the *testimonio* purports to represent reality by means of certain recognized fictional conventions. Simultaneously, it emphasizes its claim to empirical validation (Foley, 25). Testimonial narrative is supposed, therefore, to differ in emphasis from the historical novel since it privileges the truth value of its account over artistic coherence. The very name, *testimonio*, translates into the act of bearing witness, of telling the truth in a legal or religious sense (Beverley, *MC*, 14; Prada Oropeza, 10). The difference between the elegant writings of the Nobel Prize winner for literature, the Guatemalan Miguel Angel Asturias on the Maya-Quiché in Guatemala, and the narrative of the Nobel Peace laureate, the Guatemalan Indian Rigoberta Menchú, on her own people's struggle is readily apparent.[30] The difference does not lie primarily, however, in the avowed truth value of Menchú's narrative. No informant can be privileged because s/he is somehow seen as rendering a truer or more accurate testimony as the result of an experience lived. Informants, like everyone else, are limited by the "vicissitudes of memory, intention, ideology."[31] As Joan W. Scott has pointed out, experience is not the result of the unmediated relationship between language and things. Instead, all categories of analysis and articulation of experience must be seen "as contextual, contested, and contingent."[32] Such vicissitudes become doubly problematic in the *testimonio*, which offers genuine possibilities for semiotic analysis but, at the same time, effects contradictory codes that frustrate expectations regarding the notions of reader, text, and author. The reader of the *testimonio* is primarily a member of a privileged upper class who is being asked to empathize with the liminality and marginality of the uneducated native informant. Doris Sommer points out that "[e]ven if—perhaps because—the reader cannot identify with the writer enough to imagine taking her place, the map of possible identifications through the text spreads out laterally. Once the subject of the testimonial is understood as the community made up of a variety of roles, the reader is called in to fill one of them" (118). And one of the roles the reader is called to fill is spelled out in Elvia Alvarado's account, namely, to join in the struggle to overcome an oppressive class of which the reader herself/himself is a member. The text too effects conflicting codes. The data provided by the informant of the *testimonio* may be selective, but they are real, not fictional. Events that have been experienced or witnessed by the first-person informant have to be adjusted to the language and the canonized forms of the dominant culture in which they are scripted. A discussion of these forms therefore becomes necessary.

The *testimonio* has most often been associated with three literary forms: the picaresque genre, the forms of the chronicle, and autobiography. It shares with the picaresque novel a first-person narrator, a moralizing dimension, and an iconoclastic view of society (Beverley *AT*, 159–61). But the *testimonio* is not a work of fiction as is the picaresque.[33] It emphasizes real and verifiable events, and, whereas the *pícaro* rogue fends for himself/herself, the narrator of *testimonio* "fends" for an entire people. Chungara emphasizes this aspect of the *testimonio*: "I don't want anyone at any moment to interpret the story I'm about to tell as something that is only personal. Because I think that my life is related to my people. What happened to me could have happened to hundreds of people in my country . . . That's why I say that I don't just want to tell a personal story. I want to talk about my people" (15). Menchú speaks similarly: "My name is Rigoberta Menchú. I am twenty-three years old . . . I'd like to stress that it's not only *my* life, it's also the testimony of my people . . . My story is the story of all poor Guatemalans. My personal experience is the reality of a whole people" (1; emphasis hers).

The *testimonio* has also been associated with the chronicle which included counter discourses and official history in the documentation emerging from colonial Latin America (Prada Oropeza, 7–8). But this association, too, does not work and for similar reasons. There is a fundamental difference, as Doris Sommer has pointed out, between the metaphor of heroic narrative, the chronicle, which assumes an identity by substituting one signifier for another, an "I" for a "We", and the metonymy of the *testimonio*, a lateral identification that acknowledges the possible differences among an "us" as components of the whole (Sommer, 108). In

Bernal Díaz's heroic narrative, for example, he and his men become interchangeable. *The History of New Spain* begins: "I, Bernal Díaz del Castillo, . . . tell you *the story of myself and my comrades; all true conquerors . . .*" On the other hand, the "I" of the testimonio as already seen, always speaks for an impersonal "we" (Prada Oropeza, 7–8).

The third form with which the *testimonio* has been compared, (in our continuing effort to centralize the marginal), has been the memoir or autobiographical form. But this too poses problems. First, the autobiographical "I" addresses an ideal reader and, as with the picaresque and the chronicle, focuses on the singularity of the individual life being recounted.[34] The testimonial narrative, on the other hand, reveals a communal condition, "the radical loneliness of the subaltern classes" (Franco, 181). In Menchú's case, "[a]utobiography hands itself over to a struggle to decolonize the marginal subject from hegemonic forms of socio-economic, political, sexual, racial, and linguistic domination," and turns to real people to invite them to join the collective narrators in their struggle.[35] Second, autobiography is first and foremost the product of Western conventions, "determined, in all its aspects, by the resources of [its] medium."[36] It privileges selectivity, unity, and coherence achieved through the silencing of all those elements which do not fit within the formula of its particular literary discourse.[37] This view can already be traced to Book III of Plato's *Republic* where only the "artistic" could become part of literary discourse. The truth, if perceived as either ugly or unpleasant, simply had no place in narrative. The "official story," then, is most acceptable precisely because it is fabricated: "It pertains to the guardians of the city," Plato tells us, "and to them alone, to tell falsehoods, to deceive either enemies or citizens for the city's welfare."[38] The narrator of the Latin-American *testimonio*, however, is concerned with a truth repudiated by classical precedent, one that is primarily ugly and unpleasant. Consequently, she has an urgency to speak but no medium acceptable for the "truth" she wants to recount. What Western paradigm for the marriage song, the epithalamium, for example, can serve to encode Rigoberta Menchú's description of the Maya-Quiché wedding ceremony?

> The girl says: 'I will be a mother, I will suffer, my children will suffer, many of my children will die young because of the circumstances created for us by white men. It will be hard for me

to accept my children's death but I will bear it because our ancestors bore it without giving up. We will not give up either.' This is the girl's promise. The young man promises: 'I will be responsible. We will see our children die before they have grown, but we must still go on following Indian ways. . . . 'From now on we will be mother and father' (70).

It is the same with the fairy-tale script within which either Chungara or her interlocutor/editor, Moema Viezzer, has emplotted the Bolivian's story. She is described as a victimized child whose beloved mother has died and who is persecuted by a wicked stepmother who throws her out of the house. Her "savior" finds her, demands justice for her, and marries her. But being encoded in that script is ineffective since Chungara does not live happily ever after. As Mastretta's *Mexican Bolero* inverts the *Bildungsroman*, so Chungara's story begins where fairy tales end. Marriage to an abusive husband and repudiation of a society in which she cannot be integrated only foreground the distance between the fairy-tale script in which her experience has been encoded and her actual reality of hunger, poverty, torture, and death.

The third notion of *testimonio*, which frustrates literary expectations is that of author/editor. The *testimonios* we are discussing are reconstructed, organized, and edited by educated interlocutors/authors who, while they edit, necessarily reinterpret events alien to their own experience. Is the artistic reordering of the native informant's account, what Gérard Genette calls the transformation of the *récit*, the "basic story stuff," into the *discours*,[39] a rendering of the informant's *récit*, or is it, instead, a betrayal of it? The difficulty is augmented by the fact that each interlocutor/author makes different claims about the role and motivation in the process of recording the *testimonio*. The author may claim only to have recorded the native informant's *récit*, merely correcting grammatical errors and/or repetitions, as in the case of Viezzer, Burgos-Debray, Benjamin, and Dantas.[40] Or the author may emphasize that the account of the native informant has been consciously fictionalized and made into a literary artifact, as Poniatowska alleges.[41] Burgos-Debray begins Menchú's *testimonio* with an ethnographic framing of the story, informing the reader that it is she who has organized the account according to major themes arranged into sequential chapters. She admits that she has had to "insert linking passages" (Menchú, xx) and that she has transformed the original dialogue form of their interview into a monologue. The end result is that Menchú's dialogic discourse has been confined, for better or worse, within the limits established by her interlocutor who has also "cut a number of points that are repeated" and "decided to correct the gender mistakes" (xx). As a consequence of such intervention, the reader is confronted with gaps, unfilled spaces, and absences resulting from what Menchú might have said, had other and different questions been asked of her. When Burgos-Debray proclaims, "I allowed her to speak" (xx), she speaks correctly. Her manipulation of Menchú's narrative provides both a "voice" for the Maya Indian, and confines to this established framework what that voice will "say."

Critics are divided in their reactions to this method of compiling a text. David William Foster raises the issue in his discussion of Miguel Barnet's *Biografía de un cimarrón* (1966; *The Autobiography of a Runaway Slave*). He points out that this type of document presents as explicit text a narrative generated by a subtext already conditioned by the interlocutor's ethnographic interests. K. Millet views the result of an interlocutor's manipulation of the material not as the production of narrative by the native speaker, but rather, as "the textualizing of . . . [the interlocutor's] political sympathies."[42] For Gayatri Spivak it constitutes one more instance of the colonizer speaking for the subaltern.[43] On the other hand, there are critics who point out that the collaboration of an uneducated informant and an educated interlocutor brings together two classes formerly at odds, with separate interests, in a venture that unites them in a common cause or program (Beverley, *MC*, 20).[44] The native informants themselves are divided in their opinions about this cooperative work. Chungara, despite her distrust of writers in general, declares herself satisfied with her interlocutor. "That's why I want to say that I'm happy with the work method we've used. I think it's correct that you've understood and not changed what I wanted to say and interpret" (235). Menchú is much more wary, telling the reader she has deliberately kept her people's secrets hidden even from her interlocutor. How problematic the issue is becomes clear on examination of Elena Poniatowska's *Until I See You Again My Jesus*. Both the native informant's identity and the informant's story are fabricated. Poniatowska freely admits she reinterpreted, even invented, certain aspects of Josefina Bórquez's *testimonio*: "I filled in where I deemed necessary, I pruned, pieced together, changed, invented," she comments. She reports that when she read Bórquez's testimonio back to her, the latter angrily cried, "You changed everything" (García Pinto, *Historias,* 180). She called Poniatowska a liar and the text itself a lie: "You invent everything, they are pure lies, you understood nothing, the events are not like that."[45] These conflicting views also foreground the power or powerlessness of the author/interlocutor. Critics argue that the *testimonio* undermines the traditional notion of author as unique and transforms it into the function of mere compiler or "gestor" of the native informant's *récit* (Barnet, 12–42). At the same time, the interlocutor's very real power to transform the informant's *récit* has been seen as actually underwriting rather than undermining the author's role (Kerr, 370–94). Two voices are forever present in the *testimonio,* that of the native informant who narrates her account, and that of the ethnographer who gives that account "meaning." Two spaces, the literary and the cultural, two media, the oral and the written, two intentions, the political and the anthropological, are juxtaposed.[46]

The native informant's use of a literary language, and of forms to which she has not had access, is equally interesting. Menchú, for example, selects, rejects, combines whatever serves her revolutionary purposes. "Our people," she explains, "have taken Catholicism as just another channel of expression, not our one and only belief. Our people do the same with other religions" (9). Chungara is equally eclectic. Contrarieties like Catholicism and Communism, the military and motherhood, are reconciled in her account, as are others capable of actualizing her people's liberation. Menchú makes the Bible "a necessary weapon for our people" (131–32). Biblical figures like Judith and David become *exempla,* and, like them, she must at times violate her people's most treasured beliefs to save their culture. Hierarchical and patriarchal codes are consciously modified and adjusted by Menchú. Munro Edmonson's discussion of the *Popul Vuh,* the Mayan "Genesis", emphasizes that the *Popul Vuh* "is not the story of a hero: it is (and says it is) the story of a people".[47] Menchú, following the communal tradition of her cultural heritage, gives the singular hero/liberator of the Bible a collective identity. The entire people become liberators in the struggle: "We compared the Moses of those times *with us,*" she explains, who are "the Moses of today" (131; emphasis mine). Even Menchú's Spanish can be said to be in the interstices of two discourses, neither Mayan nor Spanish, both Mayan and Spanish. Her idiom is syncretic and excentric. Having learned the language from Roman Catholic nuns, she sprinkles her speech with Biblical associations. Her contact with guerrilla groups has filled her vocabulary with revolutionary terms. An autodidact, she marks her Spanish utterances with idiomatic expressions and linguistic constructions that reflect the world view of her native Quiché (Wright, viii). The concept of God, for example, is represented in Spanish as an abstract, masculine Being (as is the case in many Western languages). The Mayan culture, on the other hand, considers Mother Earth sacred and "God" as both mother and father. Menchú's God consequently becomes androgynous in the Mayan prayer: "Mother Earth, may you feed us. We are made of maize, of yellow maize and white maize . . . Father and Mother, Heart of the Sky, may you give us heat, may you give us hope . . . We, poor and humble as we are, will never abandon you" (67). This *Weltanschauung* is also translated onto the practical level. While the Spanish metonymic "father" symbolizes the family, a much larger number of presences and models is provided in the extended, indigenous Latin-American family.[48] Both mother and father become models for the Maya-Quiché community. "In our community," Menchú explains, "there is an elected representative, someone who is highly respected. He's not a king but someone whom the community looks up to like a father. In our village, my father and mother were the representatives. Well, then the whole community becomes the children of the woman who's elected" (127).

Chungara also sifts and sorts, using what serves her people's cause and discarding the rest. She thinks that religion serves capitalistic interests, that Marxism is good for her people although it lacks a spiritual dimension needed to complete the struggle successfully, and that Catholicism, in its fight against Communism, actually aids the people's oppressors. Chungara undermines all redemptive paradigms: both the paternalism of a Che Guevara who actually ignored the Bolivian "people," and the "salvation" provided by the CIA who tried to convince the people that "we do everything for you" (122). She is even skeptical of the people's unions, because "the interests of the bourgeosie really aren't our interests" (204). Chungara believes only in "the cries, the suffering and the experiences of the people . . . [because] our development must come from our own clarity and awareness" (163). Elvia Alvarado is no less forceful. She repudiates the government's attempt to "buy" her silence: "But I couldn't be happy if my belly was full while my neighbors didn't have a plate of beans and tortillas to put on the table. My struggle is for a better life for all Hondurans . . . My principles are not for sale" (98). Even the interlocutors of their stories must see their literary efforts in this context. They too must serve the revolutionary purpose. Chungara does not want the account of her people's life and suffering to be lucrative: ". . . this account of my personal experience of my people, who are fighting for their liberation . . . well, I want it to reach the poorest people, the people who don't have any money . . . It doesn't matter what kind of paper it's put down on, but it does matter that it be useful for the working class *and not only for intellectual people or for people who only make a business of this kind of thing"* (15; emphasis mine). Menchú goes further, explaining why neither reader nor interlocutor/editor must know too much. Her people, like Chungara's, must be privileged. It is they whom Menchú has primarily in mind: ". . . the Spaniards dishonoured our ancestors' finest sons, and the most humble of them. And it is to honour these humble people that we must keep our secrets. And no-one except we Indians must know it" (13). Menchú's cultural position ultimately makes her *testimonio* the most revolutionary of all the narratives discussed. The continuing silence imposed on her people from colonial times has kept intact the oppressive system she condemns in her *testimonio*. By appropriating the word, she has broken that age-old silence. By appropriating the dominant language and the means of production and publication by which this suppression has been perpetrated, she has given her people a voice. Debax's analysis of women's oppression applies to Menchú and her people. Debax points out that "[t]o reduce woman to silence is to reduce her to powerlessness; that is how the masculine will to castrate operates . . . Language, the tongue, is women's weapon."[49] Ultimately this concept of culture itself becomes one more notion this illiterate Indian woman defies in her struggle for freedom. Her *testimonio* destabilizes the traditional concept of language as power and posits, instead, the silence of her own culture as its greatest strength. "My commitment to our struggle," she reveals, "knows no boundaries nor limits . . . Nevertheless, I'm still keeping my Indian identity a secret. I'm still keeping secret what I think no-one should know. Not even anthropologists or intellectuals, no matter how many books they have, can find out all our secrets" (247). Doris Sommer aptly says that

Rigoberta Menchú knows well that no one "code fits or contains her." This "lack of fit is also the mark of her advantage as a new speaker . . . who translates unheard-of expression to express unheard-of experiences" (*Mama Blanca's Memoirs*, xxv). For Gareth Williams, Menchú's testimony is one of "embodiment." Those who, like her, were previously denied access to discourse "now speak for themselves for the first time" (82).

These humble women, who differ in race, color, and class from the other women discussed in this book, nevertheless subscribe to Victoria Ocampo's belief that "a union between politics and culture" is only possible if writers of all classes are allowed to speak. They share with Luisa Valenzuela and Carmen Naranjo a modern inversion of the age-old debate on arms and letters, whether a medium as powerful as literature may actually be powerless in a struggle that can be neither fought nor won in the pages of a literary text (Beverley, *MC*, 15). But they still continue to write.

Epilogue

Experience, Teresa de Lauretis reminds us, "is the process by which, for all social beings, subjectivity is constructed. Through that process one places oneself or is placed in social reality and so perceives and comprehends as subjective (referring to, originating in oneself) those relations—material, economic, and interpersonal—which are in fact social, and, in a larger perspective, historical."[1] I have tried to lend a gendered optic precisely to this process of subject-constitution and object-formation in the works of the women in this book. I have restricted myself to a limited sampling of their work because its sheer proliferation would have made my analysis unwieldy. Nevertheless, this representative sampling of generic reinterpretations discloses and destabilizes the gendered ideologies at work in the experience of the female characters these women portray. The genres of the romance and the sentimental novel are revalorized, as may be seen in Teresa de la Parra's *Ifigenia*, María Luisa Bombal's *The Final Mist*, and Marta Brunet's "The Child Who Wanted to Become a Picture." Popular songs that construct women as "good" when they are kept at home and "tarnished" or prone to seduction when they leave their homes are parodied, as Angeles Mastretta's *Mexican Bolero* illustrates.[2] These writers humorously invert, as Rosario Ferré does so effectively in "When Women Love Men," the common proverb in which the stock *ménage-à-trois* situation has women fighting one another for the love of a man. Through irony, these authors dismantle gendered and class positionalities, debunking their essentialism and disclosing them as merely "contextual, contested, and contingent" (Scott, 36). In order to open a space for their own discourses and subject positions they violate earlier texts and restructure space, time, and linear narrativity.[3] Precision, language, and structural cohesiveness are undermined in works like Julieta Campos's *Sabina*, Helen Parente Cunha's *Woman Between Mirrors*, and Luisa Valenzuela's *The Efficient Cat*, and silences and ruptures become significant in Griselda Gambaro's *God Does Not Want Us to be Happy*; in Campos's *Celina Or the Cats*, where Celina is deprived of a voice of her own; and in María Luisa Bombal's *The Shrouded Woman*, where the protagonist can speak only when it is too late—after she has died. The authors of all these works take upon themselves what Pierre Macherey has called "the task of *measuring silences*, whether acknowledged or unacknowledged" in a world that has deprived women of subjective utterance (87; emphasis his).

Central to the structure of these women's *Bildungsromane* is a dismantling of romance as a conciliatory genre. Theirs is no "imaginary resolution" of the contradiction of difference.[4] It is a position, instead, of enabling violence as romance's substratum. This is as true of Mastretta's *Mexican Bolero* as it is of Angel's *The Painted Bird Was Sitting in the Green Lemon Tree*, of Naranjo's *There Never Was a Once Upon a Time*, and of Parra's *Mama Blanca's Memoirs*. Parra's idyllic feminine world of bonding between a mother and her daughters is perhaps the most poignant, disclosing epistemic violence in the redefinition of the etiological tale of paradisal expulsion. Woman's *infelix culpa* is ontological: being female is seen as constituting woman's originary disobedience of the Law of the Father and her subsequent irrevocable estrangement from him. As the child narrator of *Mama Blanca's Memoirs* points out: "The matter is that we never disobeyed him [their father] but once in our life. But that single time sufficed to disunite us without scenes of violence for many years. This great disobedience took place at the hour of our birth" (21).

The Mexicans Rosario Castellanos in *The Nine Guardians* and Elena Garro in "The Tree" underline the inherent contingency and contextuality of class categories. The indigenous peoples in their works, once they become conscious of how power/knowledge relationships have worked in their object formation, reappropriate the master's tools and use them to re-construct themselves as subjects. In similar fashion, the women in Rosario Ferré's "When Women Love Men" construct their own subject positionalities. When the black prostitute Isabel La Negra inherits money, her relationship with the white Isabel Luberza ceases to be that of inferior to superior. The two women then reconstruct themselves as social equals. Class barriers, xenophobia, and misogyny are depicted as contingent categories that often operate, in Gayatri Chakravorty Spivak's words, "on crude levels of ideological reproduction" (303). In Griselda Gambaro's *Information for Foreigners*, xenophobia is transmitted in the father's bedtime story to his little girl about the "bad" Bolivians. In Carmen Naranjo's tale of misogyny "Everybody Loves Clowns," the little girl is derided for wanting to be a clown when she grows up, because, she is told, women are clowns anyway: they paint themselves and they always wear costumes. Throughout the works of these authors, therefore, the process of object formation and subject constitution is deliberately pinpointed. Repeatedly we see the "feminization" of sacrifice. The spinster Férula in Allende's *House of the Spirits* and Naranjo's "Smiling Aunts of Twentieth Street" are expected to sacrifice themselves for their mother. The little girl in Angel's *The Missus*, because she is female, must sacrifice her ambition to be an airplane pilot. Gambaro's Cledy in *To Gain Death* must sacrifice herself to her lecherous father-in-law in order to keep the family together.

The factors that produce such traffic in women are explored in Luisa Valenzuela's *Clara: Thirteen Stories and a Novel*, in Elvira Orphée's *El Angel's Last Conquest*, and in Reina Roffé's *Mons Veneris*. All three Argentines depict the commerce of women's bodies as the product of class politics, a practice sanctioned in Argentine reality as "patriotic." For example, Juan Bautista Alberdi, whose blueprint for Argentina's 1853 constitution was highly influential throughout Latin America, reiterated the slogan that "to govern is to populate."[5] On women's bodies, the body politic was to grow, and on women's bodies the morality of the country was to be sustained. Donna Guy has shown that prostitution was legalized in Argentina on this latter premise. Women's "patriotic" duty was to keep Argentine men heterosexual. "The theme of the woman who rescues the rest of the family by saving them from homosexuality," Guy explains, "was not unique to anarchist ideology and its use in 1914 foreshadowed the rationale that justified the reopening of bordellos by the Peronist government in 1955."[6] The categories of heterosexuality and homosexuality which so concerned the Peronist government are seen as merely arbitrary and contingent constructs by the women discussed in this book. In the relaxed sexual coding of Luisa Valenzuela's literary worlds, sexless José-Marías and/or María-Josés become sexually interchangeable; ubiquitous androgynes, transvestites, and cross-dressers simply defy gender markings. Hetero/homo/bisexual boundaries in Marta Traba's *Mothers and Shadows* become blurred as characters like Dolores love both men and women with equal intensity. Gender coding is rendered moot in the hilarious hermaphroditic fantasies of Griselda Gambaro's Madame X and in Carmen Naranjo's "Symbiotic Encounter," where the male becomes pregnant and the woman deserts him during his pregnancy. These women pinpoint in literature the "production" of gender categories.

Contemporary feminist/theoretical analyses focus on the contingency of such categories. For example, Marjorie Garber's fine analysis of cross-dressing discusses the real-life story of the French officer Gallimard and his Indochinese lover Song Liling.[7] Since it has been made into the highly successful theatre and film productions of *M. Butterfly*, contemporary audiences are already aware of the gendered aporia of the story. After a twenty-year liaison with the Indochinese actor/actress who has supposedly borne him a child, Gallimard discovers that his lover is actually a man. Less well known is the story Garber tells of the seventeenth-century Abbé de Choisy, French courtier, historian, and one-time ambassador to Siam whose autobiographical *Fragments* chronicle his story as a cross-dresser. The abbé repeatedly dressed as a woman, and he dressed his young mistress as a man: "Called 'the little comte,' she rode by his side in peruke and riding habit, until her pregnancy obliged him to dress her again in women's clothes. . . . It was the 'Comte' and not the 'Comtesse,' the 'husband' and not the 'wife,' who was with child" (258). And the women writers in this book apply ironic reinterpretations to just such essentialist categories. They historicize and contest the so-called natural categories of race, class, and gender and expose them as socially constructed. In so doing, they disclose what "women" as a category have in common (their femaleness) and what separates them (their racial and class identities),[8] as well as provide a deeper understanding of how such differences are produced.[9]

This problematizing of gender and class categories is evident even in the testimonial writings of Victoria Ocampo, and it becomes more obvious in the works of later writers. By her own account, Victoria Ocampo is a *mestiza*, since her grandmother was a Guaraní Indian. Her maid, Fani, on the other hand, was actually a Spaniard, a "category" in Latin America that should have made the mistress Ocampo, as a *mestiza* and a creole, inferior to her Spanish maid whose European ancestors had "colonized" Argentina. This, however, was not the case. Class and racial identities, like gender identities, are contextual. It is wealth that produces the different positionalities of these two women. Gender identities become even more blurred by the variables of race and class in the testimonial writings of the humbler women represented in this book. The collaboration between the indigenous Bolivian Domitila Barrios de Chungara and her educated interlocutor Moemi Viezzer or between the Quiché Indian Rigoberta Menchú and the anthropologist Elisabeth Burgos-Debray are cases in point. The collaboration between women of different classes and the subsequent literary results of such collaboration are seen as "products of class politics itself" (Scott, 30), undermining traditional oppositions and so becoming politically empowering. This is the view of Francine Masiello. "By giving voice to marginalized groups with little public authority or power," she remarks, "women writers [have] insinuated doubt into the binary structures that inform official history."[10] Other writers see such collaboration between classes as rendering the humbler women powerless since it underwrites the *author* of the subaltern's account. As Doris Sommer has said in another context, the effect is that the "inherited signs of a European language" which the "elusive American [read: subaltern] referent" is made to signify positions these women as objects in order to make them "literarily mature."[11] In other words, the efforts of the educated interlocutors Viezzer and Burgos-Debray to give the humbler women a voice and my own effort to include them in a book on Latin-American women, is "flattering to a First World's taste for the post-modern," and may thereby provide an "almost narcissistic pleasure of having one's ideal notions of literature mirrored back" (Sommer, 3). The alternative, however (and is it better?), is to condemn them to silence.

What is certain is that these authors go "beyond patriarchal [and even feminist] myths and perceptions" in order to problematize all categories, including the notions of "woman" and of narrative.[12] Their works represent women both as objects *and* as agents of oppression. Narrative structures are seen as both oppressive to the representation of women and capable of radical change. These women's work demonstrates, then, in the words of Rachel Blau DuPlessis, that "among the powers of the powerful is the embedding of structures of seeing, feeling, knowing, and telling—including the telling of stories—that repeat the narratives of dominance," and also that alternate structures can be created in order to effect "the changing of seeing, perceiving, and understanding"[13] of ideological categories that were once accepted as "natural."

NOTES

PREFACE

1. Quoted in Ronald Christ, "To Build Bridges: Victoria Ocampo, Grand Lady of *Sur*," *Nimrod* (Spring-Summer 1976), 136–37; hereafter cited in text.

2. See Michael Collins, *Towards Post-Modernism: Decorative Arts and Design Since 1851* (Boston: Little, Brown, 1987); Ihab Hassan, *The Postmodern Turn: Essays in Postmodern Theory and Culture* (Columbus: Ohio State University Press, 1987); Linda Hutcheon, *A Poetics of Postmodernism: History, Theory, Fiction* (New York: Routledge, 1988).

3. See Hélène Cixous, *Vivre L'Orange* (Paris: des Femmes, 1979); Hélène Cixous, "L'approche de Clarice Lispector: se laisser lire (par) Clarice Lispector a paixao segundo C. L.," *Poétique* 40 (1979), 408–19; Hélène Cixous, *Reading with Clarice Lispector*, ed. and translated by Verena Andermatt Conley (Minneapolis: University of Minnesota Press, 1990); and Verena Andermatt Conley, *Hélène Cixous: Writing the Feminine* (Lincoln, Nebraska: University of Nebraska Press, 1984), 152–54 and *passim*.

4. Monique Wittig, "The Category of Sex" in *The Straight Mind and Other Essays* (Boston: Beacon Press, 1992), 3.

5. Myriam Díaz-Diocaretz, "'I Will Be a Scandal in Your Boat': Women Poets and the Tradition," *Knives and Angels: Women Writers in Latin America*, ed. Susan Bassnett (London: Zed Books, 1990), 91–92.

6. bell hooks, *Feminist Theory: From Margin to Center* (Boston: South End Press, 1984), 28.

7. See Gayatri Chakravorty Spivak, "French Feminism in an International Frame," *Yale French Studies* 62 (1981), 84; and Domitila Barrios de Chungara, *Let Me Speak! Testimony of Domitila, a Woman of the Bolivian Mines*, ed. Moema Viezzer and tr. Victoria Ortiz (New York: Monthly Review Press, 1978), 41 and 234.

8. Lourdes Arizpe, "Interview with Carmen Naranjo: Women and Latin-American Literature," *Signs* 5, 1 (1979), 109.

9. Victoria Ocampo, "El pasado y presente de la mujer," *Testimonios VII, 1962–67* (Buenos Aires: Sur, 1967), 231–73. This essay has been translated as "Woman's Past and Present" by Doris Meyer in *Lives*

on the Line: The Testimony of Contemporary Latin-American Authors (Berkeley: University of California Press, 1988), 51–58. See 52.

10. Debra Castillo, *Talking Back: Toward a Latin-American Feminist Literary Criticism* (Ithaca: Cornell University Press, 1992), 20.

11. Adrienne Rich, "Compulsory Heterosexuality and Lesbian Existence," in *Powers of Desire: The Politics of Sexuality*, ed. Ann Snitow, Christine Stansell, and Sharon Thompson (New York: Monthly Review Press, 1983), 192.

12. Elizabeth A. Meese, *Crossing the Double Cross: The Practice of Feminist Criticism* (Chapel Hill: University of North Carolina Press, 1986), 5.

13. Francine Masiello, "Discurso de mujeres, lenguaje de poder: reflexiones sobre la crítica feminista a mediados de la década del 80," *Hispamérica* 15, 45 (1986), 56.

14. Griselda Gambaro, "Feminism or Femininity?" *Américas* 30, 12 (1978), 19.

15. Claudia Schaefer, *Textured Lives* (Tempe: University of Arizona Press, 1992), 109.

16. Hayden Herrera, *Frida: A Biography of Frida Kahlo* (New York: Harper and Row, 1983), 266. The quotation originally appeared in "They Thought I Was a Surrealist," *Time*, April 27, 1953.

17. Georg Lukács, *The Theory of the Novel*, tr. Anna Bostock (Cambridge, Mass.: MIT Press, 1977), 56.

18. Fredric Jameson, *The Political Unconscious* (Ithaca: Cornell University Press, 1981), 10.

CHAPTER 1. LATIN AMERICAN WOMEN/ WOMEN IN LATIN AMERICA

1. Charles Edward Chapman, *Colonial Hispanic America* (New York: Hafner Publishing Company, 1971), 116.

2. June Hahner, ed., *Women in Latin American History: Their Lives and Views* (Los Angeles: University of California Press, 1980), 1.

3. In so doing, the Spaniards created an even greater problem, that of class associated with race. See Chapman, 116–20, for a pertinent discussion of this issue.

4. William L. Sherman, *Forced Native Labor in Sixteenth-Century Central America* (Lincoln: University of Nebraska Press, 1979), 309–10.

5. Rosario Castellanos, *Balún Canán* (Mexico: Fondo de Cultura Económica, 1957), 7.

6. Eric Williams, *From Columbus to Castro: The History of the Caribbean, 1492–1969* (New York: Harper and Row, 1970), 67. See Williams, 293 and 299, where the mortality rate as a result of flogging is discussed. See also Barbara Bush, *Slave Women in Caribbean Society,*

1650–1838 (Bloomington: University of Indiana Press, 1990), 58–60. As Bowser points out, young children were probably left with their mothers because of their need for attention. Nevertheless, teenaged slave children were vulnerable to being sold because they had acquired salable skills. See Frederick Bowser, *The African Slave in Colonial Peru* (Stanford, California: Stanford University Press, 1974), 268–69. See also Moira Ferguson, ed., *The History of Mary Prince, a West Indian Slave, Related by Herself* (London: Pandora, 1987), 12: "I had scarcely reached my twelfth year when my mistress became too poor to keep so many of us at home; and she hired me out to Mrs. Pruden, a lady who lived about five miles off . . ." (48). Shortly thereafter Mary Prince was sold. See pages 50–3, especially the editor's note on page 53, which addresses the question of the separation of slave families.

7. Hilary McD. Beckles, *Natural Rebels: A Social History of Enslaved Black Women in Barbados* (New Brunswick, N. J.: Rutgers University Press, 1989), 141–50. For a discussion of the variety and savagery of punishments meted out by owners in Brazil, see Gerald Cardoso, *Negro Slavery in the Sugar Plantations of Veracruz and Pernambuco, 1550–1680: A Comparative Study* (Washington, D. C.: University Press of America, 1983), 101–5.

8. Charles Edmond Akers, *A History of South America*, rev. by L. E. Elliott (New York: E. P. Dutton and Company, 1930), 139–40.

9. Donald Fogelquist, "Paraguayan Literature of the Chaco War," *Modern Language Journal* 33, 8 (1949), 609.

10. Hugo Rodriguez-Alcalá, "Josefina Plá, española de América, y la poesia," *Cuadernos Americanos* 159, 4 (July–August 1968), 81.

11. Lucía Guerra-Cunningham, "Las sombras de la escritura: hacía una teoria de la producción literaria de la mujer latinoamericana," *Cultural and Historical Grounding for Hispanic and Luso-Brazilian Feminist Literary Criticism*, ed. Hernán Vidal (Minneapolis: Institute for the Study of Ideologies and Literature, 1989), 160.

12. See Evelyn Stevens, "*Marianismo*: The Other Face of *Machismo* in Latin America," *Female and Male in Latin America: Essays*, ed. Ann Pescatello (Pittsburgh: University of Pittsburgh Press, 1973), 90. See also Olivia Harris, "Latin American Women—An Overview," *Latin American Women*, ed. Olivia Harris (New York: Minority Rights Group, 1981), 4.

13. Armonía Somers, "The Fall," *Other Fires*, ed. Alberto Manguel (New York: Clarkson N. Potter, 1986), 17–18.

14. Margaret Randall, *Doris Tijerino: Inside the Nicaraguan Revolution*, tr. Elinor Randall (Vancouver: New Star Books, 1978), 35.

15. See Yvonne Jehenson, "The Pastoral Episode in Cervantes' *Don Quijote*: Marcela Once Again," *Cervantes* 10, 2 (Fall, 1990), 28, for a fuller discussion of this topic.

16. Rosario Castellanos, "The Eternal Feminine," tr. Diane E. Marting and Betty Tyree Osiek, *A Rosario Castellanos Reader*, ed. Maureen Ahern (Austin: University of Texas Press, 1988), 290–1.

17. Magdalena León and María Viveros, "Rural Women in Colombia: Invisible Labour and the Double Day," *Latin American Women*, ed. Harris, 9.

18. Helen Shapiro, "The Many Realities," *Latin American Women: One Myth—Many Realities*, ed. Patricia Flynn, Aracelly Santana, Helen Shapiro, *NACLA Report on the Americas* 14, 5 (September–October 1980),4.

19. Audrey Bronstein, *The Triple Struggle: Latin American Peasant Women* (Boston: South End Press, 1983), 30.

20. Elvia Alvarado, *Don't Be Afraid, Gringo*, ed. and tr. Medea Benjamin (New York: Harper and Row, 1987), 52. See pages 51–2 for Alvarado's description of the *campesina's* typical day.

21. Martha Paley de Francescato, "Marta Lynch: Entrevista," *Hispamérica* 10 (1975), 35. Emphasis is hers. Translation is mine.

22. Silvina Bullrich, *La Mujer Postergada* (Buenos Aires: Sudamérica, 1982), 107–8.

23. Rigoberta Menchú, *I, Rigoberta Menchú, An Indian Woman of Guatemala*, tr. Ann Wright, ed. Elisabeth Burgos-Debray (London: Verso, 1984), 38.

24. Ana Audilia Moreira de Campos, "Our National Inferiority Complex: A Cause for Violence?" *Latin American Woman: The Meek Speak Out*, ed. June H. Turner (Silver Springs, Md.: International Educational Development, 1980), 67–68.

25. Ana Bleyswyck de Carlier, "The Only Road," *Latin American Woman: The Meek Speak Out*, ed. Turner, 49.

26. Suzana Prates, "Women's Work in the Southern Cone: Monetarist Policies in Argentina, Uruguay, and Chile," *Latin American Women*, ed. Harris, 10.

27. Ximena Bünster-Burotto, "Surviving Beyond Fear: Women and Torture in Latin America," *Women and Change in Latin America*, ed. June Nash and Helen I. Safa (South Hadley, Mass.: Bergin and Garvey Publishers, 1986), 298.

28. Marysa Navarro, "The Personal is Political: Las Madres de Plaza Mayo," *Power and Popular Protest*, ed. Susan Eckstein (Berkeley: University of California Press, 1989), 246.

29. Cited in Laura P. Rice-Sayre, "Witnessing History: Diplomacy vs. Testimony," *Testimonio y literatura*, ed. René Jara and Hernán Vidal (Minneapolis: Institute for the Study of Ideologies and Literature, 1986), 64.

30. See the testimony of Cecilia Vázquez de Lutsky in Jean-Pierre Bousquet, *Las locas de la Plaza de Mayo* (Buenos Aires: El Cid, 1984),

184–91. She relates her experiences as a *desaparecida*, noting the mental and physical torture she endured. She further states that she required gynecological treatment after her release. Another woman delivered a dead baby as a result of the torture she had undergone.

31. Her article graphically describes the process by which women are physically and psychically broken by a military regime: "One of the essential ideas behind the sexual slavery of a woman in torture is to teach her that she must retreat into the home and fulfill the traditional role of wife and mother" (307). In this perverted way *marianismo* is used to carry out the political program of a repressive government.

32. Illiteracy rates for women in Latin America are much greater than for men. For example, in Bolivia, which has the highest female illiteracy in the entire area, women's illiteracy is almost twice that of men, 49% to 24.8%. In El Salvador, women's illiteracy rate is 41.1, compared to men's of 34.5%. The rate for women in Peru is 39.2%, while that for men is 16.7%. See Olivia Harris, 7, for a complete description.

33. Anna Macías, *Against All Odds* (Westport, Conn.: Greenwood Press, 1982), 3–24.

34. Doris Meyer, *Victoria Ocampo: Against the Wind and the Tide* (New York: Braziller, 1979), 41–44. Comments Meyer: "Had she known Monaco better beforehand, she said later, she would never have married him" (43).

35. Robin Morgan, ed., *Sisterhood Is Global: The International Women's Movement Anthology* (New York: Doubleday Anchor Books, 1984), 53.

36. Marta Bermúdez-Gallegos, "*The Little School* por Alicia Partnoy: el testimonio en la Argentina," *Revista Iberoamericana* 151 (1990), 463.

37. *Nunca Más: The Report of the Argentine National Commission on the Disappeared* (New York: Farrar Straus, Giroux, 1986), 426. For a detailed account of their struggle, which included arrests and the disappearances of several of their own group, see Jean-Pierre Bousquet, *Las locas de la Plaza de Mayo*. See also Marjorie Agosín, *Women of Smoke*, tr. Janice Molloy (Trenton: Red Sea Press, 1989), 33–45, and 46–48.

38. Nancy Caro Hollander, "Women: The Forgotten Half of Argentine History," *Female and Male in Latin America: Essays*, 150.

39. Elena Poniatowska, "Marta Traba o el salto al vacío," *Revista Iberoamericana* 51 (1985), 887–88. See also Bell Gale Chevigny, "A Latin American Odyssey Ends," *The Nation* (February 4, 1984), 126–28. Many of those who disappeared in Latin America in recent years were women who advocated social change, including union leaders, lawyers, doctors, professors. Agosín addresses this issue in *Women of Smoke*, 11–17.

CHAPTER 2. "TO BUILD BRIDGES"

1. Ronald Christ, "Figuring Literarily: An Interview with Victoria Ocampo," *Review—Center for Inter-American Relations* (Winter 1972), 10.

2. John King, "Victoria Ocampo (1890–1979): Precursor," *Knives and Angels: Women Writers in Latin America*, ed. Susan Bassnett (London: Zed Books, 1990), 9. Hereafter cited as King, "Precursor" in the text.

3. The following bibliographies of works by and about Ocampo are the most complete: David William Foster, "Bibliography of Writings By and About Victoria Ocampo (1890–1979)," *Revista Interamericana de Bibliografía* 39 (1980), 51–58; Doris Meyer, "Victoria Ocampo," *Spanish American Women Writers*, ed. Diane Marting (Westport, Conn.: Greenwood Press, 1989), 378–81; Fryda Schultz de Mantovani, *Victoria Ocampo* (Buenos Aires: Ediciones Culturales Argentinas, 1963), 103–11. The following works by Victoria Ocampo have been translated into English: *338171 T. E.*, tr. David Garnett (New York: E. P. Dutton, 1963; "Aries and Capricorn," *Testimonies: Alberdi and Sarmiento in Modern Argentine Life*, co-authored with Nicolás Repetto and tr. Owen Kellerman (Tempe: Arizona State University Center for Latin American Studies, 1974), 25–36; "Misfortunes of an Autodidact," "The Water Lily Pond," tr. Doris Meyer, *Contemporary Women Authors of Latin America: New Translations*, eds. Doris Meyer and Margarite Fernández Olmos (Brooklyn: Brooklyn College Press, 1983), 77–106 and 217–25; "A Selection of Essays (15) by Victoria Ocampo," Doris Meyer, *Victoria Ocampo: Against the Wind and the Tide*, 195–284; "Woman's Past and Present," tr. Doris Meyer, *Lives on the Line: the Testimony of Contemporary Latin American Authors,* ed. Doris Meyer (Berkeley: University of California Press, 1988), 49–58; "Letter to Waldo Frank," tr. Victoria Ocampo, *Review* (Spring 1974), 51–52; *Tagore on the Banks of the River Plate. Rabindranath Tagore: A Centenary Volume*, tr. Victoria Ocampo (New Delhi: Sahitya Akademi, 1961); "The Lakes of the South," tr. Harriet de Onís, *The Green Continent*, ed. Germán Arciniegas (New York: Alfred A. Knopf, 1944), 116–22; "Yesterday, Today, and Tomorrow," tr. Renata Treitel and Maralee Waidner, *Nimrod* (Spring-Summer 1976), 151–56.

4. Danubio Torres Fierro, "Entrevista a Victoria Ocampo," *Plural* (December 1975), 21.

5. Carlos Adam, "Bio-bibliografía de Victoria Ocampo," *Sur* 346 (1980), 167. Hereafter cited by author and page number within the text.

6. Victoria Ocampo, *"Sur*: ese desconocido," *Testimonios: novena serie (1971–74)* (Buenos Aires: Sur, 1975), 228.

7. See María Luisa Bastos, "Victoria Ocampo," *Latin American*

Writers, eds. Carlos A. Solé and María Isabel Abreu (New York: Charles Scribner's Sons, 1989), 2, 705. Hereafter cited as Bastos 1 in the text.

8. Nancy Kaston, "Los ensayos feministas de Victoria Ocampo," *Atenea* (1985), 50.

9. Cited in E. Rodríquez Monegal, "Victoria Ocampo por Borges, Paz, Caillois, Sackville-West, Rodríguez Monegal," *Vuelta* 3, 30 (May 1979), 40.

10. See Sylvia Molloy, *At Face Value: Autobiographical Writing in Latin America* (Cambridge: Cambridge University Press, 1991), 65. Hereafter cited by author and page within the text.

11. Magdalena García Pinto, "Entrevista: Marta Traba," *Hispamérica* 38 (1984), 45.

12. "De Victoria Ocampo a José Bergamín," *Sur* 32 (1937), 73.

13. "Sobre la metafísica del sexo," *Sur* 213–4 (July–August 1952), 161.

14. Victoria Ocampo, "A los lectores de 'Sur,'" *Sur* 268 (1961), 5.

15. John King, "Victoria Ocampo, *Sur*, y el peronismo, 1946–55," *Revista de Occidente* 37 (1984), 32. Hereafter cited as King, "El peronismo" in the text.

16. John King, "Towards a Reading of the Argentine Literary Magazine *Sur*, *Latin American Research Review* 16, 2 (1981), 65. Hereafter cited as King, "Towards a Reading" in the text.

17. María Luisa Bastos, "Escrituras ajenas, expresión propia: *Sur* y los *Testimonios* de Victoria Ocampo," *Revista iberoamericana* 46 (1980), 126. Hereafter cited as Bastos 2 in the text.

18. Stephen Barber, *Antonin Artaud: Blows and Bombs* (London: Faber and Faber, 1993), 50.

19. David Lagmanovich, "*Sur*: 40 Years," *Américas* 23, 9 (September 1971), 29.

20. María Esther Vásquez, "Victoria Ocampo, una argentina universalista," *Revista Iberoamericana* 46 (1980), 173.

21. Celia Correas de Zapata and Lygia Johnson, *Detrás de la reja* (Caracas: Monte Avila Editores, 1980), 17.

22. See Marta Gallo, "Las crónicas de Victoria Ocampo: versatilidad y fidelidad de un género," *Revista Iberoamericana* 51 (1985), 680. See also Alba Omil, *Frente y perfil de Victoria Ocampo* (Buenos Aires: Sur, 1980), 153. See also Alicia Jurado, "Victoria Ocampo, mi predecesora," *Boletín de la Academia Argentina de Letras* 46, 179–80 (1981), 83.

23. This essay, originally "Mujer: sus derechos y sus responsabilidades," appeared in *La mujer y su expresión* (Buenos Aires: Sur, 1936), 49–67. It later appeared in *Testimonios, segunda serie* (Buenos Aires: Sur, 1941), 251–67. It has been translated by Doris Meyer in *Against the Wind and the Tide*, 228–34. See 228.

24. This essay was originally published in *Testimonios: quinta serie* (Buenos Aires: Sur, 1957), 237–49. It has been translated by Doris Meyer in *Against the Wind and the Tide*, 252–62.

25. For a contrary view of Ocampo's "racism unclouded by shame," see Amy Kaminsky, "Essay, Gender, and *Mestizaje*: Victoria Ocampo and Gabriela Mistral," *The Politics of the Essay: Feminist Perspectives*, ed. Ruth-Ellen Boetcher-Joeres and Elizabeth Mittman (Bloomington: Indiana University Press, 1993), 126. In Allende's *Of Love and Shadows*, Irene Beltrán and her servant, Rosa, share an "affectionate complicity" (139). The relationships of the other women are discussed in chapters four and six.

26. This essay originally appeared in *Testimonios: quinta serie*, 108–18. It has been translated by Doris Meyer in *Against the Wind and the Tide*, 200–8.

27. Victoria Ocampo, "Mujeres en la academia," *Testimonios: décima serie* (Buenos Aires: Sur, 1978), 15. This essay has been translated as "Women in the Academy" by Doris Meyer in *Against the Wind and the Tide*, 278–84.

28. Celia Correas de Zapata, "Victoria Ocampo y Virginia Woolf: la rebeldía en el ensayo," *Ensayos Hispanoamericanos* (Buenos Aires: Ediciones Corregidor, 1978), 166.

29. Barbara Case, "On Writing, Magic, and Eva Perón: An Interview with Argentina's Luisa Valenzuela," *Ms.* (October 1983), 19. See also María-Inés Lagos-Pope, "Mujer y política en *Cambio de armas* de Luisa Valenzuela," *Hispamérica* 16, 46–47 (1987), 71–83, who speaks of the many women whose literature takes place in the context of political upheaval.

30. See Joanne Saltz, "Luisa Valenzuela's *Cambio de armas*: Rhetoric of Politics," *Confluencia* 3, 1 (1987), 61.

CHAPTER 3. "MAN'S LOVE . . .
'TIS WOMAN'S WHOLE EXISTENCE"

1. See Sylvia Molloy, "Foreword" to Teresa de la Parra, *Mama Blanca's Memoirs*, tr. Harriet de Onís and revised by Frederick H. Fornoff (Pittsburgh: University of Pittsburgh Press), 1993, xii.

2. The liberal president of Venezuela, José Gregorio Monagas, decreed the abolition of slavery in 1854. See Elizabeth Garrels, "Piedra Azul, or the Colonial Paradise of Women" in *Mama Blanca's Memoirs*, 136–49, where the author shows how Parra's "antiliberalism" idealizes the past and brackets contemporary turbulent events in Venezuela to describe an idyllic Piedra Azul, which exists "in blissful ignorance of history and material reality" (138). See also her fine study, *Las grietas de la*

ternura: nueva lectura de Teresa de la Parra (Caracas: Monte Avila Editores, 1985).

3. Rosario Hiriart, *Más cerca de Teresa de la Parra (diálogos con Lydia Cabrera* (Caracas: Monte Avila Editores, 1980), 119–20.

4. See Edna Aizenberg, "El *Bildungsroman* fracasado en Latinoamérica: el caso de *Ifigenia* de Teresa de la Parra," *Revista Iberoamericana* 51 (1985), 539–46.

5. See Gabriela Mora, "La otra cara de Ifigenia: una revaluación del personaje de Teresa de la Parra," *Sin Nombre* 7, 3 (1976), 130–44.

6. Teresa de la Parra, "Influencia de las mujeres en la formación del alma americana," *Obras completas* (Caracas: Editorial Arte, 1965), 684.

7. Quoted in Garrels, 58.

8. See Parra's "Letter to an Unknown Reader," Leysin, 29 December 1932, cited in Velia Bosch, *Esta pobre lengua viva: relectura de la obra de Teresa de la Parra* (Caracas: Ediciones de la Presidencia de la República, 1979), 222–3.

9. For more on Brunet's life and works, see Mary G. Berg, "Marta Brunet," in Diane Marting's *Spanish American Women Writers*, 53–63. See also Mary Berg, "The Short Stories of Marta Brunet," *Monographic Review/Revista Monográfica* 4 (1988), 195–206.

10. Gabriela Mora, "Una lectura de 'Soledad de la sangre' de Marta Brunet," *Estudios Filológicos* 19 (1984), 90. See also Marjorie Agosín, "La mimesis de la interioridad: 'Soledad de la sangre' de Marta Brunet y 'El árbol' de María Luisa Bombal," *Neophilologus* 63, 3 (July 1984), 386.

11. Lucía Guerra-Cunningham, *La narrativa de María Luisa Bombal: una visión de la existencia femenina* (Madrid: Editorial Playor, 1980), 19.

12. See Alberto Rabago, "Elementos surrealistas en *La última niebla*," *Hispania* 64 (March 1981), 31–40.

13. For a reading of *The Story of María Griselda* as an *antimärchen*, as a subversion of the fairy tale convention, see Marjorie Agosín, "Un cuento de hadas a la inversa: *La historia de María Griselda* o la belleza aniquilada," *Hispanic Journal* 5, 1 (1983), 141–9.

14. See, for example, *The Final Mist*, 12; *New Islands*, 88–93; *The Story of María Griselda*, 79–80; *The Shrouded Woman*, 103.

15. See Phyllis Rodríguez-Peralta, "María Luisa Bombal's Poetic Novels of Female Estrangement," *Revista de Estudios Hispánicos* 14, 1 (1980), 152.

16. See Marjorie Agosín, "Una biografía de una mujer novelada: María Luisa Bombal," *Discurso Literario* 5, 2 (1988), 325–34.

17. See Hernán Vidal, *María Luisa Bombal: La feminidad enajenada* (Barcelona: Hijos de José Bosch, S. A., 1976, 118–19.

18. Lucía Guerra-Cunningham, "Visión de lo femenino en la obra de María Luisa Bombal: una dualidad contradictoria del ser y el deber-ser," *Revista Chilena de Literatura* 25 (1985), 87–99, especially 95.

19. See Soledad Bianchi, "María Luisa Bombal o una dificil travesía (del amor mediocre al amor pasión)," *Atenea* 45 (1985), especially 181–85.

20. For an interesting analysis of the similarity of style between Brunet's *Montaña adentro* and Bombal's *The Final Mist*, see Martha Allen, "Dos estilos de novela: Marta Brunet y María Luisa Bombal," *Revista Iberoamericana* 17 (1952), 63–91.

21. See Rosario Castellanos, "María Luisa Bombal y los arquetipos femeninos," in *Mujer que sabe latin . . .* (Mexico: SepSetentas, 1973), 144–49.

22. Gabriela Mora, "Rechazo del mito en *Las islas nuevas* de María Luisa Bombal," *Revista Iberoamericana* 51 (1985), 853–65.

23. Lucía Guerra-Cunningham, "Entrevista a María Luisa Bombal," *Hispanic Journal* 3, 2 (1982), 126; Marjorie Agosín, "Mysticism and Anti-Mysticism in María Luisa Bombal's *La última niebla*," *Círculo: Publicación del Círculo de Cultura Panamericana* 11 (1982), 58. See also Gloria Gálvez Lira, "Entrevista con María Luisa Bombal," in *María Luisa Bombal: realidad y fantasía* (Potomac, Maryland: Scripta Humanística, 1986), 105–10, especially 108 where Bombal reiterates that men are the axis of a woman's life.

24. Claudia Schaefer, *Textured Lives* (Tempe: University of Arizona Press, 1992), 92.

CHAPTER 4. ARMS AND LETTERS:
THE POWER OF THE WORD

1. See Juan Gustavo Cobo Borda, "Marta Traba, novelista," *Cuadernos Hispanoamericanos* 414 (December 1984), 121–30, for an interesting overview and discussion of *Conversación al sur* and *En cualquier lugar*. See also Elia Kantaris, "The Politics of Desire: Alienation and Identity in the Work of Marta Traba and Cristina Peri Rossi," *Forum for Modern Language Studies* 25, 3 (1989), 248–64.

2. Evelyn Picon Garfield, *Women's Voices from Latin America: Interviews With Six Contemporary Authors* (Detroit: Wayne State University Press, 1985), 139. Hereafter cited as Picon Garfield, *Women's Voices* within the text.

3. Evelyn Picon Garfield, *Women's Fiction from Latin America: Selections from Twelve Contemporary Authors* (Detroit: Wayne State University Press, 19880, 214. Hereafter cited as Picon Garfield, *Women's Fiction* within the text.

4. "La sangrienta lucha que despedaza a la República Argentina," in Raquel Chang-Rodriguez and Malva E. Filer, *Voces de Hispanoamérica: Antología Literaria* (Boston: Heinle and Heinle, 1988), 171.

5. In Diana Taylor's "Afterword" to *Information for Foreigners: Three Plays by Griselda Gambaro*, ed. and tr. by Marguerite Feitlowitz (Evanston: Northwestern University Press, 1992), 161.

6. Paula L. Green, "Political Violence Is Rising As Argentina Nears Vote," *Christian Science Monitor* (22 September, 1993), 3.

7. María Sola, "*Conversación al sur*, novela para no olvidar," *Sin Nombre* 12, 4 (July–September 1982), 64–71, especially 66.

8. Oscar Montero, "'La enunciación infatigable' de *Los laberintos insolados* de Marta Traba," *Prismal/Cabral* 12–3 (Fall 1984), 93–102, especially 96.

9. See Myriam Yvonne Jehenson, "Four Women In Search of Freedom," *Revista/Review Interamericana* 12, 1 (Spring 1982), 87–99.

10. Ana Seoane, "Entretien avec Griselda Gambaro," *Cahiers du Monde Hispanique et Luso Brasilien* 40 (1983), 165.

11. See Robert Stoller, *Porn: Myths for the Twentieth Century* (New Haven: Yale University Press, 1991), and *Observing the Erotic Imagination* (New Haven: Yale University Press, 1985).

12. Janice K. McAleer, "*El Campo* de Griselda Gambaro: una contradicción de mensajes," *Revista Canadiense de Estudios Hispánicos* 7, 1 (Autumn 1982), 159–71.

13. Griselda Gambaro, *The Camp*, in William J. Oliver, *Voices of Change in the Spanish American Theatre* (Austin: University of Texas Press, 1971), 47–103. Subsequent references will be noted by page number within the text.

14. Mary Douglas, *Purity and Danger: An Analysis of Concepts of Pollution and Taboo* (New York: Praeger, 1966).

15. See Judith Malina and Julian Beck, *Paradise Now: Collective Creation of the Living Theatre* (New York: Vintage Books, 1971), and Richard Schechner, *Environment Theatre* (New York: Hawthorn Books, 1973).

16. See Dick Gerdes, "Recent Argentine Vanguard Theatre: Gambaro's *Información para extranjeros*," *Latin American Theatre Review* (Spring 1978), 11.

17. Richard Schechner, *Performance Theory* (New York: Routledge, 1988), 142.

18. Victor Turner, *From Ritual to Theatre: The Human Seriousness of Play* (New York: Performing Arts Journal), 112.

19. Elaine Scarry, *The Body in Pain: The Making and Unmaking of the World* (Oxford: Oxford University Press, 1985), 6.

20. Roffé's first novel, *Llamado al puf*, won the Sixto Pontal Ríos Prize in 1975 for the best novel by a young writer.

21. Reina Roffé, "Omnipresencia de la censura en la escritura argentina," *Revista Iberoamericana* 51 (1985), 914.

22. "El periodismo me silenció; el editor no sólo hizo desaparecer del depósito los ejemplares que quedaban, sino que al libro y a mí nos eliminó del catálogo . . . y hasta los amigos escogieron no mencionar la novela." The English rendering does not do justice to the nuances of the Spanish original.

23. Francine Masiello, "Contemporary Argentine Fiction: Liberal (Pre-)Texts in a Reign of Terror," *Latin American Review* 16, 1 (1981), 224.

24. Magdalena García Pinto, *Historias íntimas: conversaciones con diez escritoras latinoamericanas* (New Hampshire: Ediciones del Norte, 1988), 169. Hereafter cited as García Pinto, *Historias* within the text.

25. Georges Bataille, *Eroticism: Death and Sensuality*, tr. Mary Dalwood (San Francisco: City Lights Press, 1981), 61.

26. Richard Schechner, *Between Theater and Anthropology*, with Foreword by Victor Turner (Philadelphia: University of Pennsylvania Press, 1985), 231–2). In counter discourse to Schechner, Caroline Walker Bynum shows that "[m]edieval images of the body have less to do with sexuality than with fertility [the lactating madonna] and decay." See Caroline Walker Bynum, *Fragmentation and Redemption: Essays on Gender and the Human Body in Medieval Religion* (New York: Zone Books, 1992), 182.

27. René Girard, *Violence and the Sacred* (Baltimore: The Johns Hopkins University Press, 1977), 35.

28. Karen L. Laughlin, "The Language of Cruelty: Dialogue Strategies and the Spectator in Gambaro's *El desatino* and Pinter's *The Birthday Party*," *Latin American Theatre Review* 20, 1 (Fall 1986), 17–8.

29. David William Foster, *Handbook of Latin American Literature* (New York: Garland, 1987), 41.

30. Montserrat Ordoñez, "Máscaras de espejos, un juego especular: Entrevista—asociaciones con la escritora argentina, Luisa Valenzuela," *Revista Iberoamericana* 51 (1985), 516.

31. In her MLA Presidential Forum address, Valenzuela refers to *Realidad nacional desde la cama* as her "freshly minted" novel. See *Profession 91* (1991), 7.

32. See Diane Marting, "Female Sexuality in Selected Short Stories by Luisa Valenzuela: Toward an Ontology of Her Work," *Review of Contemporary Fiction* 6, 3 (Fall 1986), 53.

33. The Spanish is "Decreté que no existen"; emphasis mine. See Alfonso Callejo, "Literatura e irregularidad en *Cambio de armas*," *Revista Iberoamericana* 51 (1985), 578–79.

34. Georges Bataille, "Hemingway in the Light of Hegel," *Semiotexte* 2, 2 (1976), 1.

35. See Ana M. Fores, "Valenzuela's Cat-O-Nine Tails," *Review of Contemporary Fiction* 6, 3 (Fall 1986), 39–47.

36. Sharon Magnarelli, *The Lost Rib: Female Characters in the Spanish American Novel* (Lewisburg: Bucknell University Press, 1985), 170.

37. Roland Barthes, *S/Z*, tr. Richard Miller (New York: Hill and Wang, 1974), 112.

38. Evelyn Picon Garfield, "Interview with Luisa Valenzuela," *Review of Contemporary Fiction* 6, 3 (Fall 1986), 27.

39. "The Flowery Trick," "The Journey of Journey," "Inventory of a Recluse," *Five Women Writers of Costa Rica*, ed. Victoria Urbano (Beaumont, Texas: Asociación de Literatura Femenina Hispánica, 1976); "Why Kill the Countess?" "Ondina," *Women's Fiction from Latin America*, ed. Evelyn Picon Garfield; "And We Sold the Rain," *And We Sold the Rain: Contemporary Fiction from Central America*, ed. Rosario Santos (New York: Four Walls Eight Windows, 1988); *Nunca hubo alguna vez*, tr. Linda Britt, *There Never Was a Once Upon a Time* (Pittsburgh: Latin American Literary Review Press, 1989); and "When New Flowers Bloomed," *When New Flowers Bloomed: Short Stories by Women Writers from Costa Rica and Panama*, ed. Enrique Jaramillo Levi (Pittsburgh: Latin American Literary Review Press, 1991).

40. Picado de Bonilla, cited in Alicia Miranda Hevia, *Novela, discurso, y sociedad (diario de una multitud)* (Costa Rica: Mesén Editores, 1985), 45. Hevia does an interesting semiotic study of the novel.

41. Luz Ivette Martínez S., *Carmen Naranjo y La Narrativa Femenina en Costa Rica* (San José: Editorial Universitaria Centroamericana, 1987), 335.

42. Somers was awarded a prize for this collection of short stories in 1953 by the Uruguayan Ministry of Education and Planning.

CHAPTER 5. "TO BUILD NEW WORLDS"

1. Roland Barthes, "La Littérature Aujourd'hui," *Essais Critiques* (Paris: Seuil, 1964), 164, emphasis his. "Bien loin d'être une copie analogique du réel, *la littérature est au contraire la conscience même de l'irréel du langage:* la littérature la plus 'vraie,' c'est celle qui se sait la plus irréelle, dans la mesure où elle se sait essentiellement langage. . . ."

2. Ann Jefferson, *The Nouveau Roman and the Poetics of Fiction* (Cambridge: Cambridge University Press, 1980), 7.

3. Portions of this discussion appeared in Myriam Yvonne Jehenson, "The Dorotea-Fernando/Luscinda-Cardenio Episode in *Don Quijote*: A Postmodernist Play," *MLN* 107 (1992), 205–9.

4. Sharon Magnarelli, "Humor and Games in *El gato eficaz* by

Luisa Valenzuela: The Looking-Glass World Revisited," *Modern Language Studies* 13, 3 (1983), 81–89.

5. Martha Martínez, "Julieta Campos o la interiorización de lo cubano," *Revista Iberoamericana* 51 (1985), 793.

6. "Historia de un naufragio," *Plural* (May 1976); "Jardín de invierno," *Vuelta* 2, 21 (August 1978), 19–21. See also Beth Miller's translation of "Story of a Shipwreck," *Review—Center for Inter-American Relations* (Fall 1976), 66–68.

7. See also Julieta Campos, "Literatura y política: ¿relación o incompatibilidad?" *Texto Crítico* 4 (1976), 7–9; Julieta Campos, "¿Tiene sexo la escritura?" *Vuelta* 2, 21 (August 1978), 44–45; Julieta Campos, "Mi vocación literaria," *Revista Iberoamericana* 51 (1985), 447–50.

8. Jessica Benjamin, "Master and Slave: The Fantasy of Erotic Domination," *Powers of Desire: The Politics of Sexuality*, ed. Ann Snitow, Christine Stansell, and Sharon Thompson (New York: Monthly Review Press, 1983), 286.

9. Linda Hutcheon, *Narcissistic Narrative: The Metafictional Paradox* (New York: Methuen, 1980), 72.

10. Juan Bruce-Novoa, "Julieta Campos' *Sabina*: In the Labyrinth of Intertextuality," *Third Woman Press* 2, 2 (1984), 43–63, especially 46, 59, 60.

11. Alicia Rivero Potter, "La creación literaria en Julieta Campos: *Tiene los cabellos rojizos y se llama Sabina*," *Revista Iberoamericana* 51 (1985), 899–907. Bruce-Novoa makes similar distinctions in his article.

12. Martha P. Francescato, "Un desafío a la crítica literaria: *Tiene los cabellos rojizos y se llama Sabina*," *Revista de Crítica Latinoamericana* 7, 13 (1981), 125.

13. Hugo J. Verani, "Julieta Campos y la novela del lenguaje," *Texto Crítico* 2, 5 (1976), 132–49.

14. Evelyn Picon Garfield, "*Tiene los cabellos rojizos y se llama Sabina* de Julieta Campos," *Eco* 248 (June 1982), 172–91; see also Picon Garfield, *Women's Voices*, 77.

15. For an interesting analysis of a fear/fascination tension in Campos's work in general, see Fabrienne Bradu, "Julieta Campos, la cartografía del deseo y de la muerte," *Vuelta* 11, 128 (July 1987), 42–46.

16. Hugo J. Verani, "La narrativa de Cristina Peri Rossi," *Revista Iberoamericana* 48 (1982), 304.

17. John F. Deredita, "Desde la diáspora: entrevista con Cristina Peri Rossi," *Texto Crítico* 4, 9 (1978), 140.

18. Cristina Peri Rossi, "Literatura y mujer," *Instituto Jalisciense de Antropología e Historia* 42, 257 (1983), 505.

19. For a discussion of Peri Rossi's positive treatment of lesbian sexuality in *Lingüística general*, see Amy Kaminsky, "Gender and Exile in

Cristina Peri Rossi," *Continental Latin American and Francophone Women Writers: Selected Papers from the Wichita State University Conference on Foreign Literature, 1984–5*, ed. Eunice Myers and Ginette Adamson (Lanham, N. Y.: University Press of America, 1985), 147–59, especially 158–59.

20. Lucía Guerra Cunningham views Equis as an anti-epic hero used to contrast the tapestry with contemporary life. See "La referencialidad como negación del paraíso: exilio y excentrismo en *La nave de los locos* de Cristina Peri Rossi," *Revista de Estudios Hispánicos* 13, 2 (1989), 67.

21. For Stephen Hart, these episodes are "sordid sexual encounters" that emphasize the prostitute's battered and ugly body rather than her vulnerability. See *White Ink: Essays on Twentieth-Century Feminine Fiction in Spain and Latin America* (London: Tamesis Books, 1993), 124, 187.

22. W. H. Auden, *Collected Shorter Poems 1930–1944* (London: Faber and Faber, Ltd., 1962), 19.

23. Frank Graziano, *Alejandra Pizarnik: A Profile* (Durango, Colorado: Logbridge-Rhodes, 1987), 141.

24. See Marjorie Agosín, "Entrevista a Isabel Allende/Interview with Isabel Allende," tr. Cola Franzen, *Imagine* 1, 2 (Winter 1984), 53.

25. This view is attributed to Fabienne Bradu in Michael H. Handelsman, "*La casa de los espíritus* y la evolución de la mujer moderna," *Letras Femeninas* 14, 1–2 (1988), 57.

26. See Mario A. Rojas, "Un caleidoscopio de espejos desordenados," *Revista Iberoamericana* 51, 132–33 (1985), 917–25; Juan Manuel Marcos, "Isabel viendo llover en Barataria," *Revista de Estudios Hispánicos* 19, 2 (1985), 129–37; Juan Manuel Marcos and Teresa Méndez-Faith, "Multiplicidad, dialéctica, y reconciliación del discurso en *La casa de los espíritus*," *Los libros tienen sus propios espíritus*. Ed. Marcelo Coddou. Mexico: Universidad Veracruzana, 1986, 61–70; Linda Gould Levine, "A Passage to Androgyny: Isabel Allende's *La casa de los espíritus*" in *In the Feminine Mode: Essays on Hispanic Women Writers*, eds. Carol Maier and Noël Valis. Lewisburg: Bucknell University Press, 1990; and Marjorie Agosín's two articles: "Entrevista a Isabel Allende," 43, and especially "Isabel Allende: *La casa de los espíritus*," *Revista Interamericana de Bibliografía* 35 (1985), 448–58, where Agosín associates Clara's eccentricities and her deliberate silences with characteristics of *écriture feminine*, 451–53.

27. From October 1982 to July 1988 alone, twenty-seven editions of *The House* were published.

28. See "Los libros tienen sus propios espíritus," in *Los libros tienen sus propios espíritus: estudios sobre Isabel Allende*, ed. Marcelo Coddou, 15–20, where Allende concedes the familial recollections (15).

170 LATIN-AMERICAN WOMEN WRITERS

29. For the interaction of voices in the narrative, see James Mandrell, "The Prophetic Vision in Garro, Morante, and Allende," *Comparative Literature* 42, 3 (1990), 239–41.

30. See the fine article by Mario Rojas, "*La casa de los espíritus* de Isabel Allende: una aproximación sociolingüística," in *Los libros tienen sus propios espíritus*, 205–13. Rojas's application of Yuri Lotman's semiotic categories of *shame* and of *fear* to *The House* is very interesting in this regard. He posits that in the novel shame and/or fear are regulatory mechanisms and concludes that it is the women, not the men, who are able to rise above the resultant repressiveness (210).

31. See Ambrose Gordon, "Isabel Allende on Love and Shadows," *Contemporary Literature* 28, 4 (1987), 542. Allende herself emphasizes the obligation of all writers to serve the cause of liberty and justice. See "Los libros tienen sus propios espíritus" in *Los libros tienen sus propios espíritus*. For a contrary view of the importance of politics in Allende's works, see Willy Muñoz, "Las (re)escrituras en *La casa de los espíritus*," *Discurso Literario* 5, 2 (1988), 443–44.

32. John Krich's criticism of *The House* is found in *Mother Jones* (August/September 1985), 58. As I have pointed out, this sense of destiny as already written is a consequence of the proleptic structure of most of her novels.

33. In an excellent article, Gabriela Mora points out both the passivity of the characters in *The House* and their inability to transcend personal dramas. Consequently, Mora contends, notions of justice and freedom (which Allende pinpoints as mandatory for writers to explore) are superseded by individual interests. See "Las novelas de Isabel Allende y el papel de la mujer como ciudadana," *Ideologies and Literature* 2, 1 (1987), 60, n. 4. And Stephen Hart sees *The House* as "anti-historical and so not political" when a serious political strike is allowed to misfire because Alba has her period. See *White Ink: Essays on Twentieth-Century Feminine Fiction in Spain and Latin America*, 93–94. The identical scene takes place in *Eva Luna* where, in the midst of the guerrilla's preparation to confront the enemy, Eva Luna has her period (253).

34. The same bad taste is true of a scene Allende eroticizes in *Of Love and Shadows*. In the midst of the horror of the mine, where Irene has actually picked up the severed arm of one of the victims who were buried alive, she and Francisco retreat to a nearby hut to make love for "the ugliness of the world and the imminence of death were far away, nothing existed but the glow of their encounter" (185).

35. See Sandra M. Boschetto, "Threads, Connections, and the Fairy Tale: Reading the Writing in Isabel Allende's *La casa de los espíritus*," in *Continental, Latin American, and Francophile Women Writers*, vol. 2, eds. Ginette Adamson and Eunice Myers (Lanham: University Press of America, 1990), 58–59. Boschetto compares *The House* to the tale of

The Arabian Nights and applauds the reconciliation with which both stories end. I find Gabriela Mora's analysis more convincing. Mora reminds us of the practical danger of Alba's positing pardon and love without justice, given the political context of *The House*. Such an ending smacks, for Mora, of the same kind of propaganda promulgated by Pinochet's government: "que, como defensor de los sagrados principios de la familia cristiana, habla de amor y perdón en palabras vacías, traicionadas por los hechos" ("Las novelas de Isabel Allende," 56). ["Which, as sacred defender of Christian family values speaks of love and forgiveness in empty words, contrary to actual facts."]

36. See Patricia Klindienst Joplin, "Ritual Work on Human Flesh: Livy's Lucretia and the Rape of the Body Politic," *Helios* 17, 1 (1989), for an interesting discussion of this subject.

37. Malvia E. Filer, "Autorescate e invención en *Las andariegas* de Albalucía Angel," *Revista Iberoamericana* 51 (1985), 649–55. See also Raymond Leslie Williams, *The Colombian Novel: 1844–1987* (Austin: University of Texas Press, 1991), *passim*, for insightful discussions of Angel's novels. For *Las andariegas*, see 203–5.

38. A similar denial occurs in Carlos Fuentes's *The Death of Artemio Cruz*, tr. Sam Hilenan (New York: Farrar Straus, and Giroux, 1985), 76. As Regina and Artemio make love, they think back to their idyllic first encounter. Regina speaks of it as "a fiction that she had conjured that she [in the Spanish version it is "he"] might feel clean and innocent and sure of love. . . . her pretty lie. . . . It had no trace of truth. Neither did the truth: it was not true that he had gone into that Sinaloan pueblo just as he had gone into so many others, ready to grab the first woman who incautiously ventured outside. It was not true that a girl of eighteen had been thrown helplessly across his horse and carried back to the officers' dormitory to be violated in silence."

39. Rosario Ferré, "La cocina de la escritura," *La sartén por el mango*, eds. Patricia Elena González and Eliana Ortega (Puerto Rico: Ediciones Huracán, 1984), 148.

40. In the case of Mastretta's novel, I have provided my own translations rather than those of Wright's British-English version.

41. Franco Moretti, *The Way of the World: The Bildungsroman in European Cultures* (London: Verso, 1987), 7.

CHAPTER 6. INDIGENISTA AND *TESTIMONIO* LITERATURE: "LET ME SPEAK"

1. See Gayatri Chakravorty Spivak, "Subaltern Studies: De-constructing Historiography," *In Other Worlds: Essays in Cultural Politics* (New York: Methuen, 1987).

2. See Rosa Valdés-Cruz, *Lo ancestral africano en la narrativa de Lydia Cabrera* (Barcelona: Editoral Vosgos, 1974), 12.

3. Miriam De Costa Willis, "Folklore and the Creative Artist, " *College Language Association Journal* 27, 1 (1983), 85.

4. Cristina Guzmán, "Diálogo con Lidia Cabrera," *Zona Franca* 3, 24 (1981), 35.

5. Cited in Reinaldo Sánchez and others, *Homenaje a Lydia Cabrera* (Miami: Ediciones Universal, 1977), 16. Hereafter cited as *Homenaje* within the text.

6. Suzanne Jill Levine, "A Conversation with Lydia Cabrera," *Latin American Literature and Arts Review* 31 (1982), 13–15.

7. See Jean Franco, *Plotting Women: Gender and Representation in Mexico* (New York: Columbia University Press, 1989), 132.

8. Patrocinio Schweikert, "Reading Ourselves: Toward a Feminist Theory of Reading," *Contemporary Literary Criticism*, ed, Robert Con Davis and Ronald Schliefer (New York: Longman, 1989), 119–20.

9. Cited in Lucía Guerra, "Estrategias femeninas en la elaboración del sujeto romántico en la obra de Gertrudis Gómez de Avellaneda," *Revista Iberoamericana* 51 (1985), 713–14.

10. Franz Fanon, *Black Skin, White Masks*, tr. Charles Lam Markmann (New York: Grove Press, 1967), 8.

11. Rosario Hiriart, "En torno al mundo negro de Lydia Cabrera," *Cuadernos Hispanoamericanos* 120 (1980), 438–40.

12. Rosario Castellanos, "La novela mexicana y su valor testimonial," *Juicios Sumarios* 1 (México: Biblioteca Noven, 1984), 122.

13. Sandra Messinger Cypess, "*Balún Canán*: A Model Demonstration of Discourse as Power," *Revista de Estudios Hispánicos* 19 (1985), 10.

14. Emmanuel Carballo, "Elena Garro," *Protagonistas de La Literatura Mexicana* (Mexico City: Ediciones del Ermitaño, 1985), 490.

15. See Cynthia Duncan, "La culpa es de los Tlaxcaltecas," in *El cuento del siglo XX*, ed. Emmanuel Carballo (New York; Empresas Editoriales, 1964), 443–58.

16. See Sandra Messinger Cypess, "The Figure of La Malinche in the Texts of Elena Garro," *A Different Reality: Studies in the Works of Elena Garro*, ed. Anita Stoll (Lewisburg: Bucknell University Press, 1990), 117–35, for a discussion of how the female protagonists in both *Recollections* and "The Tlaxcalans Are to Blame" are patterned on the Malinche archetype and how Garro subverts that archetype.

17. Irwin Stern, ed., *Dictionary of Brazilian Literature* (New York: Greenwood Press, 1988), 244.

18. *New York Times Book Review* (May 24, 1992), 7.

19. Sara Castro-Klarén and others, eds., *Women's Writing in Latin America: An Anthology* (Boulder: Western Press, 1991), 78.

20. Luisa Valenzuela, "The other face of the phallus," *Reinventing the Americas: Comparative Studies of Literature of the United States and Spanish America*, ed. Bell Gale Chevigny and Gari Laguardia (Cambridge: Cambridge University Press, 1987), 243.

21. John Beverley, "Anatomía del testimonio," chapter seven of *"Del Lazarillo" al Sandinismo: estudios sobre la función ideológica de la literatura española e hispanoamericana* (Minneapolis: Institute for the Study of Ideologies and Literature, 1987), 14. Hereafter cited as Beverley, *AT* within the text.

22. Barbara Harlow, *Resistance Literature* (New York: Methuen, 1987).

23. For a highly informative article and pertinent bibliography, see David William Foster, "Latin American Documentary Narrative," *PMLA* 99 (1984), 41–55.

24. See Gloria Ardaya Salinas, "The Barzolas and the Housewives' Committee," *Women and Change in Latin America*, ed. June Nash, Helen I. Safa, and others (South Hadley, Massachusetts: Bergin and Garvey Publishers, 1986), 326–43.

25. Chandra Mohanty, "Under Western Eyes: Feminist Scholarship and Colonial Discourses," *Feminist Review* 30 (Autumn 1988), 61–88.

26. Edward Saïd, *Orientalism* (New York: Pantheon Books, 1978).

27. Françoise Ega, *Lettres a une noire* (Paris: Editions L'Harmattan, 1978. "On te lit par curiosité, moi, je ne lirai jamais tout ce que tu as écrit, je le sais."

28. See Octavio Paz, *Posdata* (Mexico City: Siglo Veintiuno, 1970, tr. as *The Other Mexico: Critique of the Pyramid* (New York: Grove Press, 1972); "A cinco años de Tlatelolco," in *El oro filantrópico*, ed. Octavio Paz (Mexico City: Joaquín Mortiz, 1979); Carlos Fuentes, "La disjuntiva mexicana," *Tiempo mexicano* (Mexico City: Joaquín Mortiz, 1971); "Mexico and Its Demons," a review of *The Other Mexico: Critique of the Pyramid*, *The New York Review of Books* 20 (1973), 16–21; María Luisa Mendoza, *Con él, conmigo, con nosotros tres* (Mexico; Joaquín Mortiz, 1971). For a comprehensive review of the literature dealing with the events of Tlatelolco, see Dolly J. Young, "Mexican Literary Reactions to Tlatelolco—1968," *Latin American Research Review* 20, 2 (1985), 71–85. See also Bell Gale Chevigny, "The Transformation of Privilege in the works of Elena Poniatowska," *Latin American Review* 13, 2 (1985), 49–62, especially 57 and *passim*. This work is hereafter cited as Chevigny, "The Transformation of Privilege" within the text.

29. Elena Poniatowska, *Massacre in Mexico*, tr. Helen Lane with a foreword by Octavio Paz (New York: Viking Press, 1975), vii–viii.

30. John Beverley, "The Margin at the Center: On *Testimonios* (Testimonial Narrative)," *Modern Fiction Studies* 35, 1 (1989), 14. Hereafter cited as Beverley, *MC* within the text. See also Renato Prada

Oropeza, "De lo testimonial al testimonio: nota para un deslinde del discurso-testimonio," *Testimonio y literatura*, ed. René Jara and Hernán Vidal (Minneapolis: Institute for the Study of Ideologies and Literature, 1986), 7–21. I am grateful to Brian Morgan for providing me with this reference.

31. Elzbieta Sklodowska, "La forma testimonial y la novelística de Miguel Barnet," *Revista/Review Interamericana* 12, 3 (1982), 379.

32. Joan W. Scott, *Feminists Theorize the Political*, ed. Judith Butler and Joan W. Scott (New York: Routledge, 1992), 22–40.

33. For a fine recent discussion of picaresque literature, see Peter Dunn, *Spanish Picaresque Fiction: A New Literary History* (Ithaca: Cornell University Press, 1993).

34. Georges Gusdorf, "Conditions and Limits of Autobiography," *Autobiography: Essays Theoretical and Critical*, ed. James Olney (Princeton: Princeton University Press, 1980), 29.

35. Gareth Williams, "Translation and Mourning: The Cultural Challenge of Latin American Testimonial Autobiography," *Latin American Literary Review* 21, 4 (1993), 83.

36. Paul de Man, "Autobiography as Defacement: Fiction in Autobiography," *Studies in the Art of Self-Invention*, ed. Paul John Eakin (Princeton: Princeton University Press, 1985), 185.

37. Pierre Macherey, *A Theory of Literary Production*, tr. Geoffrey Wall (London: Routledge and Kegan Paul, 1978), 155.

38. Plato, *The Republic*, tr. and ed. by A. D. Lindsay (New York: E. P. Dutton, 1957), Book III, 8607.

39. See Shlomith Rimmon, "A Comprehensive Theory of Fiction," *PTL: A Journal of Descriptive Poetics and Theory of Literature* 1 (1976), 33–62.

40. Robert Levine points out that Dantas, de Jesús's agent and mentor, refused to publish her stories and poetry, which she thought more significant than her diaries. Further, despite her objections, Dantas published portions of her notebook in a newspaper story, telling the readership, "I am not bringing you a newspaper story but a revolution." De Jesús complained that he so vastly altered her subsequently published texts that they were no longer hers, a charge he consistently rejected. That he did delete statements is evident through the ellipses appearing in the narratives. The significance of these facts is that Dantas, who claimed merely to have regularized de Jesús's writing, profited both professionally and monetarily from this venture. While he and de Jesús were supposed to share the royalties from her writing, she ultimately saw little of her money. He, in contrast, was promoted to the position of bureau chief of *O Cruzeiro*, a popular weekly magazine. See "The Cautionary Tale of Carolina María de Jesús," *Latin American Research Review* 29, 1 (1994), 55–83.

41. See Barnet, "La canción de Rachel," appendix to *La novela testimonio: socio-literatura* (Barcelona: Editorial Estela, 1970), 125–50. He insists that such "fictionalizing" is essential to the writing of *testimonios*.

42. K. Millet, "Framing the Narrative: The Dreams of Lucinda Nahuelhual," *Poética de la población marginal: sensibilidades determinantes*, ed. James Romano (Minneapolis: Prisma Institute, 1987), 425.

43. Gayatri Chakravorty Spivak, "Can the Subaltern Speak?" *Marxism and the Interpretation of Culture*, ed. Cary Nelson and Lawrence Grossberg (Urbana: University of Illinois Press, 1988), 271–313.

44. See also Cynthia Steele, "The 'Other' Within: Class and Ethnicity as Difference in Mexican Women's Literature," *Cultural and Historical Grounding*, 320–22.

45. "Usted inventa todo, son puras mentiras, no entendió nada, las cosas no son así." Elena Poniatowska, "Testimonios de una escritora: Elena Poniatowska en micrófono," *La sartén por el mango: encuentro de escritoras latinoamericanas*, ed. Patricia Elena González and Eliana Ortega (Rio Piedras, P. R.: Ediciones Huracán, 1984), 160. Poniatowska does the same in her reconstruction of Angelina Beloff's love affair with the Mexican artist Diego Rivera and in the memoirs of Gaby Brimmer, a young Mexican victim of cerebral palsy: "Poniatowska chooses to circumvent, displace, in some instances contradict, and otherwise 'censor' or edit any 'official' perspectives of these women . . ." (Schaefer, 83).

46. Adriana Rosman, lecture at Columbia University, 1990.

47. Munro Edmonson, *The Book of Counsel: The Popul Vuh of the Quiché Maya* (New Orleans: Tulane University Press, 1971), xiv.

48. Sara Castro-Klarén, "The Novelness of a Possible Poetics for Women," *Cultural and Historical Grounding*, 164.

49. Quoted in Christine Brooke-Rose, "Woman as Semiotic Subject," *The Female Body in Western Culture*, ed. Susan Rubin Suleiman (Cambridge: Harvard University Press, 1986), 205–16.

EPILOGUE

1. Teresa de Lauretis, *Alice Doesn't* (Bloomington: Indiana University Press, 1984), 159.

2. What Donna Guy has said of the Argentine tango applies to the Mexican bolero. See Donna Guy, "Tango, Gender, and Politics" in *Sex and Danger in Buenos Aires: Prostitution, Family, and Nation in Argentina* (Lincoln: University of Nebraska Press, 1991), 141–74, especially 150–51.

3. See Doris Sommer, *Foundational Fictions: The National Romances of Latin America* (Berkeley: University of California Press,

1991), 121, for the way Gertrudis Gómez de Avellaneda accomplishes this in *Sab*.

4. See Fredric Jameson, "The Structural Study of Myth," in *The Political Unconscious: Narrative as a Socially Symbolic Act* (Ithaca: Cornell University Press, 1981), for whom romance solves the dilemma of difference by "something like a semic evaporation," 118.

5. Juan Bautista Alberdi, "Las Bases y Puntos de Partida para la Organización Política de la República Argentina" (1852), cited in Sommer, *Foundational Fictions*, 15.

6. Donna J. Guy, *Sex and Danger in Buenos Aires: Prostitution, Family, and Nation in Argentina* (Lincoln: University of Nebraska Press, 1991), 159.

7. Marjorie Garber, *Vested Interests: Cross-Dressing and Cultural Anxiety* (New York: Routledge, 1992).

8. See Elizabeth V. Spelman, *Inessential Woman: Problems of Exclusion in Feminist Thought* (Boston: Beacon Press, 1989), 113.

9. See Christina Crosby, "Dealing with Difference," in *Feminists Theorize the Political*, 130–43.

10. Francine Masiello, *Between Civilization and Barbarism: Women, Nation, and Literary Culture in Modern Argentina* (Lincoln: University of Nebraska Press, 1992), 11.

11. Doris Sommer is actually speaking of Gertrudis Gómez de Avellaneda's *Sab* and how Sab is introduced through a series of negatives, *Foundational Fictions*, 117. Questions of language maturity, of different registers, are seen as contextual in these women's works. The lower-class Vicente Cochocho's sixteenth-century Spanish which the children use in *Mama Blanca's Memoirs* is corrected as vulgar by the children's English nanny and by their mother. The little girls learn later on, however, that they were right in loving "the flavor of the noble, vintage Spanish that comprised Vicente's vocabulary. . . . Vicente's Spanish was that of the Golden Age" (72–73).

12. Marianne Hirsch, "Review Essay: Mothers and Daughters," *Signs* 7 (Autumn 1981), 221.

13. Rachel Blau DuPlessis, *Writing Beyond the Ending: Narrative Strategies of Twentieth-Century Women Writers* (Bloomington: Indiana University Press, 1985), 196–97.

SELECTED BIBLIOGRAPHY

I. PRIMARY SOURCES

Allende, Isabel. *La casa de los espíritus.* Tr. Magda Bogin. *The House of the Spirits.* 1985. New York: Bantam Books, 1993.

———. *Los cuentos de Eva Luna.* Tr. Margaret Sayers Peden, *The Stories of Eva Luna.* New York: Atheneum, 1991.

———. *De sombra y amor.* Tr. Margaret Sayers Peden, *Of Love and Shadows.* New York: Alfred A. Knopf, 1987.

———. *Eva Luna.* Tr. Margaret Sayers Peden, *Eva Luna.* New York: Alfred A. Knopf, 1989.

———. *El plan infinito.* Tr. Margaret Sayers Peden, *The Infinite Plan: A Novel.* New York: Harper Collins Publishers, 1993.

Alvarado, Elvia. *Don't Be Afraid, Gringo.* Tr. and ed. Medea Benjamin. New York: Harper and Row, 1987.

Angel, Albalucía. *Las andariegas.* Barcelona: Argos Vergara, 1984.

———. *Estaba la pájara pinta sentada en el verde limón.* Bogotá: Instituto colombiano de cultura, 1975.

———. *Misiá señora.* Barcelona: Argos Vergara, 1982.

Barrios de Chungara, Domitila. *"Si me permiten hablar . . ."*: Testimonio de Domitila una mujer de las minas de Bolivia.* Tr. Victoria Ortiz, *Let Me Speak! Testimony of Domitila, A Woman of the Bolivian Mines.* Ed. Moema Viezzer. New York: Monthly Review Press, 1978.

Bombal, María Luisa. "La última niebla," "Las islas nuevas, " "El árbol." Tr. Richard and Lucía Cunningham, "The Final Mist," "The New Islands," "The Tree," *New Islands and Other Stories.* Ithaca: Cornell University Press, 1982. 3–47.

———. *La amortajada.* Tr. María Luisa Bombal, *The Shrouded Woman.* New York: Farrar, Straus and Company,1948.

———. "La historia de María Griselda." Tr. María Luisa Bombal, "The Story of María Griselda," *The Shrouded Woman.* New York: Farrar, Straus, and Company, 1948.

Brunet, Marta. *Obras completas.* Santiago: Zig-Zag, 1963.

Campos, Julieta. *Celina, o los gatos.* México: Siglo XXI, 1968.

———. *La imagen en el espejo.* México City: Universidad Autónoma de México, 1965.

———. *El miedo de perder a Euridíce.* México: Joaquín Mortiz, 1979.

————. *Muerte por agua*. México: Fondo de Cultura Económica, 1965.

————. *Tiene los cabellos rojizos y se llama Sabina*. Mexico: Joaquín Mortiz, 1974.

Cabrera, Lydia. *Ayapá: cuentos de Jicotea*. Spain: Ediciones Universal, 1971.

————. *Por qué . . . cuentos negros de Cuba*. Madrid: RAMOS, Artes Gráficas, 1972 (2nd ed.).

Castellanos, Rosario. *Balún Canán*. Tr. Irene Nicholson, *The Nine Guardians*. New York: Vanguard, 1960.

————. "El eterno femenino." Tr. Diane E. Marting and Betty Tyree Osiek, "The Eternal Feminine," *A Rosario Castellanos Reader*. Ed. Maureen Ahern. Austin: University of Texas Press, 1988.

Cunha, Helena Parente. *Mulher no espejo*. Tr. Fred P. Ellison and Naomi Lindstrom, *Woman Between Mirrors*. Austin: University of Texas Press, 1989.

Ferré, Rosario. *Papeles de Pandora*. Mexico: Editorial Joaquín Mortiz, 1976.

Gambaro, Griselda. "El campo." Tr. William J. Oliver, "The Camp." *Voices of Change in the Spanish American Theatre*. Austin: University of Texas Press, 1971. 47–103.

————. *Dios no nos quiere contentos*. Buenos Aires: Editorial Lumen, 1979.

————. *Ganarse la muerte*. Buenos Aires: Ediciones de la Flor, 1976.

————. *Lo impenetrable*. Tr. Evelyn Picon Garfield, *The Impenetrable Madame X*. Detroit: Wayne State University Press, 1990.

————. *Información para extranjeros*. Ed. and tr. Marguerite Feitlowitz, *Information for Foreigners: Three Plays by Griselda Gambaro*. Evanston: Northwestern University Press, 1992. Also contains *Las paredes* (*The Walls*) and *Antigona Furiosa*.

Garro, Elena. *Los recuerdos del porvenir*. Tr. Ruth L. C. Simms, *Recollections of Things to Come*. Austin: University of Texas Press, 1987.

————. *La semana de colores*. Xalapa: Universidad Veracruzana, 1964.

Jesús, Carolina María de. *Quarto de despejo: diario de uma favelada*. Tr. David St. Clair, *Child of Darkness: The Diary of Carolina María de Jesús*. New York: E. P. Dutton and Company, Inc., 1962.

Lynch, Marta. *La alfombra roja*. Buenos Aires: Fabril, 1962.

————. *Los dedos de la mano*. Buenos Aires: Sudamericana, 1976.

————. *Informe bajo llave*. Buenos Aires: Sudamericana, 1983.

————. *No te duermas, no me dejes*. Buenos Aires: Sudamericana, 1985.

————. *La penúltima versión de la Colorada Villanueva*. Buenos Aires: Sudamericana, 1978.

————. *La Señora Ordoñez*. Buenos Aires: Jorge Alvarez, 1967.

————. *Al vencedor*. Buenos Aires: Losada, 1965.

Mastretta, Angeles. *Arráncame la vida*. México: Ediciones Oceano, 1985. Tr. Ann Wright, *Mexican Bolero*. New York: Viking Press, 1989.

Menchú, Rigoberta. *Me llamo Rigoberta Menchú y así me nació la conciencia*. Tr. Ann Wright, *I, Rigoberta Menchú: An Indian Woman in Guatemala*. Ed. Elisabeth Burgos-Debray. London: Verso, 1984.

Mendoza, María Luisa. *Con él, conmigo, con nosotros tres*. Mexico: Joaquín Mortiz, 1971.

Naranjo, Carmen. *Camino al mediodía*. San José: Editorial Costa Rica, 1968.

———. *Diario de una multitud*. San José: Editorial Universitaria Centromamericana, 1974.

———. *Hoy es un largo día*. San José: Editorial Costa Rica, 1974.

———. *Nunca hubo alguna vez*. Tr. Linda Britt, *There Never Was a Once Upon a Time*. Pittsburgh: Latin American Literary Review Press Series, 1989.

———. *Ondina*. San José: EDUCA, 1983. Also found in Evelyn Picon Garfield, *Women's Literature from Latin America: Selections from Twelve Contemporary Authors*. Detroit: Wayne State University Press, 1988.

———. *Los perros no ladraron*. San José: Editorial Costa Rica, 1966.

———. *Responso por el niño Juan Manuel*. San José: Editorial Conciencia Nueva, 1971.

———. *Sobrepunto*. San José: Editorial Universitaria Centroamericana, 1985.

Ocampo, Victoria. *Autobiografía I: El archipiélago*. Buenos Aires: Ediciones Revista Sur, 1979.

———. *Autobiografía II: El imperio insular*. Buenos Aires: Ediciones Revista Sur, 1980.

———. *Autobiografía III: La rama de Salzburgo*. Buenos Aires: Ediciones Revista Sur, 1981.

———. *Autobiografía IV: viraje*. Buenos Aires: Ediciones Revista Sur, 1982.

———. *Autobiografía V: Versailles-Keyserling; Paris-Drieu*. Buenos Aires: Ediciones Revista Sur, 1983.

———. *Autobiografía VI: Sur y Cía*. Buenos Aires: Ediciones Revista Sur, 1984.

———. *Testimonios I*. Madrid: Revista de Occidente, 1935.

———. *Testimonios II*. Buenos Aires: Sur, 1941.

———. *Testimonios III*. Buenos Aires: Sur, 1946.

———. *Soledad sonora*. Buenos Aires: Sudamericana, 1950.

———. *Testimonios V*. Buenos Aires: Sur, 1957.

———. *Testimonios VI*. Buenos Aires: Sur, 1963.

———. *Testimonios VII*. Buenos Aires: Sur, 1967.

———. *Testimonios VIII*. Buenos Aires: Sur, 1971.

————. *Testimonios IX.* Buenos Aires: Sur, 1975.

————. *Testimonios X.* Buenos Aires: Sur, 1977.

Orpheé, Elvira. *La última conquista de El Angel.* Tr. Magda Bogin, *El Angel's Last Conquest.* New York: Ballantine Books, 1985.

Parra, Teresa de la. *Obra (narrativa, ensayos, cartas).* Eds. Velia Bosch and Julieta Fombona. Caracas: Biblioteca Ayacucho, 1982.

————. *Obras completas.* Caracas: Editorial Arte, 1965.

————. *Las memorias de Mamá Blanca.* Tr. Harriet de Onís, *Mama Blanca's Memoirs.* Revised by Frederick H. Fornoff. Pittsburgh: University of Pittsburgh Press, 1993.

————. *Ifigenia, diario de una señorita que escribió porque se fastidiaba.* 1924. Lima: Ediciones Antartida, 1960. Tr. Bertie Acker *Iphigenia: The Diary of a Young Lady Who Wrote Because She Was Bored.* Austin, Texas: University of Texas Press, 1994.

Peri Rossi, Cristina. *Indicios pánicos.* Montevideo: Nuestra América, 1970.

————. *La nave de los locos.* Tr. Psiche Hughes, *The Ship of Fools.* Great Britain: Allison and Busby, 1989.

————. *Una pasión prohibida.* Barcelona: Seix Barral, 1986.

Piñón, Nélida. *A república dos sonhos.* Tr. Helen Lane, *The Republic of Dreams.* New York: Alfred A. Knopf, 1989.

————. *A doce cancâo de Caetana.* Tr. Helen Lane, *Caetana's Sweet Song.* Alfred A. Knopf, 1991.

Pizarnik, Alejandra. *Arbol de Diana.* Buenos Aires: Sur, 1962.

————. *La condesa sangrienta.* Buenos Aires: López Crespo Editorial, 1971.

————. *El infierno musical.* Buenos Aires: Siglo XXI Argentina, 1971.

————. *Extracción de la piedra de locura.* Buenos Aires: Editorial Sudamericana, 1968.

————. *Textos de sombra y últimos poemas.* Ed. Olga Orozco and Ana Becciú. Buenos Aires: Editorial Sudamericana, 1982.

————. *Los trabajos y las noches.* Buenos Aires: Editorial Sudamericana, 1965. Excerpts of Pizarnik's work are translated in Frank Graziano, *Alejandra Pizarnic: A Profile.* Durango, Colorado: Logbridge-Rhodes, 1987.

Poniatowska, Elena. *Hasta no verte, Jesús mío.* Mexico City: Era, 1969.

————. *La noche de Tlatelolco.* Tr. Helen Lane, *Massacre in Mexico.* New York: Viking Press, 1975.

Randall, Margaret. *Doris Tijerino: Inside the Nicaraguan Revolution.* Tr. Elinor Randall. Vancouver: New Star Books, 1978.

Roffé, Reina. *Monte de Venus.* Buenos Aires: Ediciones Corregidor, 1976.

Somers, Armonía. "El derrumbamiento." Tr. Alberto Manguel, "The Fall." *Other Fires: Short Fiction by Latin American Women,* ed. Alberto Manguel. New York: Clarkson N. Potter, Inc., 1986.

————. *La mujer desnuda*. Montevideo: Ediciones Tauro, 1966 (third edition).

Traba, Marta. *Conversación al sur*. Tr. Jo Labanji, *Mothers and Shadows*. London: Reader's International, 1986.

Valenzuela, Luisa. *Aquí pasan cosas raras*. Tr. Helen Lane, *Strange Things Happen Here: Twenty-Six Short Stories and a Novel*. New York: Harcourt, Brace, Jovanovich, 1979. Contains translation of *Como en la guerra*.

————. *Cambio de armas*. Tr. Deborah Bonner, *Other Weapons*. New Hampshire: Ediciones del Norte, 1985.

————. *Cola de lagartija*. Tr. Gregory Rabassa, *The Lizard's Tail*. New York: Farrar, Straus, Giroux, 1983.

————. *Como en la guerra*. Tr. Helen Lane, *He Who Searches*. Elmwood Park, Illinois: Dalkey Archive Press, 1987.

————. *Donde viven las águilas*. Buenos Aires: Celtia, 1983.

————. *El gato eficaz*. México: Joaquín Mortiz, 1972. Tr. Evelyn Picon Garfield, "The Efficient Cat" in *The River Styx* 14 (1984), 87–89; "The First Feline Vision" in *Antaeus* 48 (1983), 75–78. *El gato eficaz* has not been translated in its entirety.

————. *Hay que sonreir*. Buenos Aires: Américalee, 1966.

————. *Novela negra con Argentinos*. Tr. Toby Talbot, *Black Novel (With Argentines)*. New York: Simon and Schuster, 1992.

————. *Realidad nacional desde la cama*. Buenos Aires: Grupo Editor Latinoamericano, 1990. This novel has not been translated.

II. GENERAL WORKS

A. Books

Agosín, Marjorie. *Women of Smoke*. Tr. Janice Molloy. Trenton: Red Sea Press, 1989.
Collection of essays, many of which deal with the political instability of Latin America and its effect on women.

Beverley, John. *"Del Lazarillo" al Sandinismo: estudios sobre la función ideológica de la literatura española e hispanoamericana*. Minneapolis: Institute for the Study of Ideologies and Literature, 1987.
Examines the *testimonio* as a literary form.

Bousquet, Jean-Pierre. *Las locas de la Plaza de mayo*. Buenos Aires: El Cid Editor, 1984.
Records the efforts of the Argentine mothers of "the disappeared" to find out about their children.

Brodzki, Bella and Celeste Schenck, eds. *Life/Lines: Theorizing Women's Autobiography*. Ithaca: Cornell University Press, 1988.

Examines the autobiography as a literary genre in several cultures. Contains Doris Sommer's excellent essay on the Latin American *testimonio*.

Castillo, Debra. *Talking Back: Toward a Latin American Feminist Literary Criticism*. Ithaca: Cornell University Press, 1992.
Considers strategies of Latin American women writers through investigation of specific texts. Fine discussion of the work of Luisa Valenzuela.

Foley, Barbara. *Telling the Truth: The Theory and Practice of Documentary Fiction*. Ithaca: Cornell University Press, 1986.
Discusses the theory and practice of various types of documentary literature, including the historical novel and the African American documentary novel.

Franco, Jean. *Plotting Women: Gender and Representation in Mexico*. New York: Columbia University Press, 1989.
Contains good discussion of Poniatowska's *Hasta no verte, Jesús mío*.

Harlow, Barbara. *Resistance Literature*. New York: Methuen, 1987.
Considers the types of literary texts produced in Third World liberation movements.

Jara, René and Hernán Vidal, eds. *Testimonio y literatura*. Minneapolis: Institute for the Study of Ideologies and Literature, 1986.
Contains series of articles dealing with various views on *testimonio*.

Macías, Anna. *Against All Odds*. Westport, Conn.: Greenwood Press, 1982.
Interesting and useful history of feminism in Mexico.

Molloy, Sylvia. *At Face Value: Autobiographical Writing in Spanish America*. Cambridge: Cambridge University Press, 1991.
Investigates autobiographical texts of nineteenth and twentieth centuries. Especially good examination of Ocampo's *Autobiography*.

Morgan, Robin, ed. *Sisterhood is Global: The International Women's Movement Anthology*. New York: Doubleday Anchor Books, 1984.
Source book for statistical data on Latin America as well as other parts of the world.

Nash, June and Helen I. Safa. *Women and Change in Latin America*. South Hadley, Mass.: Bergin and Garvey Publishers, Inc., 1986.
Seventeen essays on life of contemporary Latin American women, including economic and political status.

Solé, Carlos and María Isabel Abreu, eds. *Latin American Writers*. New York: Charles Scribner's Sons, 1989.
Bio-bibliographical articles on current Latin American authors.

B. Articles

Araújo, Helena. "Narrativa femenina latinoamericana." *Hispamérica* 11, 32 (1982), 23–34.
Compares narrative of the Latin American woman writer to Scheherezade, who tells a story in order to live. Discusses various women writers who have attempted to overcome the oppression of Latin American culture.

Beverley, John. "The Margin at the Center: On *Testimonios* (Testimonial Narrative)." *Modern Fiction Studies* 35, 1 (1989), 11–28.
Studies distinctions between *testimonio*, life history, *novela-testimonio*, and documentary fiction.

Masiello, Francine. "Discurso de mujeres, lenguaje de poder: reflexiones sobre la crítica a mediados de la década del 80." *Hispamérica* 15, 45, (1986), 53–60.
Good overview of feminist criticism.

Mohanty, Chandra. "Under Western Eyes: Feminist Scholarship and Colonial Discourses." *Feminist Review* 30 (Autumn, 1988), 61–88.
Excellent critique of basic analytical presuppositions present in feminist discourse concerning Third World women.

Williams, Raymond Leslie. *The Colombian Novel: 1844–1987*. Austin: University of Austin Press, 1991.
Overview of the development of the novel in Colombia. Addresses regionalism, *La Violencia*, and other important issues. Of particular interest is the chronology of Colombian authors.

III. WORKS ABOUT SPECIFIC WOMEN AUTHORS

A. Books

Basnett, Susan, ed. *Knives and Angels: Women Writers in Latin America*. London: Zed Books, Ltd., 1990.
Thirteen essays about contemporary Latin American authors, including Ocampo, Castellanos, Poniatowska, Gambaro, and Bombal.

Bosch, Velia. *Esta pobre lengua viva: relectura de la obra de Teresa de la Parra*. Caracas: Ediciones de la Presidencia de la República, 1979.
Discusses *Ifigenia* in terms of text and in relation to the life of Parra. Includes excerpts from Parra's correspondence as well as bio-bibliographical material.

Correas de Zapata, Celia and Lygia Johnson. *Detrás de la reja*. Caracas: Monte Avila Editores, 1980.

Overview of twentieth century Latin American women writers with excerpts corresponding to stages of a woman's life.

García Pinto, Magdalena. *Historias íntimas: conversaciones con diez escritoras latinoamericanas*. New Hampshire: Ediciones del norte, 1988. Introductory essay on Latin American women's writing; interviews with ten well-known women authors; bibliography of their major works. Excellent resource book.

Garrels, Elizabeth. *Las grietas de la ternura: nueva lectura de Teresa de la Parra*. Caracas: Monte Avila Editores, 1985. Discusses *Mama Blanca's Memoirs* as Parra's vehicle for advancing her feminist ideas.

González, Patricia Elena and Eliana Ortega. *La sartén por el mango: encuentro de escritoras latinoamericanas*. P.R.: Ediciones Huracán, 1984. Ground-breaking series of papers originally given at 1982 Colloquium on Latin American women writers. Features presentations by Traba, Molloy, Ferré, Poniatowska, etc.

Guerra-Cunningham, Lucía. *La narrativa de María Luisa Bombal: una visión de la existencia femenina*. Spain: Editorial Playor, 1980. Critical study of Bombal's major works.

Hiriart, Rosario. *Más cerca de Teresa de la Parra (diálogos con Lydia Cabrera)*. Caracas: Monte Avila Editores, 1980. Explores Parra's career as revealed through conversations with her life companion, Lydia Cabrera. Contains extensive bibliography by and about Parra.

Magnarelli, Sharon. *The Lost Rib: Female Characters in the Spanish-American Novel*. Lewisburg: Bucknell University Press, 1985. Very good discussion of the portrayal of women by nineteenth and twentieth century authors, both female and male. Contains chapter on Valenzuela's *El gato eficaz*.

Marting, Diane, ed. *Spanish American Women Writers*. Westport, Conn.: Greenwood Press, 1989. Very useful bio-bibliographical accounts for fifty Spanish American women writers. Does not deal with Brazilian writers.

———. *Women Writers of Spanish America: an Annotated Bio-Bibliographical Guide*. New York; Greenwood Press, 1987. Indispensable reference guide for research in Spanish American women authors. Like Marting's 1989 volume (see above), however, does not include Brazilian writers.

Meyer, Doris, ed. *Lives on the Line: The Testimony of Contemporary Latin American Authors*. Berkeley: University of California Press, 1988.

Excerpts of essays which were written between 1960–86 by female and male authors. They document Latin American intellectual life during this period.

————. *Victoria Ocampo: Against the Wind and the Tide.* New York: Braziller, 1979.
Sympathetic treatment of Ocampo. Contains fifteen essays from *Testimonios* translated by Meyer.

————, and Margarite Fernández Olmos, eds. *Contemporary Women Authors of Latin America: New Translations.* 2 vols. Brooklyn: Brooklyn College Press, 1983.
Contains translated excerpts from works of current Latin American women writers, as well as extensive commentary.

Picon Garfield, Evelyn, ed. *Women's Fiction from Latin America: Selections from Twelve Contemporary Authors.* Detroit: Wayne State University Press, 1988.
Along with translations of such authors as Somers, Traba, Cabrera, Valenzuela, etc., book contains very useful bibliography of works by and about each writer.

————. *Women's Voices from Latin America: Interviews with Six Contemporary Authors.* Detroit: Wayne State University Press, 1985.
Extremely helpful book. Interviews and follow-up questions with Somers, Garro, Campos, Orphée, Valenzuela, Traba. Comprehensive biographical and bibliographical material included.

Stoll, Anita. *A Different Reality: Studies in the Work of Elena Garro.* Lewisburg: Bucknell University Press, 1990.
Contains Cypess's fine essay on the figure of La Malinche in Garro's narratives.

Valdés-Cruz, Rosa. *Lo ancestral africano en la narrativa de Lydia Cabrera.* Barcelona: Editorial Vosgos, S. A., 1974.
Discusses Cabrera's work in studying African influences on Cuban literature, especially folklore.

Zea, Gloria, ed. *Marta Traba.* Bogotá: Museo de Arte Moderno de Bogotá, 1984.
Lavish tribute to Marta Traba, published after her death. Contains extensive bibliography, as well as excerpts from interviews and numerous articles.

B. Articles

Adam, Carlos. "Bio-bibliografía de Victoria Ocampo." *Sur* 346 (1980), 125–79.
Traces Ocampo's career through excerpts from her writings and speeches.

Agosín, Marjorie. "La mimesis de la interioridad: 'Soledad de la sangre' de Marta Brunet y 'El árbol' de María Luisa Bombal." *Neophilologus* 68, 3 (1984), 380–88.
Discusses Chileans Bombal and Brunet as pioneering feminist writers through an examination of their works.

Aizenberg, Edna. "El *Bildungsroman* fracasado en Latinoamérica: el caso de *Ifigenia* de Teresa de la Parra." *Revista Iberoamericana* 51 (1985), 539–46.
Investigates *Ifigenia* in terms of the masculine notion of the *Bildungsroman* as set forth by Cynthia Steele and Martin Swales.

Allen, Martha. "Dos estilos de novela: Marta Brunet y María Luisa Bombal." *Revista Iberoamericana* 17 (1952), 63–91.
Discusses Brunet's *Montaña adentro* y *Bestia dañina* and Bombal's *La última niebla* and *La amortajada*.

Araújo, Helena. "El tema de la violación en Armonía Somers y Griselda Gambaro." *Plural* 15, 179 (1976), 21–23.
Discusses the portrayal of sexual violence in the works of Somers and Gambaro.

Arizpe, Lourdes. "Interview with Carmen Naranjo: Women and Latin American Literature." *Signs* 5, 1 (1979), 98–110.
Contains biographical material and revelatory interview about Naranjo's views on writing and feminism.

Bastos, María Luisa. "Escrituras ajenas, expresión propia: *Sur* y los *Testimonios de Victoria Ocampo. Revista Iberoamericana* 46 (1980),123–37.
Provides background material on *Sur* and discusses various topics associated with Ocampo's *Testimonios*.

Berg, Mary G. "The Short Stories of Marta Brunet." *Monographic Review/Revista Monográfica* 4 (1988), 195–206.
Describes Brunet's short fiction as she herself categorized it.

Boschetto, Sandra M. "Threads, Connections, and the Fairy Tale: Reading the Writing in Isabel Allende's *La casa de los espíritus.*" *Continental, Latin-American, and Francophile Women Writers*. Ed. Ginette Adamson and Eunice Myers. Lanham: University Press of America, 1990. 51–63.
Compares fairy tale motifs, particularly those located in *The Thousand and One Nights*, to motifs found in Allende's most famous work.

Bradu, Fabienne. "Julieta Campos: la cartografía del deseo y la muerte." *Vuelta* 11, 128 (1987), 42–46.
Explores circular structure of Campos's novels and her emphasis on death.

Bruce-Novoa, Juan. "Julieta Campos' *Sabina*: In the Labyrinth of Inter-textuality." *Third Woman Press* 2, 2 (1984), 43–64.
Very insightful feminist analysis. Looks at possible sources for Campos's experimental novel.

Callejo, Alfonso. "Literatura e irregularidad en *Cambio de armas*, de Luisa Valenzuela." *Revista Iberoamericana* 51 (1985), 575–80.
Examines the real/unreal aspects of Valenzuela's text.

Case, Barbara. "On Writing, Magic, and Eva Perón: An Interview with Luisa Valenzuela." *Ms.* (October 1983), 18–20.
Valenzuela discusses *The Lizard's Tail* and what it means to be a woman writer in Argentina.

Chevigny, Bell Gale. "A Latin American Odyssey Ends." *The Nation* (February 4, 1984), 126–28.
Biographical article about Marta Traba and Angel Rama, written shortly after their deaths.

———. "The Transformation of Privilege in the Works of Elena Poniatowska." *Latin American Review* 13, 2 (1985), 49–62.
Discusses Poniatowska's revolutionary works, especially *Massacre in Mexico*, in contrast with her conservative, privileged, aristocratic background.

Christ, Ronald. "Figuring Literarily: An Interview with Victoria Ocampo." *Review—Center for Inter-American Relations* (Winter 1972), 5–13.
Wide-ranging interview in which Ocampo talks about her sister Silvina, her imprisonment, *Sur*, and feminism.

Cobo Borda, Juan Gustavo. "Marta Traba, novelista." *Cuadernos Hispanoamericanos* 414 (December 1984), 121–30.
Focuses on *En cualquier lugar* and its relationship to *Conversación al Sur*.

Cypess, Sandra Messinger. "*Balún Canán*: A Model Demonstration of Discourse as Power." *Revista de Estudios Hispánicos* 19 (1985), 1–15.
An excellent study of the "strategies of power" in the novel as they pertain to the relationship between oppressor and oppressed.

DeCosta Willis, Miriam. "Folklore and the Creative Artist: Lydia Cabrera and Zora Neale Hurston." *College Language Association Journal* 27, 1 (1983), 81–90.
Comparative study of the two authors. Offers critical analysis of specific texts.

Duncan, Cynthia. "'La culpa es de los Tlaxcaltecas': A reevaluation of Mexico's Past Through Myth." *Crítica Hispánica* 7 (1985), 105–20.

Examines the story with attention paid to aspect of time and memory. Also shows how Garro makes use of both myth and history in creating her text.

Feal, Rosemary Geisdorfer. "Spanish American Ethnobiography and the Slave Narrative Tradition: *Biografía de un cimarrón* and *Me llamo Rigoberta Menchú.*" *Modern Language Studies* 20, 1 (1990), 100–11. Examines the two texts as ethnobiographical writings, pointing out the complexities of truth claims and verisimilitude.

Filer, "Autorescate e invención en *Las andariegas* de Albalucía Angel." *Revista Iberoamericana* 51 (1985), 649–55. Examines the book in light of Angel's statement that "the battle of sex is the battle of texts."

Gallo, Marta. "Las crónicas de Victoria Ocampo: versatilidad y fidelidad de un género." *Revista Iberoamericana* 51 (1985), 679–86. Critical analysis of Ocampo's *Testimonios*.

García Pinto, Magdalena. "Entrevista: Marta Traba." *Hispamérica* 38 (1984), 37–46. Traba discusses her career as art critic and feminist writer, as well as her ideas on *escritura femenina* in general.

Guzmán, Cristina. "Diálogo con Lidia Cabrera." *Zona Franca* 3, 24 (1981), 34–8. Cabrera talks about her studies and about writing in general.

Hancock, Joel. "Elena Poniatowska's *Hasta no verte Jesús mío*: The Remaking of the Image of Woman." *Hispania* 86, 3 (1983), 353–59. Examines Jesusa Palancares as Poniatowska's attempt to expose and debunk stereotypes of women.

Hiriart, Rosario. "En torno al mundo negro de Lydia Cabrera." *Cuadernos Hispanoamericanos* 120 (1980), 433–40. Excellent bio-critical article. Contains information about renewed interest in African culture in the 1920s.

Jurado, Alicia. "Victoria Ocampo: mi predecesora." *Boletín de la Academia Argentina de Letras* 46, 179–80 (1981), 81–95. Jurado's speech at induction into Argentine Academy. She lauds Ocampo as writer.

Kerr, Lucille. "Gestures of Authorship: Lying to Tell the Truth in Elena Poniatowska's *Hasta no verte Jesús mío.*" *MLN* 106 (1991), 370–94. An excellent article which argues that the *novela-testimonio* reaffirms the importance of the author's role, redefining that role by making the author's responsibilities as much investigative as editorial.

King, John. "Towards a Reading of the Argentine Literary Magazine *Sur.*" *Latin American Research Review* 16, 2 (1981), 57–78. Historical and critical analysis of Victoria Ocampo's *Sur*.

————. "Victoria Ocampo, *Sur*, y el peronismo, 1946–55." *Revista de Occidente* 37 (1984), 30–44.
Critical discussion of content of *Sur*'s articles during Perón's régime.

Kantaris, Elia. "The Politics of Desire: Alienation and Identity in the Work of Marta Traba and Cristina Peri Rossi." *Forum for Modern Language Studies* 25, 3 (1989), 248–64.
A comparative study of the works by these two writers who both were exiled from their homelands. Their texts, according to Kantaris, "examine the mechanisms which appear to link the monopoly of power to the process of alienation" (248).

Lagmanovich, David. "*Sur*: 40 Years." *Américas* 23, 9 (September 1971), 10–14.
Reviews history of *Sur*, noting Latin American and foreign authors whose works appeared in the journal.

Lagos-Pope, María Inés. "El testimonio creativo de *Hasta no verte Jesús mío*." *Revista Iberoamericana* 56 (1990), 243–53.
Examines text as an example of a *novela-testimonio*.

Laughlin, Karen L. "The Language of Cruelty: Dialogue Strategies and the Spectator in Gambaro's *El desatino* and Pinter's *The Birthday Party*. *Latin American Theatre Review* 20, 1 (Fall 1986), 11–20.
Investigates notion of cruelty as it applies not only to the characters in the plays but also to the spectators in the audience.

Levine, Robert M. "The Cautionary Tale of Carolina María de Jesús." *Latin American Research Review* 29, 1 (1994), 55–83.
Biographic article revealing the seldom admitted social bias against African-Brazilians. Points out that others, rather than de Jesús, benefitted from her literary efforts.

Levine, Suzanne Jill. "A conversation with Lydia Cabrera." *Latin American Literature and Arts Review* 31 (1982), 13–5.
Cabrera talks about her work, Cuba, her early years in France. Includes short story, "Time Fights the Sun and the Moon Consoles the Earth."

Martinez, Martha. "Julieta Campos o la interiorización de lo cubano." *Revista Iberoamericana* 51 (1985), 793–97.
Alleges Campos's work has been overlooked by critics because it is apolitical. Offers overview to several of her best known works.

McAleer, Janice K. "*El campo* de Griselda Gambaro: una contradicción de mensajes." *Revista Canadiense de Estudios Hispánicos* 7, 1 (Autumn 1982), 159–71.
Excellent analysis of the sign systems employed in *El campo*, how they communicate their message, and how the contradiction of information essential for the final vision of the work arises.

Méndez-Faith, Teresa. "Sobre el uso y abuso de poder en la producción dramática de Griselda Gambaro." *Revista Iberoamericana* 51 (1985), 831–41.
Examines several of Gambaro's plays with reference to political repression in Argentina.

Montero, Oscar. "La 'enunciación infatigable' de *Los laberintos insolados* de Marta Traba." *Prisma/Cabral* (Fall 1984), 93–102.
Discusses the novel in terms of the Homeric Ulysses myth.

Mora, Gabriela. "Una lectura de 'Soledad de la sangre' de Marta Brunet." *Estudios Filológicos* 19 (1984), 81–90.
Studies Brunet's text in terms of feminist response to patriarchal oppression in Chilean culture.

———. "La otra cara de Ifigenia: una revaluación del personaje de Teresa de la Parra." *Sin Nombre* 7, 3 (1976), 130–44.
Highly informative article. Compares text of *Ifigenia* to Parra's recorded principles of writing.

Ordoñez, Montserrat. "Máscaras de espejos, un juego especular." *Revista Iberoamericana* 51 (1985), 511–19.
Interview with Valenzuela, using word-association as basis for responses.

Paley de Francescato, Martha. "Marta Lynch: Entrevista." *Hispamérica* 10 (1975), 33–44.
Wide-ranging interview in which Lynch talks about her literary beginnings, influences, works. She offers thoughts on politics and public opinion.

Peri Rossi, Cristina. "Literatura y mujer." *Instituto Jalisciense de Antropología e Historia* 42, 257 (1983), 498–506.
Rejects notion that there is a particular "literatura femenina."

Picon Garfield, Evelyn. "Interview with Luisa Valenzuela." *Review of Contemporary Fiction* 6, 3 (1986), 25–30.
The subject is Valenzuela's fiction.

———. "*Tiene los cabellos rojizos y se llama Sabina,* de Julieta Campos." *Eco* 248 (June 1982), 172–91.
Excellent discussion of the novel as an *opera aperta* ("open work") as defined by Umberto Eco.

Poniatowska, Elena. "Marta Traba o el salto al vacío." *Revista Iberoamericana* 51 (1985), 883–97.
Biographical and critical article on Traba, published after her death. Focuses on Traba's self-comparison to Joan of Arc.

Saltz, Joanne. "Luisa Valenzuela's *Cambio de armas*: Rhetoric of Politics." *Confluencia* 3, 1 (1987), 61–6.
Discusses political events influencing *Cambio de armas*.

Seoane, Ana. "Entretien avec Griselda Gambaro." *Cahiers du Monde Hispanique et Luso Brésilien* 40 (1983), 163–5.
Gambaro responds to questions about her dramatic works.

Sola, María. "'Conversación al Sur,' novela para no olvidar." *Sin Nombre* 12, 4 (July–September 1982), 64–71.
Examines the novel using Traba's phrase "so as not to forget" as a starting point for the discussion.

———. "'Escribo como mujer': trayectoria de la narrativa de Marta Traba." *Sin Nombre* 14, 3 (April–June 1984), 101–14.
Examines Traba's ideas on *escritura femenina* as reflected in her fictional works and her critical essays.

Vásquez, María Esther. "Victoria Ocampo, una argentina universalista." *Revista Iberoamericana* 46 (1980), 167–75.
Laudatory review of Ocampo's literary career.

Verani, Hugo J. "Julieta Campos y la novela del lenguaje." *Texto Crítico* 2, 5 (1976), 132–49.
Excellent article. Posits that language itself is the focus of Campos's literary experiments, especially *Sabina*.

———. "La narrativa de Cristina Peri Rossi." *Revista Iberoamericana* 48 (1982), 303–16.
Discusses Peri Rossi's work in light of the changes in rhetorical categories in Latin American literature.

Williams, Gareth. "Translation and Mourning: The Cultural Challenge of Latin American Testimonial Autobiography." *Latin American Literary Review* 21, 41 (1993), 79–99.
Uses the *testimonios* of Menchú and Chungara to examine the politically motivated discursive practices of such texts.

INDEX